Towards a Global Mu

How do we explain the globalized musical world in which we find ourselves in the early twenty-first century and how did we arrive here? This extraordinary book outlines an understanding of the human musical story as an intercultural—and ultimately a transcultural—one, with travel and trade as the primary conditions and catalysts for the ongoing development of musical styles.

Starting with the cultural and civilizational precedents that gave rise to the first global trading and travel network in both directions across the Afro-Eurasian Old World Web in the form of the Silk Road, the book proceeds to the rise of al-Andalus and its influence on Europe through the Iberian peninsula before considering the fusion of European, African, and indigenous musics that emerged in the Americas between c. 1500 and 1920 as part of Atlantic culture and the New World Web, as well as the concurrent acceleration of globalism in music through European empires and exoticism. The book concludes by examining the musical implications of our current Age of Instantaneous Exchange that technology permits, and by revisiting the question of interculturality and transculturality in music.

Mark Hijleh has taught music at the university level for 25 years. Currently Provost and Professor of Music at The King's College in New York City, he holds an MA in World Music with distinction from the University of Sheffield; the DMA in Composition from Peabody Conservatory of Johns Hopkins University; the MM in Composition and Conducting from Ithaca College; and the BS in Music with Honors from William Jewell College. Hijleh has spoken and written about world music theory and history through the College Music Society, Analytical Approaches to World Music, the *Journal of the Royal Asiatic Society*, and the Society for Ethnomusicology. He also studied shakuhachi with Ronnie Nyogetsu Reishin Seldin and Black music with Dominique Rene DeLerma.

Towards a Global Music History

Intercultural Convergence, Fusion, and Transformation in the Human Musical Story

Mark Hijleh

Routledge
Taylor & Francis Group

LONDON AND NEW YORK

First published 2019
by Routledge
2 Park Square, Milton Park, Abingdon, Oxon OX14 4RN

and by Routledge
52 Vanderbilt Avenue, New York, NY 10017

First issued in paperback 2020

Routledge is an imprint of the Taylor & Francis Group, an informa business

British Library Cataloguing-in-Publication Data
A catalogue record for this book is available from the British Library

Library of Congress Cataloging-in-Publication Data
Names: Hijleh, Mark, author.
Title: Towards a global music history: intercultural convergence, fusion,
and transformation in the human musical story / Mark Hijleh.
Description: Abingdon, Oxon; New York, NY: Routledge, 2019. |
Includes bibliographical references and index.
Identifiers: LCCN 2018042997 | ISBN 9781138088733 (hardback) |
ISBN 9781315109688 (ebook)
Subjects: LCSH: Music–History and criticism. | World history. |
Intercultural communication–History. | Music and globalization.
Classification: LCC ML160 .H605 2019 | DDC 780.9–dc23
LC record available at https://lccn.loc.gov/2018042997

ISBN 13: 978-0-367-66336-0 (pbk)
ISBN 13: 978-1-138-08873-3 (hbk)

Typeset in Times New Roman
by Deanta Global Publishing Services, Chennai, India

To Kelley, Hannah, and Noah
S.D.G.

Contents

PART III
The Global Web and continuous transformation,
since c. 1920 CE   181

Figures

Music examples

Acknowledgments

To my intrepid editor, Heidi Bishop: You will ever have my most profound admiration and gratitude for your vision and entrepreneurial spirit that translated into support for this project. Likewise, this book would not have materialized without the gracious votes of confidence I have felt for many years from Jeremy Begbie and Jonathan P.J. Stock. I am grateful to my colleagues at The King's College, New York, for their support and encouragement; especially to professors Henry Bleattler, Steele Brand, Joseph Loconte, Amity Shlaes, and David Tubbs for your inspiring interest and insights. My wife Kelley Hijleh and mother-in-law Lucille Ruth graciously and sacrificially read drafts and provided extremely helpful suggestions. To the many other scholars who are courageously advancing a global perspective on musicology—among them Michael Church, Patrick Savage, Michael Tenzer, and Godfried Toussaint—I am most grateful for your trailblazing work. The fond memory of Rob Schultz (1977–2016), visionary co-founder and tireless promoter of the *Analytical Approaches to World Music* enterprise, is ever before us.

Mark Hijleh
New York

1 Introduction

Global musicianship and global musicology

How and why do Italian bel canto singing, Anglo-Celtic jigging and reeling, Latin dance forms from the tango to the Macarena, modal (maqam) improvisation in the Middle East and the Balkans, toasting and rapping in the Caribbean and the United States, Central European polka, the bell-patterns of West African drumming, the timbre-rich droning of Australian aboriginal music, and the colotomic processes of Javanese gamelan cross so many cultural boundaries with such energy, boundaries at which so much else comes to an abrupt halt?

—Martin Stokes (2004:76)

In my musical journey I have had the opportunity to learn from a wealth of different musical voices...and have wondered how these complex interconnections occurred and how new musical voices were formed from the diversity of these traditions.[1] Whatever we might think the present is, it has come from deep interconnections among people. This continuum, as a historical view, is a metaphor. In the life of creativity and invention, purity doesn't really exist...When you look back through world history, there have been many instances of increasing globalization—it's inevitable, and continuous. Now it is simply moving more swiftly.[2]

—Yo-Yo Ma

As of this writing, it would be difficult to deny the global musical influence of Chinese-American cellist Yo-Yo Ma (b. 1955). Though coming to prominence from within the Western European tradition, Ma has for more than two decades been an ambassador for what could be called Global Musicianship: a set of perspectives, concepts, and competencies with which twenty-first-century musicians might thrive in a musical world that is increasingly multicultural, intercultural, transcultural—in short, a more "global" musical world.[3] Global musicianship encompasses music theory and analysis, music history, and music performance. Ethnomusicologist and composer Michael Tenzer suggests that such a disposition constitutes

a response to economic and cultural transformation making it desirable for musicians to acquire competence not just passively hearing, but contemplating and integrating any music. The well-established ethnomusicological model of bi- or tri-musicality is inadequate to describe us anymore; we are approaching multi- or a virtual pan-musicality. For many this is already a fact of life, and not just for composers: trumpet players do salsa, Corelli, free jazz, and mariachi all in the same week, and the iPod shuffle mode compresses infinite musics, cultures, eras, and locales for listening with consummate effortlessness.

(2006:34)

In this light, the idea that music history ought to remain more or less entirely focused on the contributions of Western Europe—however considerable and commendable those may be—seems ill-advised. And yet that is too often what continues to transpire in collegiate music history curricula at the time of this writing. Certainly, more attention is now paid to a broader plurality of musics, but these are either still seen as peripheral rather than central to musical education, or at best understood to be set apart from one another at levels of remove that preclude the possibility of human musical universality. Such a situation creates a less than ideal context in which students may pursue the sort of competence Tenzer describes—and perspectives are not inconsequential to motivations. As a result, prospective music faculty are not always being prepared to serve their own future students as well as they could.

Tangible physical evidence of human musical activity, in the form of bone flutes, goes back at least 35,000–45,000 years, but there is no reason not to believe that humans were musical from the very beginning, since every human culture today includes music. However, global music history cannot be merely a review of every musical culture that has ever been (as if that were possible). All histories reflect choices, and the one outlined here posits that the human musical story is best understood, in twenty-first-century retrospect, from a global developmental perspective in the context of intercultural convergence, with travel and trade as the primary defining conditions and catalysts. The speed and effect of these intercultural convergences have increased as developing technologies have enabled them over time, eventually approaching the level of instantaneous musical exchange, fusion, and global transculturality that we observe today. This is a captivating story, one that provides a plausible, manageable framework for overall understanding of the human musical journey, a framework into which students and scholars may delve deeper with regard to any one music or group of musics.

This study is by no means the first aiming to address the topic. In 1980, under the auspices of UNESCO, an attempt to write a world music history was undertaken,[4] but never came to fruition. This may be because, as in other such attempts, certain overly restrictive priorities of ethnomusicology held sway, with proponents insisting on emphasizing cultural distinctives between musical traditions—a disposition that leads to a collection of musical histories rather than a coherent global music history. A clear example of this phenomenon can be seen in a recent attempt titled *The Cambridge History of World Music* (Bohlman 2013), which gingerly approaches the issues from the perspectives of multiple focused scholars and their specializations, with some trepidation about intercultural exchange that seems to have led to considerable reticence about any transcultural trajectory. Thus we have benefitted from increasingly detailed histories of various musics across time and space, but not as yet from a truly global music history.[5]

This book is not a collection of musical histories. Indeed it is not a comprehensive history of any particular musical culture, but rather a history of a certain metaculture—one that has been advancing, retreating, and advancing again from within the global milieu that has emerged over the past five thousand years. The term "global" is thus used advisedly here. Though perpetually under suspicion, the concept of globalization as interpreted in this book nevertheless provides a coherent thesis: that the cultures of humankind have been increasingly shaped by one another on an accelerating trajectory as travel and communication speeds have increased. With such a state comes increasing interdependence, since the evident inter/transcultural results are otherwise incomprehensible. This does not mean that difference has been erased (as if it could be), but rather that isolation is practically impossible. Thus, with instantaneous exchange now comes constant transformation—which is intercultural to begin with—leading to new transcultural phenomena. The nature of this issue will be revisited in Chapter 10 at the end of the book, after examples of its evidence in human history from roughly 3500 BCE to the present have been reviewed.

In such a milieu, and with such hindsight, a coherent theory is needed by which a single global music history might reasonably be conceived. Moreover, as I have argued previously (Hijleh 2012), there is a practical dimension to the question of how music history should be written and presented in the context of the education of both musicians and thoughtful musical connoisseurs in our time. No one can learn all of the special histories of every musical culture, least of all students in the formative stages of their development (i.e., through the undergraduate years). A single, manageable narrative is needed for the development of global musicianship for a global age. *Twenty-first-century musicians can and should become experts in understanding human musical history as a history of synthesis.* This is both an imperative and a dilemma. In that sense, we are actually in need of a global musicology, a synergy of theoretical/analytical and historical perspectives and tools for how music has evolved as globalization has unfolded over millennia.

There have been three particularly pivotal inter/transcultural convergences that can be seen as defining the shape of human musical history. Each has led to the next in some ways, and each was part of the acceleration into this age of global instantaneous exchange in which we of the twenty-first century find ourselves. Two of these convergences coalesced in the Afro-Eurasian Old World and the third in the New World of the Americas. The first unfolded from about 200 BCE to 900 CE along a collection of developing trade pathways across the heart of Central Asia, one of which dipped further south into Indian and Persian territory, that came to be called the Silk Road. This Road was anchored by two great empires on either end—Rome in the West and Han China in the East—but encompassed a wide variety of cultures in between that had considerable impact. The second convergence arose in North Africa, the Iberian peninsula, and further north into other parts of Europe from about 700 to 1500 CE, emerging and spreading from what the Arabs called *al-Andalus*. And the third sprang dramatically from about 1500 CE in the Americas with the full flowering of Atlantic culture, proceeded to accelerate into and through the twentieth century, and finally exploded into the current transcultural age.[6] For the purposes of defining a global music history, the musical cultures of all regions are best considered in the context of their respective roles within any or all of these pivotal convergences. Western European music history, for example, is most important in the scheme of convergences two and three rather than in isolation. The issues surrounding the difficult but inevitable choices this approach demands are explored later in this chapter.

This book, to some degree in combination with my previous volume *Towards a Global Music Theory*, is meant to serve the global musicianship project by helping to form and inform global musicologists.[7] The ability to see a wide range of pitch schemes, rhythmic features, musical textures, and processes as individual cultural expressions of qualified human music universals across many times and spaces, as suggested in *Towards a Global Music Theory*, aids in demonstrating how fusion and subsequent transformation emerge out of the interchange of distinctive musical cultures over time. However, it is important to distinguish further the notion of a global music *history* from any sense of a global musical *style*. In the thesis of this book, styles are being constantly forged and reforged through the processes of intercultural convergence, fusion, and transformation—and in fact, one could argue that certain styles dominate globally in certain eras—but no one absolutely global style has emerged or is yet clearly emerging as a result. History thus far has demonstrated that human cultural products remain resistant to the kind of massive consolidation that would be required for a global musical style to coalesce for very long. Therefore "transcultural" here does not imply the consolidation of any single style. Rather, it is shorthand for the specific expressions of these musical universals in various combinations. Because there is a dynamic boundary between interculturality and transculturality in that sense, the term "inter/transcultural" is used freely in this study to capture the resulting tensions.

Global music history: sources, people, and defining characteristics

What constitutes an established musical culture? And how is its history preserved? In a sweeping global context, a broad range of sources must be understood as legitimate. These might include:

- Literary description: When one considers how much more of history can be gleaned from written sources—that is, from the time that language, communication, and eventually music itself appeared in written forms—one understands why this classic element has held sway in making difficult choices.[8] Music history, like much other history, benefits greatly from the preserved written word, a compilation of countless eons of speech just as musical notation normally reflects music in its elemental—and much more important—incarnation as sound. There are visual depictions and other anthropological evidence that tells us much, but the most helpful of these do not appear to pre-date written sources.

- Visual depiction: Music being performed, music being experienced—pictures of these moments can provide priceless insights into the way music has been manifested in particular times and places.
- Organology (musical instrument design and use): This turns out to be at or near the top in order of importance for tracing ways in which qualified musical universals are manifested historically within and across cultures, since some instruments actually survive archaeologically while others can be recreated from visual depiction or even literary description. Several chapters that follow will therefore feature spotlights on individual instruments or categories that represent such developments throughout global music history, though how instruments were actually played is not always entirely clear. Likewise, though the nature of singing across the ages cannot be so readily captured as with instruments, many questions about the development of singing style are highly relevant, and will be addressed as evidence permits.
- Theoretical principles: Some cultures—starting with the ancient Sumerians, Babylonians, and Greeks—left evidence of pitch, rhythmic, and formal principles for their musics. These are very often encoded jointly in the associated organologies. By the time of the second pivotal convergence, treatises on music theory are more common and often more detailed, though these later theories owe much to basic acoustic principles established very early on.
- Pitch and/or rhythmic notation: This has been considered something of a convenient dividing line with regard to the implications of written vs. oral traditions. Certainly historical evidence comes differently in each of those contexts. One is left with a number of foundational questions, though, including: How much *can* music notation capture? How much *should* it? The issue of fixedness arises in many instances as a result. Into the twentieth century, sound recording technology becomes a critical part of that issue as well, as does both the promise and the limits of attempting to capture orally oriented musics through notated transcription.
- Living oral/performance tradition: Outside of written notation or sound recording, preserved performance traditions offer much insight. However, the fact that these evolve(d) over time at varying rates—a phenomenon that reinforces the evolutionary nature of music generally—must be considered. Moreover, observation—and certainly its interpretation by the observer—can color results. Therefore, though observation of preserved traditions is valuable, it cannot be considered definitive with regard to preservation. Rather, it is definitive of music as a living tradition and not a fixed one, no matter how much practitioners may insist on the latter.

In addition, several contextual roles of music embedded in cultures can usefully be kept in mind throughout. Each of these could serve as the basis for a separate book; in this study they serve simply as passing contexts to the broad outline of the story:

- Music and religion
- Music and work
- Music and entertainment
- Music and social ritual
- The historically rare concept of "absolute" music for contemplative listening

These categories can overlap significantly. "Absolute" music is typically a goal of art music, yet religious music intended for contemplation also often has the highest artistic standards in mind. Much music is entertaining even though it may have other goals.

In this context, dealing with genres is often more useful than dealing with repertoire. Though a few key examples of repertoire will be addressed in this study, a global music history will not necessarily yield a global music literature in the way a specific musical history from a specific culture might. Similarly, though reference to individual musicians and others who had profound effects on the course of musical developments is essential to the narrative, and though each chapter will highlight certain stories in the midst of the larger sweep, the global musicologist does not find a collection of figures who constitute a pantheon of global musicians. Or perhaps it is more accurate to say that this is true until the point in history is reached in which such figures began to be in near-term dialogue with one another in a globalized context, i.e., within the last 120 years or so. In that light, global repertoires and communities of globalized musicians will likely continue to develop and emerge.

Global regions: an overview of their roles and contributions

All regions of the world are important to the human musical story. Yet the influence of each on the *global* musical story, and the extent and the timing of that influence, varies greatly. The following provides a broad introductory overview of how each region and its cultural and commensurate musical contributions fit into the proposed paradigm, integrating chronology, geography, and force and depth of impact.

- The Nile-Indus corridor (McNeill and McNeill 2003) served as a key locus from which human civilization emerged, in Mesopotamia, Egypt, and the Indus Valley. This in turn provided context for the development of Central Asia as a transcultural hub. During the same eras, the Mediterranean–Aegean region (Greece and Rome) was developing—and in that context some of the first questions arise as to the level of inter/transcultural musical activity. Within this larger milieu, West Asian characteristics also formed, though very likely not as independently as may sometimes be presumed.
- North Africa and its connection to the Iberian peninsula was a critical locus from earliest times. Its later impact through France and into the rest of Western Europe as the latter came of age into the thirteenth century CE can and should be seen in tandem with the role of the Byzantine empire as an East-West mitigator.

- Though very ancient in the scope of human history, the expanded global influence of sub-Saharan (and especially West) African musics began later, in the European Colonial period in the Americas. Coupled with some earlier intercultural exchange along East African coastal areas, these musics cannot be disputed in their centrality to global music history. The emergence of a globalized New World (Central and South America, the Caribbean, North America), its truly hybrid music, and their worldwide exportation into the current age of instantaneous exchange—an age in which geography no longer defines "region" due to the nature of technology—was at the heart of this development.
- Meanwhile, in this context, East/Southeast Asia and Australasia/Oceania provide significant challenges due to their relative global isolation until the European Colonial period, though China was more exceptional in this regard because of the Silk Road.

In light of these perspectives, a different way of organizing a book like this might have been to consider the musical implications of Atlantic culture (the civilizations facing the Atlantic Ocean from both directions, and their encounters) and Pacific culture (civilizations facing the Pacific Ocean), with the rest of Afro-Eurasia in the middle as an anchor. The challenge for such a paradigm, as attractive as it may be, is that it masks the true flow of global musical history, which does begin with the sweep of inwardly looking Afro-Eurasia but then proceeds largely in an Atlantic-oriented direction and very little in a Pacific-oriented direction. The major countries of East and Southeast Asia, for example, including Australia and even Hawaii, exerted far more influence on music history via their role in Central Asian and later Atlantic culture than through any sort of clear Pacific paradigm. This is true even to the extent that, though the Americas were likely originally populated by Pacific peoples of various kinds, indigenous Americans only influenced global music history significantly in Mexico and further south—until the musical world was already globalized, allowing Pacific and native North American musics to join the conversation substantially. Even then, these cultures were profoundly redirected by the power of the other two super-regions and their histories. This is not a popular view in a world highly sensitized to maintaining and celebrating cultural difference rather than taking a clear-eyed view of cultural—in fact, inter/transcultural—influence, but it does offer a highly coherent explanation for the trajectories that can be observed.

Yet another way of organizing the subject might simply have been to follow human technological developments and their implications for musicking. This too is highly attractive, though it would likely give too little weight to aspects of culture that are more intangible—including religion or at least "spirituality" broadly defined, which turns out to be one of the most consistent contexts out of which human musics arise.[9] Music includes too many mysteries to be understood entirely naturalistically, again not always an especially popular perspective at present. One could also write a very interesting book on the roles of women evident in a global musical story that, even late in its trajectory, tends to be dominated by the names of men. That book should be written, and it is in many ways precisely the kind of project that could arise from the implications of the outline of this book, but it will only be touched on herein.

Beautiful musical histories on the global periphery—until later

It is thus inevitable that some wonderful musics figure more substantially in the global musical story only much later in history, when all musics began to be in dialogue. An example of this is Japanese *shakuhachi* music, which arose c. 650 CE, developed slowly over 500 years, and culminated in a revival during the eighteenth century (see Lee 1992 for details)—until wider travel and audio recording in the twentieth century resulted in its distinctive sound quality being appropriated frequently into media music as an exoticism, such as for films.[10] In that sense, the shakuhachi genre may represent a global history in miniature. Any number of other musics likewise gain a more significant place with the coming of accelerating travel and trade. These and every other human music of which we have evidence display particular manifestations of qualified musical universals that can and should be considered in the beautiful mosaic, even as the nature and extent of the respective global impact of each continues to evolve.

Three examples are particularly interesting in this regard, each in a different way. The first may be one of the oldest distinctive major musical cultures to arise intact while achieving a significant level of awareness from outsiders: the musics of the various forest peoples of Central Africa. Isolated from the majority of the wider world until at least the mid-to-late nineteenth century, the musics of tribes such as the BaAka (Aka) and the Mbuti developed relatively undisturbed and remained representative of more ancient sensibilities much longer than other comparable examples. Anthropologist Colin Turnbull, whose 1961 study *The Forest People* is considered seminal to the ethnomusicology of the Mbuti, noted in 1955:

> The [Mbuti] preserve a way of life and thought that is essentially their own...In music [they remain] unaffected not only by the more distant influences, but even by the practices of [more local neighbors]...The cultural isolation of the [Mbuti] is all the more remarkable in view of the close relationship in which they live with their Bantu masters.
>
> (1955:23–24)

Both Turnbull (1955:23) and Gerhard Kubik (2000:268) point out that these forest peoples have tended to influence their neighbors musically with their distinctive polyphony and yodeling style, rather than the other way around, emphasizing the preservation of its distinctiveness. Writing on the basis of her research from the 1980s, Michelle Kisliuk is careful to note that BaAka nearer to urban centers in their homeland "include in their repertory a form that mixes together hymns from various Christian sects, pop-song snippets from the radio, and rhythms and melodies from [a neighboring culture]" (2000:291)—that is, acknowledging that global influence has been unavoidable late in the twentieth century.

Yet even so, communities of other BaAka remained deeper in the forest with less such influence, and that when outside sources arrived in their midst, these were recontextualized rather rapidly (2000:298–306). This relatively one-way musical influence—from Central African forest peoples outward—remained intact late in the twentieth century and into the twenty-first.[11] Thus the global effect of this music and its place in the globalized milieu has come rather late in the historical trajectory.

Likewise, the legacies of Oceania—Australia, Melanesia (including New Guinea), Micronesia, and Polynesia (including New Zealand and Hawai'i), encompassing perhaps 25,000 islands and 30 million people (Kaeppler 1998:2)—are worthy of note, even if their ultimate influence on global musical history has not been as a strong. The surviving traditional cultures in the region may date back as far as 65,000 years, and they may very well have been the source of musics brought by some of the oldest colonists to the American Pacific coasts (see Chapter 4): The oldest audio recording of Oceanic music, a Samoan responsorial dance-song made at the World's Columbian Exposition in Chicago in 1893 (Kaeppler and Love 1998:1036), features a steady pulse and two or possibly three pitches (approximately C, D, and perhaps G, quite possibly an anhemitonic pentatonic subset) repeated many times in a rhythmically straightforward (unsyncopated) phrase that shares much with some Native North American musics. Yet these musics simply were not situated in the flow of developments that seems to have shaped the most coherent narrative. A substantial history of the music(s) of Oceania is difficult to write precisely because these were until relatively recently (no earlier than c. 1500 CE) significantly isolated from the larger currents of world history. Meanwhile, modern history has created a strong intercultural musical context in the region (Kaeppler 1998:6) that is reflective of the trajectory of global music history—but has not as yet itself contributed to that trajectory substantially. As a representative case study, Australian music provides a good example of the history of region, one to which this book will return to near the end (Chapter 10) because of its contextual and comparative value in the proposed paradigm.

Finally, the traditional music of Indonesia falls somewhere along the continuum of prominence in the global story, for it remained distinctive yet in dialogue with other musics for some time, even into the twentieth century, moving in and out of more globalized contexts. Balinese *gamelan gong kebyar*, for example, "is twentieth-century music in the genuine sense that many of its features, though naturally girded by time-tested, inherited musical practices, were invented and developed after 1900" (Tenzer 2000:4). It is probably true, though, that kebyar takes less from the past century than from the many centuries before. Even the indigenous elements of Indonesian music (and those of many other Southeast Asian cultures) were likely heavily influenced by Indian and probably Chinese musics relatively early into the first millennium (Fletcher 2001:268–281). And this is to say nothing of the effect of European settlers from the seventeenth century onward. Thus Indonesian music has been both a globally and a locally focused music at different times and in different ways.

The realities of these examples take nothing away from the intrinsic value or beauty of musics less determinative of global music history, nor from the people who conceive(d) and practice(d) them, but must be acknowledged as the natural result of looking through a lens based on global intercultural consequence. And that thought leads to another one about inclusion and what is often associated with its concerns—the matter of (in)justice.

A word on creativity and injustice

The musical story in this book is more inclusive than what has typically been put forward as music history. Yet there are at least two ways in which twenty-first-century citizens may feel uncomfortable as the coalescence of a global music history over millennia is examined. First, throughout the history of humanity on this planet, and not least in the convergences highlighted in this book, all was not sweetness and light. Suffering and injustice mark the human story. One fervently wishes that those who suffered tragedies might have been spared. But the human spirit and the dynamism of its musical expression have prevailed nevertheless. Indeed, some of the most important developments in global musical history have arisen out of the worst religious, political, and economic tensions and injustices. While it is logical to assume that a certain amount of order and agency is neces-sary for artistic development, even situations in which people were forced into lives of bare survival have featured music, sometimes the most interesting music. Life was very hard for many along the Silk Road, in medieval al-Andalus, and in the Americas since 1500 CE. People enslaved and brutalized one another. Even in the best of conditions, exploitation of one kind or another was often a fact of life. All of this tragically continues today, yet life-giving musical development has also continued. Intercultural convergence, fusion, and transformation do not come easily; living together in diversity is not for the faint of heart. But a global music history demonstrates that the greatness which can emerge from such a milieu is an authentic part of the enduring human legacy. Speaking of the origins of the Blues in the United States, Robert Palmer offers an excellent example: "Black American music as it was sung and played in the rural South was both a continuation of deep and tenacious African traditions and a creative response to a brutal, desperate situ-ation" (1981:39).

Second, the loss of specific musical cultures as they converge, fuse and trans-form into something different might be mourned. Yet economist Tyler Cowen emphasizes that the effect of economic globalization on the arts

> illustrates Joseph Schumpeter's metaphor of capitalist production as a gale of 'creative destruction'...Cross-cultural exchange, while it will alter and disrupt each society it touches, will support innovation and creative human energies...The world as a whole has a broader menu of choice, but older synthetic cultures must give way to newer synthetic cultures...The 'creative destruction' of the market...creates a plethora of innovative and

high-quality creations in many different genres, styles, and media…
Cross-cultural contact often mobilizes the creative fruits of an ethos before
disrupting or destroying it.

(2002:11, 17, 18, 55)

As Cowen aptly demonstrates, this phenomenon is readily apparent across music
history as part of cultural history, and more so since technology has made it
increasingly possible to observe over the course of a single lifetime. Nor has justice prevailed in the process: a survey of successful artistic movements across
time and space reveals that "the benefits of cultural exchange usually have come
from dynamic settings in great imbalance, rather than from calm or smoothly
working environments" (Cowen 2002:7). In these environments, individual people are hurt and specific cultures are absorbed or destroyed. A global music history acknowledges that culture is not static, and there is a cost to its dynamism.
Yet out of these fires arise the fresh moments of musical history that in time
come to define it until the next instance of creative destruction. In our time, these
moments come continuously, perhaps challenging the very notion of "music history" itself. Thus the costs of the resultant injustice are even greater in one sense,
while at the same time more opportunity for human musical expression is created
than ever before. In this second sense, human beings are as free musically now as
they ever have been.

Robert Baron and Ana Cara (2011), and some of their colleagues, have
essentially argued as well for the creatively positive possibilities of "creolization," which they define more broadly than the original meaning attached to
Latin American cultural studies: it is a "universal process that occurs anywhere
cultures encounter one another," and can be understood as offering "a critical
way of conceptualizing the emergence of cultural phenomena borne out of the
necessity to negotiate cultural differences and to resist dominance by asserting a
new local voice…Creolization is cultural creativity in process" (2011:3–4). This
clearly echoes Cowen's economic analysis, and it is at the heart of why this book
embraces an unflinching look at how global music history arose all too often, but
still successfully, from unjust milieus.

This touches also on the question surrounding what sort of historiography is
most illuminating for a global music history. To some degree, the famous dictum
that history is written by the victors cannot be avoided, but the writing of cultural
history can, should, and often does stand as something of a contrast to political-
military history. The final "victors" of culture are not always the political-military
victors. Despite borders and edicts, artistic expression has been more fluid. Indeed,
the argument of this book is that music's greatest energy comes precisely from
inter/transculturality, which must breach or at the very least severely push against
borders of many kinds. The victors of global music history are often very different
from the power-based victors of so-called traditional history, if one is willing to
adjust one's lenses. At heart, this is a book about the heroic genius of the human
musical spirit manifested across its fascinating and inspiring global history.

Notes

1 Quoted in Kim 2009:60.
2 Quoted in Keller 2007.
3 See also Hijleh 2012, Chapter 1.
4 See Vandor 1980; luminaries such as Nketia and Touma contributed in their areas of specialty, and work on the project continued at least through 1984 (Brook and Bain 1984).
5 Bruno Nettl has taken a thorough and interesting look at the relationships between Western music history, world music histories, world music history (writ larger), and ethnomusicology more than once recently (2010, 2013). I am deeply indebted to a number of authors who have courageously paved the way on this topic of late, especially Peter Fletcher for his monumental *World Musics in Context* (2001), to Patrick Savage and Steven Brown for reviving and updating the pursuit of "comparative musicology" (2013), and to Michael Church (2015) for bringing together eminent thinkers to consider key questions and findings. (And even Bohlman's 2013 collection of essays provides much value.) In addition, Peter van der Merwe came to many conclusions entirely consistent with my own in his *Origins of the Popular Style* (1989) decades earlier than almost all of these—but stopped short of their implications for a fully globalized music history.
6 In some ways, this final convergence is a continuously present one, and may signal the end of "music history" *per se*, though perhaps other transculturalities yet unimagined will emerge that propel the story further.
7 Andrew Brown and the other contributors to his volume *Sound Musicianship* (2012) provide further useful analysis and support for this general idea.
8 Bauer (2007:xxv–xxvii) make this general point about history and written sources in an especially well-nuanced way.
9 See Fletcher 2001, which both begins and ends with more or less this same insight.
10 The shakuhachi is used to considerable historical, cultural, and emotional effect, for example, in John Williams's score to the 1987 film *Empire of the Sun*.
11 Recording groups such as Deep Forest and Baka Beyond popularized key elements of the Central African forest peoples' style starting in the 1990s, while in 2003 pianist Pierre-Laurent Aimard wove together indigenous performances with African-inspired, rhythmically oriented works by contemporary Western composers György Ligeti and Steve Reich on a performance/recording event titled *African Rhythms*.

References

Baron, Robert, and Ana Cara (eds.). 2011. *Creolization as Cultural Creativity*. Jackson, Mississippi: University of Mississippi Press.

Bauer, Susan. 2007. *The History of the Ancient World*. New York: W.W. Norton.

Bohlman, Philip (ed.). 2013. *The Cambridge History of World Music*. New York: Cambridge University Press.

Brook, Barry, and David Bain. 1984. "Music in the Life of Man: Theoretical and Practical Foundations." *Yearbook for Traditional Music* 16: 155–165.

Brown, Andrew (ed). 2012. *Sound Musicianship: Understanding the Crafts of Music*. Newcastle upon Tyne: Cambridge Scholars Publishing.

Church, Michael (ed.). 2015. *The Other Classical Musics*. Woodbridge, Suffolk: Boydell and Brewer.

Cowen, Tyler. 2002. *Creative Destruction: How Globalization is Changing the World's Cultures*. Princeton, New Jersey: Princeton University Press.

Fletcher, Peter. 2001. *World Musics in Context*. New York: Oxford University Press.

Hijleh, Mark. 2012. *Towards a Global Music Theory*. Farnham, Surrey: Ashgate.

Kaeppler, Adrienne. 1998. "Profile of Oceania." In Kaeppler, Adrienne, and J. Love (eds.), *The Garland Encyclopedia of World Music, Volume 9: Australia and the Pacific Islands*, New York: Garland, 2–6.

Kaeppler, Adrienne, and J. Love (eds.). 1998. *The Garland Encyclopedia of World Music, Volume 9: Australia and the Pacific Islands*. New York: Garland.

Keller, Johanna. 2007. "Yo-Yo Ma's Edge Effect." *Chronicle of Higher Education (The Chronicle Review)* 5329: B10.

Kim, Young Yun. 2009. "The Identity Factor in Intercultural Competence." In Deardorff, Darla (ed.), *The SAGE Handbook of Intercultural Competence*, Los Angeles: Sage Publications, 53–65.

Kisliuk, Michelle. 2000. "Music Life in the Central African Republic." In Stone, Ruth (ed.), *The Garland Handbook of African Music*, New York: Garland Publishing, 291–306.

Kubik, Gerhard. 2000. "Central Africa: An Introduction." In Stone, Ruth (ed.), *The Garland Handbook of African Music*, New York: Garland Publishing, 260–290.

Lee, Riley. 1992. *Yearning for the Bell: A Study of Transmission in the Shakuhachi Honkyoku Tradition* (unpublished doctoral dissertation). Sydney, Australia: University of Sydney.

McNeill, J.R., and William McNeill. 2003. *The Human Web*. New York: W.W. Norton.

Nettl, Bruno. 2010. *Nettl's Elephant: On the History of Ethnomusicology*. Urbana, Illinois: University of Illinois Press.

Nettl, Bruno. 2013. "On World Music as a Concept in the History of Music Scholarship." In Bohlman, Philip (ed.), *The Cambridge History of World Music*, New York: Cambridge University Press, 23–54.

Palmer, Robert. 1981. *Deep Blues*. New York: Penguin.

Savage, Patrick, and Steven Brown. 2013. "Toward a New Comparative Musicology." *Analytical Approaches to World Music* 22: 148–197.

Stokes, Martin. 2004. "Music and the Global Order." *Annual Review of Anthropology* 33: 47–72.

Tenzer, Michael. 2000. *Gamelan Gong Kebyar: The Art of Twentieth-Century Balinese Music*. Chicago: University of Chicago Press.

Tenzer, Michael. 2006. "Introduction: Analysis, Categorization, and Theory of Musics of the World." In Tenzer, Michael (ed.), *Analytical Studies in World Music*, New York: Oxford University Press, 3–38.

Turnbull, Colin. 1955. "Pygmy Music and Ceremonial." *Man* 55: 23–24.

van der Merwe, Peter. 1989. *Origins of the Popular Style: The Antecedents of Twentieth-Century Popular Music*. New York: Oxford University Press.

Vandor, Ivan (ed.). 1980. "Towards a World Music History." *The World of Music* 22: 3.

Part I

The Afro-Eurasian Old World Web, c. 3500 BCE–1500 CE

2 Precedents to the Silk Road

[Prince] Gudea made the temple of Ningirsu to rise like the sun in his majesty... In the holy place was its lyre which sounded [like] a bellowing bull... To fill the front court of Eninnu with the joy of the flute, to banish the gloom of the city from the house of comfort with the stringed instrument, to quiet the heart, to soothe [the emotions], to dry tears in the eyes that weep, to diminish sorrows; [yet also] the raging of the lord like the sea, like the cleansing Euphrates, like a storm whose rumblings are sacred... [Prince Gudea], the builder of Eninnu, installed his beloved lyre Ushumgal-kalam-ma in the highest place for the lord Ningirsu... He brought Ushumgal-kalam-ma, the lyre, the cymbal, all roaring like a storm.

—From Gudean Cylinder inscriptions, Lagash, Sumer, c. 2100 BCE
(adapted from quotation in Price 1927)

David... set apart... [men] under the supervision of their father for the music of the temple of the LORD, with cymbals, lyres and harps, for the ministry at the house of God... Along with their relatives—all of them trained and skilled in music for the LORD—they numbered 288... Make music to the LORD with the harp, with the harp and the sound of singing, with trumpets and the blast of the ram's horn— shout for joy before the LORD, the King.

—Hebrew Bible, 1 Chronicles 25:1–7 and Psalm 98:5–6, relating
events traditionally dated to c. 1000 BCE

[The Egyptians] have one song about Linos—who is also sung about in Phoenicia, Cyprus and elsewhere, though by a different name—that is just like the one sung by the Hellenes about Linos. Among the many things I wonder about Egypt, I especially wonder where they got this song; apparently they have sung it since ancient times.

—Herodotus, *Histories* II:79 (Greece, c. 440 BCE)

The nymphs of heaven... desire to look upon Guttila the Musician... The maidens of the gods... wish to hear your music, Master... For the space of a week the Bodhisatta played [his seven-stringed harp] to them, and his music surpassed the music of heaven.

—From the Guttila Jātaka, Buddhist India, c. 400 BCE
(adapted from Rouse 1895)

Figure 2.1 Detail of wall painting showing two different types of lutes and double-tubed wind instrument, Theban tomb of Nebamun, Egyptian Dynasty XVIII, c. 1350 BCE.

Global music pre-history

How might we define the most useful point of entry for a global music history? Since intercultural convergence, fusion, and transformation are proposed as the key elements in this particular musical story, identifying when those processes first arose and how they began to affect human musical development is the first order of business. Chapter 3 of this study addresses the question by suggesting that the rise of the Silk Road, running back and forth in both directions through Central Asia, provided exceptionally fertile ground that encouraged the acceleration of global musical exchange. And yet there is significant human history that pre-dates such times. In this context, key evidence of musical origins in Afro-Eurasia prior to about 200 BCE can be understood as precedents to the Silk Road, the critical inputs leading to that first pivotal convergence. Examination of these precedents also reveals much else that is useful in understanding the story of human musicality.

As noted earlier, every known human culture has music, and there is therefore no reason to doubt that human beings were musical from their origins. What this really means, however, is far from simple. Derek Bickerton, for example, notes that

> the whole process by which the human species developed...includes acquisition of language, of music, of mathematics, of logic, of self-consciousness; all those traits that either have no equivalent in other species or that are developed to a degree unknown in other species. It would be bizarre to suppose that all of these capacities developed autonomously and independently, without constantly influencing one another.
>
> (2000:161)

Much interest (and controversy) surrounds the relationship between music, language, and communication as early human traits, especially since it is logical to assume that at least a substantial part of the earliest music came in vocal form.[1] The research makes clear, however, that there is little consensus around how language, music, and communication work in tandem now, let alone how they may have functioned within the human brain early in its history, and it is appropriate to recognize that *meaning* does not flow from musical sound in the same ways as from words.[2]

In any case, the question of how far back one might reach to find the earliest days of humanity is not crucial for the purposes of a global music history as envisioned in this volume. Many arguments are being made today about the musicality of early humanity in comparison to non-human animals, for example.[3] But that discussion is not something on which this history depends for its salience, because this is a history about the cross-cultural nature of human musical development and not the psycho-physical details of intrinsic human musicality. This history assumes the view that human musical expression did originally and now continues to reside first in fundamental physicalities—including the rhythmic movement of the body and the acoustics of the singing voice. But that too is not definitive for making historical choices, because evidence of musical instruments appears to date from well before such a distinction would have significant cultural meaning: at least 35,000–40,000 years ago and still counting backward as new discoveries are made.[4] So, for all practical historical purposes, humanity has always been singing, dancing, and making and playing instruments, with and without words, for various purposes of communication or merely for entertainment.

All of this is pre-history for music as for other purposes. Humans have had culture, including music, from the beginning. However, a useful distinction between "culture" and "civilization" in human history can be made that suggests that while music itself is a cultural feature, music *history* is more richly understood in a civilizational context. J.R. McNeill and William McNeill call this context "The Human Web," noting that "the exchange and spread of...information, items, and inconveniences, and human responses to them, is what shapes history" (2003:4). Whether music itself is "information" might be a matter of debate, but it is clear that where items and information are exchanged and spread, music is among the things that accompany these human activities.

J.M. Roberts (2004:2, 36) draws the distinction between culture and civilization by suggesting that the latter means "the interaction of human beings in a very creative way, when, as it were, a critical mass of cultural potential and a certain surplus of resources have been built up...[, releasing] human capacities for development at quite a new level," noting further that after about 1500 BCE "there are no civilizations to be explained which appear without the stimulus, shock or inheritance provided by others which have appeared earlier" (2004:42). Like the McNeills, Roberts implicitly argues that it is travel and trade (understood broadly) among peoples with real differences that provide the context for this cross-cultural feature of civilization (2004:43–45). More specifically, Roberts notes that

> It is in [western Asia and the eastern Mediterranean] that the stimulating effects of different cultures upon one another first became obvious and no doubt it is much of the story of the appearance of the earliest civilizations there...The Fertile Crescent was to be for most of historic times a great crucible of cultures, a zone not only of settlement but of transit, through which flowed an ebb and flow of people and ideas. In the end, this produced a fertile interchange of institutions, language and belief from which stems much of human thought and custom today.
>
> (2004:45)

Roberts explicates further the roots of this "cradle of civilization," emphasizing the importance of foundational linguistic groups that intermixed over time in the Fertile Crescent: by about 4000 BCE these included Hamitic (from Africa north of the Sahara), Indo-European (from southern Russia into Europe and Iran), and true Caucasian (from Georgia) lines, with one of the most important additional dynamics resulting from Semitic peoples (from the Arabian peninsula) integrating into the region over the subsequent millennium (2004:47).

Perhaps less clear, especially in this context, is the history of the peoples who migrated much earlier and much further east, including those that crossed over what was then the land bridge of Beringia into the Americas.[5] In any case, East Asian peoples were to remain relatively isolated until the rise of the Silk Road proper, and those in the Americas profoundly isolated from the rest of the world for much longer than that. We will return to the relevant musical features and contributions of these cultures in due course.

Meanwhile, there is ample evidence of extensive Bronze Age cultural exchange and interdependence beginning c. 3500 BCE, the effects of which are even more striking in light of the Bronze Age collapse of c. 1206–1150 BCE. In the preface to his study of that historical moment, Eric Cline notes that

> discussing "collapses" and comparing the rise and fall of empires is not a new idea; ...[many scholars have considered] how a single empire or a single civilization came to an end—the Romans, the Maya, the Mongols, and

so forth. Here [c. 1177 BCE], we are considering a globalized world system with multiple civilizations all interacting and at least partially dependent upon each other. There are only a few instances in history of such globalized world systems; the one in place during the Late Bronze Age and the one in place today are two of the most obvious examples.

(2014:xvi)

In this context we may posit a global music pre-history, a set of precedents to the Silk Road that commenced with the relatively well-documented Sumerian musical culture of southern Mesopotamia c. 3500 BCE and focused on the interaction of civilizations along the Nile-Indus corridor in various ways through c. 200 BCE, when the stability of Rome and Han China gave rise to the first full iteration of the Silk Road itself.

Musical characteristics and interactions across early civilizational centers

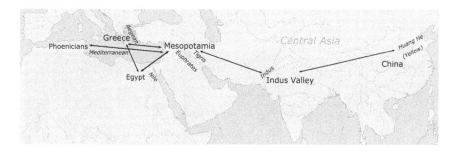

Figure 2.2 Map of early civilizational centers.

Roots: Mesopotamia, Egypt, the Mediterranean-Aegean and the Indus Valley

Others have provided extended studies on what we know of the earliest musics in various individual civilizations, such as Lise Manniche's explication of ancient Egyptian music (1991), Francis Galpin's study of Mesopotamian music (1937), and Giovanni Comotti's treatise on music in Greek and Roman culture (1979). The full details of these topics need not be repeated here. Rather, careful examination of the evidence in such studies reveals a plausible case for shared musical elements between Egyptian, Mesopotamian, and Mediterranean–Aegean cultures in the ancient world (likely with at least some contemporaneous connections to the Indus Valley). These shared elements include scalar material based on acoustic understanding of stopped strings and tubing lengths built on ratios of 3:2 (pure/perfect 5ths[6]) using similar chordophones and flutes, as indicated in Sumerian, Babylonian, and Greek treatises and implied pictorially in Egypt; Curt Sachs (1943:63–100) and more recently Peter Fletcher (2001:77–88, 118–124) have previously charted successful paths towards this perspective. West (1994) documents the tuning systems of Babylonian lyres—dating back to at least c. 1800 BCE and possibly as early as c. 2200 BCE—as heptatonic/diatonic resulting from 3:2 ratios in precisely the same way as what is now termed Pythagorean tuning, and Marcelle Duchesne-Guillemin goes further in linking these discoveries to Greek music itself (1967; 1984:84–85).

Illuminating comparative transcriptions are found in the sources named above—though necessarily produced with some speculation. For example, M.L. West (1994:177), eschewing any attempt to recreate rhythm from scant evidence, transcribes the pitch sequences of one Hurrian hymn melody (c. 1250–1200 BCE) in which all seven diatonic pitches are included, oriented in their arrangement as what today is called "Dorian" mode. Meanwhile Duchesne-Guillemin presents transcriptions (with rhythm) of Ugarit, Jewish, and Syro-Chaldean chant side by side (1984:29–32), showing correspondences.

Comparisons of musical depictions on Mesopotamian artifacts such as the Royal Standard of Ur (c. 2600–2400 BCE) and in literary sources with those on Egyptian tombs and in proto-Greek figurative and literary arts in the same broad range of dates make plain the shared musical perspectives, especially organologically (Manniche 1991; Comotti 1979:5).[7]

Figure 2.3 Detail of harp from Royal Standard of Ur (left); detail of Greek chordophones from amphora (right).

The harps, lyres, flutes, and sometimes reeds featured in these sources constitute the most obvious physical modeling of mathematical-musical pitch ratios, which is why they figure so prominently and so early in the story alongside vocal music. These instrument designs would most likely have led musicians towards similar basic pitch and timbral results upon which to build. And as they encountered their counterparts in the intercultural contexts suggested by this chapter, they would naturally have explored an expanding set of expressive micro-tonal and micro-timbral variations. As West summarizes it, "when one surveys the development and spread of musical instruments in the eastern Mediterranean and western Asia between 3000 and 500 BC, it appears natural to see the whole area as a cultural continuum, with much regional variety and individuality of musical practice but *no fundamental antinomies*" (1994:179, emphasis added). Another way to put this is that fundamental similarities provided the grounding upon which individual cultural varieties might exert mutual influence.

Less is known about the relationships between the rhythmic features of these early musics. Manniche (1991) cites Hans Hickman's theory of the "chironomist"—a sort of conductor or leader, usually a singer who is not playing an instrument—as depicted in Egyptian musical scenes, noting that these figures may be directing the performers' hand positions and resultant pitch structures, or the rhythmic/metrical material, or both. More is known about Greek musical rhythm after c. 800 BCE, as treatises indicate the relationships to poetic metrical structures (Comotti 1979:12). This raises the question of how vocal musics in all these cultures developed, though it is reasonable to assume that language exerted a profound rhythmic influence on each context—as is readily observable in the many ways existing vocal musics conform rhythmically to the languages in which they are written.[8] In a situation in which travel and trade were the key milieus in which musics would be shared interculturally, it is not unlikely that the cadences of various languages were experienced. Any other speculation on rhythm, including in Mesopotamian music and music as described in the Hebrew scriptures, relies on imagining what might have created the moods, from contemplative to raucous, that are extant in visual and written depictions of musical contexts (religious worship, civic celebrations, dance festivals, displays of virtuosity, etc.).

Within the same broad time frame, at more of a remove on the Eastern outskirts of the Nile-Indus corridor, lies clear evidence of a flourishing Indus Valley civilization in Harappa and Mohenjo-Daro, near what is now Pakistan, beginning c. 2500 BCE (Bauer 2007:104–109). This area had robust land and sea trade routes with contemporaneous Mesopotamia (Kishore and Ganpati 2003:6). While the musical details of this early civilization are not as clear as in the Fertile Crescent, Prem Kishore and Anuradha Ganpati (2003:10) suggest tenuous allusions to its religious music in the later Rig Veda (c. 1500–500 BCE). Reis Flora notes that "it is reasonable to conjecture that the four categories [of musical instruments] identified in the *Natyasastra*[9] had already been in use among the people of the fertile Indus river valley for over two millennia," from the time of Harappa and Mohenjo-Daro (2000:319). Flora identifies these categories, in order of cultural prominence, as chordophones, membranophones, idiophones, and aerophones, and notes that both rattles and small vessel flutes have been recovered from these city sites (2000:319–322). During this same period, Egyptians venerated their sistrums and other similar rattles as instruments of religious significance (Manniche 1991:62–63).

In all these instances, music was (and is) important to religious purposes. And because the interchange of Hamitic, Semitic, and Caucasian peoples was a foundational developmental feature of early intercultural history, it is also important that the same sorts of musical elements throughout this corridor are featured prominently in the long and well-documented history of the Hebrews. While there is significant dispute about the value of the Old Testament as a concurrent historical document, it is clear that music was important to Hebrew culture from its origins. The first figure in the Hebrew bible upon which there is wide consensus regarding external historic verifiability is king Ahab, c. 853 BCE (1 Kings 17; 2 Chronicles 18; Kurkh Monolith inscription of Assyrian Shalmaneser III). This is after the story of Solomon, whose famous father King David is noted for his musical prowess on the harp or lyre (1 Samuel 16:15–23). However, the traditional date of the much earlier Hebrew patriarch Abraham's birth is c. 2100 BCE, and historians such as Susan Bauer (2007:127) see the Masoretic text from which that date and other early events are derived as having historical, even chronological value.[10] Moreover, Abraham's (Abram's) city of origin is listed as Ur, within the same Sumerian area noted above.

Beyond this context, we cannot date the lifespan of the first musical figure whose personal identity is recorded for us in the Hebrew Bible: a Semite named Jubal, son of Lamech and Adah, of the line of Cain and the seventh generation after the biblical first people Adam and Eve. The text declares simply that Jubal was "the father of all those who play the lyre and flute" (Genesis 4:21), and provides a genealogical record that places him well before Abraham (and thus ostensibly prior to 2100 BCE). Alas, we know nothing of Jubal's musical profile other than what is written in the verse above. Nevertheless, it is interesting that Jubal's musical distinctive is an instrumental rather than a vocal one, and the mention of lyre and flute specifically is significant in light of the extant organological evidence noted earlier.

As demonstrated in the quotes that introduce this chapter, Old Testament passages about music for religious worship—such as 1 Chronicles 25:1–7, relating events traditionally dated to c. 1000 BCE—parallel descriptions of Mesopotamian worship in important ways. The geographical proximities of these cultural groups, along with numerous Old Testament passages about the interactions of Hebrews with surrounding Semitic societies (including Egypt), strongly suggest cross-pollination. Fletcher draws an interesting parallel between the Jewish use of the ram's horn (*shofar*),[11] the Buddhist use of the conch shell, and the use of the kudu horn in sub-Saharan Africa as a signaling "trumpet" in religious contexts, noting also that the member of the Levite tribe identified in the scriptural passages above were employed as prized musicians along the Nile-Indus corridor (2001:135). Sachs provides evidence from the Talmudic Tamid from Babylonian times of their musical prowess and elaborate culture, and spends considerable time outlining the details of the melodic structures used (1943:61, 79–95).

Out of the Bronze Ages: expansions as the corridor strengthens

Around c. 1000 BCE, the Mediterranean world was undergoing a profound re-formation after the Bronze Age collapse referenced earlier. One key culture in that restoration was that of the Phoenicians, fierce Semitic traders who began their colonization of North Africa and the formation of Carthage around the same time. This development would lead to important intercultural connections through Iberia into the rest of Europe, resulting in profound influences well into the age of al-Andalus (see Chapter 5). The Phoenicians and their famous port cities of Tyre and Sydon in Asia minor were well known to both the Hebrews and the Egyptians, and thus they participated fully in the same intercultural milieus featured throughout this chapter. Tyre itself would eventually become an important destination on the Western end of the Silk Road (see Chapter 4).

Musically, these broad regional interactions had been going on for some time. Manniche (1991:37–38) reproduces an image, appearing on an Egyptian tomb at Beni Hassan (12th Dynasty, Middle Kingdom, c. 1990–1800 BCE), of a bedouin man carrying what is clearly a West Asian lyre, and goes on to note another example:

> During the course of the 13th Dynasty [c. 1800–1650 BCE] merchants and artisans from the areas of Phoenicia and Canaan arriving in Egypt had settled there, and early migrants built their dwellings in the ruins of an old palace. One of these was found on excavation to contain a set of three hand drums. They are of a type known in modern Egypt as *darabukka*, a clay pot open at the lower end, with a membrane glued or laced to the upper rim. This drum is scarcely represented in ancient Egypt.
>
> (1991:38–39)

Today the *darabuka* and very similar drums such as the African *djembe* remain ubiquitous throughout the region (and, increasingly, throughout the rest of the world).

With regard to how the Aegean civilizations came to be within this same sphere, Scott Noegel notes that

> it is generally recognized that, during the Bronze Age, the Minoan civilization of Crete played a formative role in shaping the cultural contours of what was later to become Mycenaean Greece…However, it is also known that the Minoan civilization was itself greatly shaped by contacts with Egypt and with the civilizations of the eastern Mediterranean, including Mesopotamia.
>
> (2006:26)

This is important to discussion of the profile and role of the classical Greek civilization that emerged by c. 800 BCE, eventually giving rise to the intercultural Hellenistic world of Alexander the Great that can in turn be seen to have led to the Silk Road. Roberts sums up well the near certainty that these classical Greeks shared in (and in some instances inherited) the Nile-Indus milieu:

> Slaves may and foreign residents must have been among the many channels by which the Greeks continued to be influenced by the Near East long after

civilization had re-emerged in the Aegean. Homer[12] had already mentioned the *demiourgoi*, foreign craftsmen who must have brought with them to the cities of the Hellenes not only technical skill but the motifs and styles of other lands...When the Persians took Egypt in 525 [BCE], Greeks fought on each side. Some of these men must have returned to the Aegean, bringing with them new ideas and impressions. Meanwhile, there was all the time a continuing commercial and diplomatic intercourse between the Greek cities in Asia and their neighbors. The multiplicity of day-to-day exchanges resulting from the enterprise of the Greeks makes it very hard to distinguish native and foreign contributions to the culture of archaic Greece. One tempting area is art; here, just as Mycenae had reflected Asian models, so the animal motifs which decorate Greek bronze work, or the postures of goddesses such as Aphrodite, recall the art of the Near East. Later, the monumental architecture and statuary of Greece was to imitate Egypt's...Although the final product, the mature art of classical Greece, was unique, its roots lie far back in the renewal of ties with Asia in the eighth century [BCE]. What is not possible to delineate quickly is the slow subsequent irradiation of a process of intercultural interplay which was by the sixth century [BCE] working both ways, for Greece was by then both pupil and teacher.

(2004:177)

The famed Greek musical-mathematician Pythagoras (c. 560–470 BCE) reportedly explored Egyptian and Babylonian science that would correspond to the pitch acoustics noted earlier (Comotti 1979:27). In the following generation, Aristoxenus of Tarentum (fl. 335 BCE), peripatetic philosopher and pupil of Aristotle, penned the *Elements of Harmony* from which comes our earliest and most directly consolidated theoretical understanding of ancient Greek music.[13] However, Comotti makes clear that "the Greeks...did not know harmony, in the modern sense of the term, or polyphony; their music expressed itself through pure melodic line alone," and that "the rhythm of the musical performance was conditioned by the metrical form of the [poetic] verse" (1979:12). Aristonxenus himself opens the *Elements of Harmony* by noting that "the branch of study that bears the name Harmonic is to be regarded as one of the several divisions or special sciences embraced by the general science that concerns itself with Melody," and then makes reference to "the profounder speculations which confront us when scales and keys are enlisted in the service of poetry" (Macran 1902:165). This monophonic approach (which at least theoretically included microtonal elements), focused on singing and sometimes on dance in religious rituals (as depicted visually), along with the ubiquity of the lyre (kithara) and the aulos (double-piped wind instrument) for accompaniment, highlights the similarities with other nearby cultures over time. That is, the interculturality (perhaps even transculturality) of musical practices was a critical part of regional musical development as the Aegeans joined the Nile-Indus corridor milieu. This point has tended to be lost in musical histories of Western Europe, in which the Greeks are characterized primarily as having brought forward the elements that led to Western harmony and polyphony, when in fact they also reflected the musical practices of the known world in and prior to their own time.[14]

It is important to reiterate here that these features are best understood as precedents to the transcultural transformational artistic nexus that arose with the Silk Road several centuries later. The level of musical sharing suggested would naturally have evolved in that direction as travel and trade networks strengthened, becoming more extended and more efficient.

Musical developments blossomed even further East and South as well, with the most reliable sources appearing a little earlier than the rise of classical Greece, and continuing thereafter. These developments included some of the "qualified universal" features (see Hijleh 2012:8–9) of the Nile-Indus-Aegean sphere, but also some that were more independent.

In India, after the disappearance of the much earlier Indus Valley civilization previously noted, the foundational religious-musical texts Rig Veda ("hymns of praise") and Sama Veda ("knowledge of song [melodies]"), the Mahabharata (including the Bhagavad Gita), and the Ramayana all date from at least c. 1500–500 BCE. The veena (seven-stringed chordophone in various forms) and the flute both figure prominently along with singing in these foundational texts, which are themselves composed to be chanted, establishing the full infusion of music with the history, culture, and religious perspectives of India at various levels throughout. Kishore and Ganpati simply state that, based on the nature of these works, "the Aryans had a great love of music and song and constantly chanted and sang hymns" (2003:10). Fletcher notes that "the Vedic Sanskrit of the Rigveda show correspondences with the Old Iranian language of the Avesta (the Persian Scriptures); and both show correspondences with Hittite," suggesting that Vedic culture owed something to the West Asian contexts explored earlier in this chapter, though he also cautions that this is far from certain (2001:95). As Hinduism emerged from this early Indian context, a number of its cosmological elements affected the development of its music, not least the concept of time as cyclic rather than as progressive (see, e.g., Clayton 2000:10–26), and of pitch as emanating from *shruti* (at first "that which is heard," but later the essences of *unheard* musical notes; see Fletcher 2001:244–246). Both of these are inextricably wedded to religious aims around the idea of the interconnectedness of humanity with the universe. This Hindu perspective was in marked contrast to the Greek view—as Fletcher puts it, "where Indians believed that sound emanates from immaterial ether, Greeks believed that sound emanates from impact" (2001:126). For the Greeks, that is, sound came from a series (rather than a cycle) of articulated interactions that create linear form. In many ways this distinction remains the most profound one between the musical sensibilities of East and West, adding a great deal of dynamism to the story of global musical development even to the present day.[15]

Within early Indian societies, Buddhism arose as something of a reform to Hinduism. While there are deep differences, the two belief systems therefore share some of the same cosmological underpinnings that result in shared musical features, particularly around the creation of meditative states. Bo Lawergren (1994) details the role of music in the life of the Buddha, born Siddhartha Gautama

c. 565 BCE into something of a privileged family. Siddhartha was surrounded by music and other sensual pleasures, but later renounced such pursuits for an asceticism designed to lead to enlightenment. As will be discussed in Chapter 4, a number of complexities emerged around cultural and artistic expressions as Buddhism developed into a Central and East Asian religion through the new millennium CE. Within 200 years of the death of the Buddha, for example, an account of the homage paid to him by followers mentions "dancing, and hymns, and music,...garlands and perfumes" (Lawergren 1994:228), an obvious softening of the rejection of music and other sensual delights.

Even further East, from its place outside the original Nile-Indus-Aegean corridor, Chinese *civilization* dates back to at least c. 2000 BCE, though, like many of the earliest civilizations, aspects of its *culture* are much older. Interestingly, in his study of China in world history, Paul Ropp observes "that all the great civilizations except China's have been melting pots of many divergent peoples, languages and cultures" (2010:xi, reflecting Diamond 1999). Not until the advent of the Silk Road did China begin to influence music history as part of a more global melting pot, even as it developed contemporaneously with classical Greece. Ropp points out one profound difference that clearly influenced Chinese culture and its musical orientation:

> In contrast to so many other societies, the early Chinese accepted the world and human existence as facts of life that needed no supernatural explanation or divine creator...[, thus crediting] advancements in civilization to human beings, not to gods or divinities. This optimistic humanism became one of the distinctive aspects of Chinese thought and culture up to modern times. It stands in sharp contrast to the ancient Greek fascination with tragedies, to the jealous tribal God of Judaism, Christianity, and Islam, and to the elaborate metaphysical speculations of Indian mystics.
>
> (2010:2)

This may help to explain the early (and ongoing) technological achievements of the Chinese, as well as their attitudes towards music as a human activity in a material world, though the later arrival of Buddhism would color that perspective.

The first reference to China's most ancient and ethically foundational chordophonic instrument, the *guqin* (seven-stringed zither) or simply *qin*, is found in the *Shujing* (Book of History) and the *Shijing* (Book of Odes), dated to c. 1000–600 BCE (Kouwenhoven 2015:113) during the first half of the approximately 900-year rule of the Zhou dynasty. Out of this era arose Confucius (551–479 BCE), who established the centrality of ritual and music to honor ancestors, elaborate government and court structures, and philosophical non-religious foundations of order—and was known to be a qin player. The ethos of the qin as directly preserved historically reflects the formal seriousness of Confucianism that pervades Chinese cultural roots. The instrument has strings normally tuned to C-D-F-G-A-C-D—mode three of world (anhemitonic) pentatonic, arising from the most fundamental stack of 3:2 ratios (see Hijleh 2012:70–71)—and is strongly associated with the natural world, and with its assumed ability to "sound the cosmos" …[Players] foster a dream of spiritual communion with nature,…[aspiring] to attain wisdom and redemption with their art, and through it to live in blissful harmony with their environment.

(Kouwenhoven 2015:105)

Regarding the relationship between this ethos and the ubiquitous pentatonicism in Chinese music, Fletcher notes that

perhaps because of the persistent association of pitch with cosmological concepts,…the five pitches of the anhemitonic pentatonic scale (C-D-E-G-A), based on four steps of a fifth, in sequence, in quasi-Babylonian cycle-of-fifths procedure, became the backbone structure of the music.

(2001:333)

These lofty concepts, though, do not tell the whole story, for early Chinese musical culture also featured "rowdy dance spectacles and extravaganzas, as the tomb statues of disfigured drumming and singing dwarves show" (Kouwenhoven 2015:114). As will be explored in subsequent chapters, this mix of musical sensibilities proves important to understanding musical development along the Silk Road and indeed through every era of global musical history—that is, art musics and vernacular (popular) musics tend to be concurrently present and mutually influential.

The Hellenistic world and the seeds of the Silk Road

Within a century or two of the end of Zhou rule, Old World interculturality was enhanced by the establishment of the Hellenistic world forged by Alexander the Great and his associates starting c. 330 BCE. This world stretched from the Nile-Mediterranean-Aegean regions across Central Asia (Bactria and Sogdiana, which were to lie in the heart of the Silk Road, as well as Persia) and on to the outskirts of India (Taxila, which connected it culturally with a wide swath of central India even though Alexander advanced no further). In some ways, it was more of a culmination than a revolution. Kishore and Ganpati (2003:31) remind us, for example, that "India had already come into contact with Greece when Cyrus the Great of Persia (558–535 BCE) conquered the Greek cities of Asia Minor," and both Xinru Liu (2010:1–3) and Ropp (2010:8–9) make clear that the Chinese had a history of contact with a wide variety of Central Asian peoples long before Alexander arrived. Liu states simply that "it was the nomads on the Central Asian steppe who brought West and East together" (2010:1).

Alexander's empire did not survive his death in 323 BCE, and was immediately split into several kingdoms ruled by his closest generals and their descendants. Nevertheless, the Hellenistic aftermath of Alexander's conquests created both a vision and more robust economic conditions for trade and cultural exchange across Afro-Eurasia. Alexander himself had tried to encourage cultural synthesis by marrying a Bactrian (Sogdian) princess, Roxanne, and embracing Persian customs—including, one must imagine, Persian music. Bactria was perhaps the most far-flung region to remain significantly Hellenized despite falling to Central Asian tribes by c. 127 BCE and eventually embracing both Zoroastrianism and Buddhism, all of which makes it especially important to the Silk Road history that followed. From the other direction, East to West, it is interesting that China sought diplomatic relations with the Parthians after the latter (who had been part of Achaemenid Persia) reemerged from under the rule of the descendants of Seleucus (one of Alexander's generals) and pushed their territorial boundaries all the way back to the Euphrates (Roberts 2004:224–225). Meanwhile, the Mauryan (Indian) king Asoka (r. 269–232 BCE) built government buildings "in the Persian style," which likely influenced the many Buddhist *stupas* (temples) he also commissioned, "sent Buddhist missionaries to preach the concept of *dharma* [*dhamma*; essentially 'beneficent, non-violent righteousness'] in Egypt and [Greek] Macedonia,...maintained friendly relations with the rulers of the Hellenistic world," and presided over adoption of many Greek customs among his subjects (Kishore and Ganpati 2003:38–39). Thus the stage was set for a continuous stream of Greco-Persian, Indian, and Chinese influences in both directions across Central Asia, as well as much to be gained by these civilizations from Central Asian tribes.

Just as importantly, however, Alexander and his successors established the conditions under which a deeply Hellenized Rome would unite the western third of Afro-Eurasia, extending it further West across the rest of North Africa, Iberia, and into the heart of Europe. The flourishing of Alexandria in Egypt under the Ptolemies was itself one of the most important cultural milestones of the ancient world, preserving and further developing knowledge—including musical theory and practice—on the basis of what the Greek homeland had accomplished, but in a new intercultural context.[16] Hellenized Byzantium, strategically located on the Bosporus and the Black Sea, also served to bridge East and West geographically and culturally, eventually becoming the seat of Rome and an important source for early Christian and Western European music (see, e.g., Wellesz 1961:28–31). First, however, these dynamic loci of intercultural civilization were to play a role in the rise of what eventually became known as the Silk Road.

Spotlight: The global ubiquity of hand drumming

The use of the hands to beat out rhythms seems elemental to human musicality. The construction of instruments to color and amplify these rhythmic motions—drums—must certainly have arisen early. Membranophones and the wooden frames or cylinders across which the skins were stretched, along with the slit drum—a hollowed log with an opening cut into it to enhance resonance—could not have survived the millennia as some bone flutes have, but nevertheless likely came earlier (Blades 2005:44–45). The evidence is in the ubiquity of hand drums both pictorially from earliest times and in the oldest living traditions, especially in Asia and Africa.

Two morphological types of hand drums seem to have dominated global music history: goblet-shaped and bowl-shaped. The Middle Eastern/North African *darabuka* and the West African *djembe* referred to earlier in this chapter are examples of the first type. The djembe in particular has emerged within the last several decades as a global instrument, and likely began to spread through West Africa early in music history due to *Numu* blacksmiths among the Maninka people (Charry 2000:193, 213).

North Indian *tabla* (played in pairs) constitute perhaps the best-known example of hand-played bowl drums, and have a long association with spoken syllables that define the strokes. One stone relief in the Bhaja caves of western India, dating to the second century BCE, appears to depict a musician playing a pair of hand drums that could be precursors of the tabla. Interesting comparisons can be made between tabla and the small pairs of Cuban bongos, though the latter are not closed-bottom bowls and also clearly have strong African ties.

Two other common types of hand drums should also be mentioned: frame-constructed and hourglass-shaped. Frame drums, especially round shapes, appear most commonly in African and Arabic cultures, perhaps because of considerable cross-pollination between cultures from both regions. The North African *bandir* and the Persian-Arab *daf*, for example, can be quite similar both in construction and performance. Hourglass drums played with the hands include the Indian *deru* and the Japanese *tsuzumi*. One particularly interesting hand drum in which the hourglass shape is carved inside a tapering cylindrical outer body is the Indonesian *kendang*, a part of *gamelan* ensembles (Tenzer 2000:48). Finally, hand drums made from clay or other earthenware are also popular due to their distinctive sounds; the Nigerian (Igbo) *udu* and the South Indian *ghatam* are among the most frequently encountered of these.

Notes

1 See in Nils Wallin, et al., 2000, e.g., Bickerton; Brown; Frayer and Nicolay; Hauser; Marler; Merker; Molino; Richman; and Ujhelyi.
2 DeNora (1986) provides an interesting take on and a good summary of this point.
3 See again, e.g., Wallin et al., 2000.
4 See, e.g., Conard, et al., 2009. One could also speculate on the first archer's bows, from which experience of pitch from the chordophonic twang of the stretched "string" might first have been noticed; there is secondary evidence of the use of bows and arrows some 70,000+ years ago (see, e.g., Wayman 2012). Finally, the physical conditions needed to produce musical sounds from idiophones like hollow gourds or membranophones with stretched skins are so rudimentary that it is difficult to imagine that they too did not arise very early in human experience, though the materials involved would not have survived the necessary millennia.
5 See, e.g., extended analysis in Steven Oppenheimer (2004).
6 The topic of what I have elsewhere (Hijleh 2012) called the "world pentatonic" pitch collection/structure, otherwise known as anhemitonic pentatonic, and the ubiquity of it and its subsets in indigenous musics worldwide is treated effectively by Mieczyslaw Kolinski (1957). Extension of this same principle yields the diatonic and chromatic scales, leading all the way up the stack to a useful 52-note set with many levels of microtonality that can, conceptually at least, accommodate a wide variety of known pitch approaches in world musics.

7 A great deal of organological correspondence across considerable time and space, based on foundational acoustic principles, is provided pictorially by Carl Engel (1875).

8 Aniruddh Patel (2006), for example, affirms at least some key connections between language and musical rhythm, though the full nature of this relationship is not clear.

9 Because its author, Sage Bharata Muni, lived during the rise of the Silk Road proper, the *Natyasastra* will be discussed further in Chapter 3.

10 In addition, see Daniel Pioski (2015) regarding the historicity of King David in relationship to other contemporaneous local cultures that have been documented.

11 *Yovel*, akin to the name Jubal, is the Hebrew word for "ram."

12 Likely flourished between c. 1102 and 850 BCE.

13 Aristoxenian ideas have sometimes been seen as in tension with those of the Pythagoreans, but Norman Cazden (1958) has shown how they are rather more complementary, and reconcilable at a fundamental level. The essence of this issue can also be dealt with by accepting pure ratios as basic to the perception of consonance and dissonance while at the same time recognizing the contextual variability of timbre and tuning in musical performance, leading to an expanded theory of pitch and a much larger master pitch set out of which global musical subsets tend to arise and which can encompass a wider variety of microtonalities (see Hijleh 2012:59–108).

14 M.L. West explores this issue effectively in the Epilogue to his *Ancient Greek Music* (1992:386–390). Henry G. Farmer (1930:117–129) offers further analytical interpretation of evidence reinforcing the notion that Greek musical advances were intertwined with earlier West Asian knowledge.

15 Lewis Rowell 1979 also details the many subtleties of ancient Greek, Indian, and Chinese conceptions of musical time.

16 See, e.g., Sachs 1943:212–213 and Comotti 1979:83. Sachs (1943:71), citing a description by the historian Josephus in his *Antiquities of the Jews*, also suggests the potential for intriguing correspondences between the tuning design of first-century CE Egyptian harps and the Greek tetrachordal genera, allowing for some variance in microtuning.

References

Bauer, Susan. 2007. *The History of the Ancient World*. New York: W.W. Norton.

Bickerton, Derek. 2000. "Can Biomusicology Learn from Language Evolution Studies?" In Wallin, Nils, Bjorn Merker, and Stephen Brown (eds.), *The Origins of Music*, Cambridge, Massachusetts: MIT Press, 153–163.

Blades, James. 2005. *Percussion Instruments and Their History* (Revised ed.). Westport, Connecticut: The Bold Strummer (orig. published 1970 by Faber and Faber, London).

Cazden, Norman. 1958. "Pythagoras and Aristoxenos Reconciled." *Journal of the American Musicological Society* 11(2/3): 97–105.

Charry, Eric. 2000. *Mande Music: Traditional and Modern Music of the Maninka and Mandinka of Western Africa*. Chicago: University of Chicago Press.

Clayton, Martin. 2000. *Time in Indian Music*. London: Oxford University Press.

Cline, Eric. 2014. *1177 B.C.: The Year Civilization Collapsed*. Princeton, New Jersey: Princeton University Press.

Comotti, Giovanni (trans. Munson, Rosaria). 1979 [1991]. *Music in Greek and Roman Culture*. Baltimore, Maryland: Johns Hopkins University Press.

Conard, Nicholas, Maria Malina, and Susanne Münzel. 2009. "New Flutes Document the Earliest Musical Tradition in Southwestern Germany." *Nature* 460: 737–740.

Curry, Daniel. 1880. "Musical Instruments of All Ages." In Curry, Daniel (ed.), *National Repository, Volume VII*, New York: Phillips and Hunt, 289–297.

DeNora, Tia. 1986. "How Is Extra-Musical Meaning Possible? Music as a Place and Space for 'Work'." *Sociological Theory* 4(1): 84–94.

Duchesne-Guillemin, Marcelle. 1967. "Survivance orientale dans la designation des cordes de la lyre en Grece?" *Syria* 44: 233–246.

Duchesne-Guillemin, Marcelle. 1984. "A Hurrian Musical Score from Ugarit: The Discovery of Mesopotamian Music." *Sources from the Ancient Near East* 2(2): 67–94.

Engel, Carl. 1875. *Musical Instruments (No. 5, South Kensington Museum Art Handbooks, William Maskell, ed.).* London: Chapman and Hall.

Farmer, Henry George. 1930. *Historical Facts for the Arabian Musical Influence.* London: William Reeves.

Fletcher, Peter. 2001. *World Musics in Context.* New York: Oxford University Press.

Flora, Reis. 2000. "Classification of Musical Instruments." In Arnold, Alison (ed.), *The Garland Encyclopedia of World Music, Vol.5, South Asia: The Indian Subcontinent,* New York: Taylor and Francis, 319–330.

Galpin, Francis. 1937 [1970]. *The Music of the Sumerians, and Their Immediate Successors the Babylonians and Assyrians.* Cambridge: Cambridge University Press. [Reprinted: New York: Da Capo Press.]

Hijleh, Mark. 2012. *Towards a Global Music Theory.* Farnham, Surrey: Ashgate.

Kishore, Prem, and Anuradha Ganpati. 2003. *India: An Illustrated History.* New York: Hippocrene Books.

Kolinski, Mieczyslaw. 1957. "The Determinants of Tonal Construction in Tribal Music." *The Musical Quarterly* 43(1): 50–56.

Kouwenhoven, Frank. 2015. "China: The Guqin Zither." In Church, Michael (ed.), *The Other Classical Musics,* Woodbridge, Suffolk: Boydell and Brewer, 105–125.

Lawergren, Bo. 1994. "Buddha as a Musician: An Illustration of a Jataka Story." *Artibus Asiae* 54(3/4): 226–240.

Liu, Xinru. 2010. *The Silk Road in World History.* New York: Oxford University Press.

Macran, Henry (trans.). 1902. *The Harmonics of Aristoxenus.* Oxford: Clarendon Press.

Manniche, Lise. 1991. Music and Musicians in Ancient Egypt. London: British Museum Press.

McNeill, J.R., and William McNeill. 2003. *The Human Web.* New York: W.W. Norton.

Noegel, Scott. 2006. "Greek Religion and the Ancient Near East." In Ogden, Daniel (ed.), *The Blackwell Companion to Greek Religion,* London: Blackwell, 21–37.

Oppenheimer, Stephen. 2004. *Out of Eden: The Peopling of the World.* London: Constable and Robinson.

Patel, Aniruddh. 2006. "Musical Rhythm, Linguistic Rhythm, and Human Evolution." *Music Perception* 24(1): 99–104.

Pioske, Daniel. 2015. *David's Jerusalem: Between Memory and History.* New York: Routledge.

Price, Ira. 1927. *The Great Cylinder Inscriptions A and B of Gudea.* Leipzig: J.C. Hinrichs'sche Buchhandlung.

Roberts, J. M. 2004. *The New Penguin History of the World* (4th ed.). New York: Penguin.

Ropp, Paul S. 2010. *China in World History.* New York: Oxford University Press.

Rouse, W.H.D. (trans.). 1895. "Guttila-Jātaka. " In Cowell, E.B. (ed.), *The Jātaka, or Stories of the Buddha's Former Births, Vol II,* Cambridge: Cambridge University Press, 172–178.

Rowell, Louis. 1979. "The Subconscious Language of Musical Time." *Music Theory Spectrum* 1: 96–106.

Sachs, Curt. 1943 [2008]. *The Rise of Music in the Ancient World*. New York: W.W. Norton. [Reprinted: Mineola, New York: Dover.]

Tenzer, Michael. 2000. *Gamelan Gong Kebyar: The Art of Twentieth-Century Balinese Music*. Chicago: University of Chicago Press.

Wallin, Nils, Bjorn Merker, and Stephen Brown (eds.). 2000. *The Origins of Music*. Cambridge, Massachusetts: MIT Press.

Wayman, Erin. 2012. "Early Bow and Arrows Offer Insight into Origins of Human Intellect." *Smithsonian.com*. Accessed 8-30-2016 at http://www.smithsonianmag.com/science-nature/early-bow-and-arrows-offer-insight-into-origins-of-human-intellect-112922281.

Wellesz, Egon. 1961. *A History of Byzantine Music and Hymnography* (2nd ed.). London: Oxford University Press.

West, M.L. 1992. *Ancient Greek Music*. London: Oxford University Press.

West, M.L. 1994. "The Babylonian Musical Notation and the Hurrian Melodic Texts." *Music and Letters* 75(2): 161–79.

3 The first pivotal convergence

The Silk Road, c. 200 BCE–900 CE

[The Silk Road was] the Internet of antiquity.

—Yo-Yo Ma (quoted in Keller 2007)

Figure 3.1 Map of key locations, first pivotal convergence.

Phase I: The Road emerges, c. 200 BCE–200 CE

As suggested in Chapter 2, the Silk Road arose from the seeds of Alexander the Great's Hellenistic empire, which had brought significant musical cross-pollination across the Mediterranean-Aegean, Egyptian, Persian, and Indian worlds. Within 125 years of Alexander's death (i.e., by about 200 BCE), the western half of Central Asia was dominated by the legacies of Hellenistic society coupled with Persian/Iranian cultural remnants and the heterogenous Parthians on the rise. Meanwhile large sections of the eastern half of Central Asia were home to the nomadic equestrian Yuezhi and Xiongnu[1] tribes to the north and the powerful Mauryans in what is today India and Pakistan. The emergent Silk Road was at its inception anchored by Rome in the West and Han China in the East, with the capital of the latter at Chang'an (modern Xi'an). The musical story of this Road is tri-partite, with a shift in emphases over time. At first it is about the centers of gravity exerted by Rome and China respectively, about the relationship between them as mediated by those in the middle, and about the relationships each had with those mediators. Later it is just as much about those in the middle itself as about the civilizations at either end (Figure 3.1).

There is scant direct evidence about music along the Silk Road. Much must be derived by extension from what is known about visual art, religion, and politics, about the stories of people and their journeys, and about the effects seen on cultures that are better documented.

As Rome began to expand and flourish further while Greece faded, between about 300 and 150 BCE, the Romans, as they did with most of the cultures they absorbed, assimilated the cultural products of the Greeks. Thus the classical Greek musical legacy was transferred almost wholesale over to Rome. Giovanni Comotti notes that "because of the increasingly close ties between Roman and Greek civilizations, after the start of the third century BC[E] there no longer appeared to be substantial differences between the forms of musical expression in the two cultures" (1979:7). Little more need be said about the state of music in Rome itself as the Silk Road began to rise: it was essentially Hellenized, and this was reflected also in the cultural commerce between Rome and the Hellenistic stronghold of Alexandria in Egypt, where Greek learning and music had flourished further. Egypt was a Roman province from c. 30 BCE, but had been culturally Greco-Roman for much longer, even as it remained connected in some ways to its ancient musical past. These conditions facilitated the continuation of the inter/transcultural milieu of which Greece had been a part as well as the energy it both brought to and took from areas of the world outside of the Mediterranean–Aegean complex.

China's more traditionalist mindset discouraged an outcome similar to that of Rome, though China did have increasing contact with Central Asian tribes, some of it peaceful and some warlike, but all of it culturally enriching. The addition of Taoism (arose c. 300 BCE) to Confucian thinking offered a more mystical connection to the spirit world of ancestors through the metaphysical concepts of yang and yin. At the same time, the Taoist goal of being in harmony with the "Way" focused less on Confucian social order and more on nature, including sound. Yang was represented by pitch intervals of rising fifths, which is the likely conceptual reason reinforcing an anhemitonic pentatonic scale (henceforth called "world pentatonic" in this study; see Chapter 2, note 6) as the basis for the predominant pitch collection, along with Chinese acoustic experiments with lengths of tubing: By c. 40 BCE the Han musician and court official Ching Fang had demonstrated the 53-tone perfect fifth (3:2) spiral that practically returns to an octave equivalence (McClain 1979:208). This pentatonic collection was also regularly extended to all seven diatonic tones and even further into the dodecaphonic collection, though more often as ornamental rather than structural (Fletcher 2001:330–333).

Not all music that interested the Chinese courts came directly from court or temple musicians. Yumei Wang (2012) details how the folksongs of the Zhou-era *Shijing* (Book of Odes) and the Han-era *yuefu* were systematically collected by the courts with the goal of keeping them as authentic as possible (especially the later Han *yuefu*) so that the rulers could understand the expressions of the common people. Some 5000 *yuefu* dating from the Han through the T'ang periods were compiled by Guo Maoqian in the eleventh century CE. Unfortunately, the music to which these song-poems were set has been lost, though Wang presents evidence that their basic rhythms and pitch contours can be understood from their poetic structures and Chinese language tones (2012:31–47). The eight traditional instruments specified as possible accompanying ensembles in these sources— *sheng* (reed-based mouth organ), *di* (bamboo transverse flute), *jiege* (castanet), *qin* (see Chapter 2), *se* (twenty-five-stringed chordophone), *pipa* (Chinese– Central Asian lute discussed further in this chapter), and *zheng* (a zither different from the qin)—reflect a full range of pitch and timbral possibilities, though the repertoire was also sung without accompaniment.

Both ancient Greek and ancient Chinese philosophies embraced the ethical power of music, though the Chinese saw this power as being manifested through physical effects on the body while the Greeks (namely Plato) saw it as something more metaphysical. The Greek approach was more theoretical, the Chinese more practical (Wang 2004). This is fascinating in that Hellenistic musical culture was in practice just as sensuous and materialistic—perhaps because of the complexities of the Greco-Roman integration—as Chinese musical culture was philosophical, and suggests that the complex dynamics between theory, praxis, sensuality, and philosophy were qualified human musical universals from very early on in the story. This is reinforced by the way music has been used in religious, work, entertainment, and aesthetic contexts across time and space, not least through the millennia across the cultures of Eurasia.

Certainly, the power and influence of both Rome and Han China as civilizational centers in this era should not be underestimated. Yet formal and informal musical activity continued to develop within the cultures between these two anchors across the Eurasian sweep. Two of the most important of these were Persia and India, both of which had ancient roots.

Ancient Persian (Achaemenid, c. 550–331 BCE) musical traditions came into dialogue with Greek ideas during the conquests of Alexander in Central Asia. However, all but the faintest direct glimpse of the musical culture of ancient Persia may have been lost (Farhat 1990:3). Anything meaningful to be gleaned must likely be pieced together from the general cultural-artistic environment that flourished, which was considerable, and from later sources. The strongest evidence from art and architecture suggests that the Achaemenid Persians synthesized styles from the many cultures with which they came in contact and ultimately consolidated, including the Medes, Assyrians, Egyptians, and Asiatic Greeks. Bo Lawergren (2009), for example, comments on several instances of visual depiction of musical scenes from Elam (Assyria) that include harps, lutes, lyres, double-pipes, and possibly small percussion. This would in essence represent the Nile–Mediterranean–Aegean musical context discussed in Chapter 2. Herodotus, Xenophon, and other Greeks also comment on singing women in the Achaemenid court, a precursor to later roles found in Arab culture.

The history of ancient Iran/Persia in the *Shahnameh* (written c. 1000 CE), the fading of the Seleucids and rise of the Parthians (247 BCE–224 CE), and insights from the religious rituals of Zoroastrianism—which dominated Persia from at least the sixth century BCE and are known to us through the *Zend Avesta* and Herotodus's *Histories*—also contribute to understanding of the sphere under discussion. In the *Zend Avesta*, Jamshid (Yima) is given a golden horn[2] by the Zoroastrian deity Ahura Mazda, with which Jamshid expands the earth for the increase of its creatures. In the *Shahnameh*, meanwhile, Jamshid is a great king who brings all the elements of art and invention to humankind for a Golden Age. A later episode has Rustam (Rostam), another of the heroes in the *Shahnameh*, finding a *tanbur* (ubiquitous Central Asian long-necked plucked chordophone) during one of his seven trials, and accompanying his own song of lament. In keeping with a variation on this tale, in which Rustam finds the tanbur in a tree and is able to play it without practice, the instrument or one of its many cousins (*barbat, dutar, oud*) is still featured as an accompanying instrument in modern dramatic performances of the *Shahnameh*. Taken together, these stories suggest the invention and practice of music in a context of legendary power, happiness, and plenty, corresponding to the generally positive disposition of this culture towards music prior to the coming of Islam.

Both Persia and India shared Indo-Aryan linguistic roots, and therefore likely at least some musical foundations as well. These foundations would have been formed in the pre-historic times discussed previously, but they would also have facilitated inter/transcultural musical sharing along the Silk Road. On the basis of modern performances in combination with analysis of older descriptive texts, for example, Peter Fletcher notes that the

> syllabic style [of Zoroastrian chant] contrasts with the rhythmically freer, more ornamented and melismatic style of chanting Samaveda, used by Hindus in India; but the use in both styles of varied reiterations of simple three- or four-note melodies, within a compass of approximately a fourth, is common in epic and scriptural chant throughout the world.
>
> (2001:93)

In this context, the further development of music in India was thus highly consequential to the Silk Road as well. Bharata Muni, one of India's earliest recorded musicologists, is traditionally understood to have been the author of the arts treatise *Natyasastra*. The difficulties surrounding the dating of this work are immense, with scholars suggesting its appearance as early as 200 BCE or as late as 500 CE, though in any case the roots of the work almost certainly go back hundreds of years earlier and Bharata's role may involve as much codification as origination. In it, Bharata details fundamental theories of pitch in the form of the 22 *shrutis* and how these are used to build intervals that distinguish pitch and heptatonic modes (Jairazbhoy 1975). Laurence Picken (2000:202) makes the interesting comment that six of the seven ancient pitch collections (sub-modes of the parent scales) in this system include two notes considered weaker, which, when eliminated, effectively produce world pentatonic collections (there is also reference to this in the *Natyasastra* Chapter 27), while three other sets may be seen as possible bases for Indonesian *pelog* and *slendro* modes. Such correspondences provide further evidence of theoretical connections between Old World musics along the Silk Road. Bharata also elucidates theories of rhythmic patterns and cycles (*tala*[3]) in *Natyasastra* Chapter 31, which Abhinavagupta (c. 950–1020 CE) later explicitly situates within the Indian cosmology of creation, dissolution, and rebirth cycles by way of the rhythmic terminology used (Rowell 1979:101). Central to both Hinduism and Buddhism, this cosmology on the one hand distinguished Indian music from that of other cultures (especially Greece); on the other hand, it profoundly influenced the music of Buddhism that flowed out of India into Central Asia and eventually China. Bharata explicates the *tala* in the context of both vocal and instrumental music, but just as fundamentally in the context of poetry and drama; Victor Mair (2008) has discussed how concepts of auditory aesthetics in Chinese and Indian poetry were likely mutually influential and not of a kind with the West.

China looking west

As the Han "looked west" during the early days of the Silk Road (Liu 2010:1–19), it discovered and became enamored with the powerful horses cultivated by the Yuezhi and Xiongnu, while these tribes in turn became enamored with silk finery from China that could set apart Central Asian nobility. In this atmosphere, China came to be profoundly influenced by Central Asian tribes and their cultures: "Several Han emperors became very fond of nomadic dress, food, music, and dance, and such attractions spread to many in the Han social elite as well... They imported many things from Central Asia, including... musical instruments" (Ropp 2010:28). There is evidence of the transmission of Central Asian music ("Hengchui qu", or "songs with horizontal flutes") to Chang'an as a result of the well-known journey into Central Asia of the Han emissary Zhang Qian, c. 130 BCE (as recorded later by the historian Siam Qian). Records also indicate that additional music was created on the basis of this material for military processions by Emperor Wu's court musician Li Yannian, and that use of this music lasted into the Eastern Han phase of the empire after the turn of the millennium (Knechtges and Chang 2010:370). The following comment from the aforementioned *yuefu* compiler Guo Maoqian (eleventh century CE) makes this clear:

> The origin of Guchui naoge is unknown, but it had such a name when the army [was] stationed in the north since Han Dynasty. Hujia [Mongolian reed

whistle] is beaten to be accompanied with Xiao [vertical bamboo flutes and pan pipes] which does not mean the Ba-Yin [traditional eight instruments used by the Chinese]. Hengchuiqu [was] also called Guchui at its beginning. It is played on the horse back, so it is military music. Northern ethnic groups all play music on the horse back, thus the music of northern ethnic groups is sorted into the catalog of Guchui since Han Dynasty.

(adapted from translation in Wang 2012:40)

A fascinating musical figure from this early period was Wang Zhaojun (Wang Qiang), a skilled musician and cultured Han bride sent to appease the Central Asian Xiongnu c. 33 BCE. So powerful is her story—though continuously expanded and embellished over the centuries—that she is named as one of the legendary Four Beauties of ancient China, of which three, including Wang Zhaojun, have some basis in historical fact. Her story is one of the most retold of these, especially in artistic contexts. As a "woman of the palace" (a royal concubine), Wang Zhaojun would have been trained in music for the purposes of entertainment and edification, and she is traditionally associated with a high level of skill on the *pipa*. Though it has become one of the most emblematic of Chinese instruments—with tradition holding that it was invented for another Han princess, Liu Xijun, sent in 108 BCE to marry a chieftain of the Wusun (who lived near the Yuezhi)—Picken (1955) argues compellingly that the pipa emerged during the first or second century CE from Gandharan influence in Central Asia. In an updated dramatic version titled *Autumn in the Han Palace*, written and set in later Yuan China by Ma Zhiyuan (c. 1250–1321 CE), Wang Zhaojun is depicted playing her pipa, but other stories and general historic context suggest she is more likely to have played an earlier form of lute which would later have been subsumed under the pipa concept. Still, that the Central Asian pipa became the form associated with the stories and with Chinese instrumental virtuosity to this day is noteworthy for the purposes of this study.

Also important is that in Wang Zhaojun we have an early example of a theme in global music history that reappears with some regularity across time, space, and culture: the story of women whose opportunities for musical excellence were only available in what must be called sexualized contexts—as courtesans, political brides, slaves, and prostitutes, though often in ways that carried more dignity and influence than might be expected from a twenty-first-century perspective. It is a testament to the power of music that musical skills should be desired in such contexts. This tradition continued along the Silk Road; later, the *qiyan* of early Arabic/Islamic culture and the geishas of Japan constitute other examples.

The famous Great Wall marked both a series of entrances to Han territory for goods traveling east and a line of defense against Xiongnu raiders. The further outpost of this Wall, the Gate of Jade, lay near Dunhuang, an ancient settlement which would in time become a center of Buddhist culture along the Silk Road. The Yuezi, with which the Han had peaceful cultural congress (in contrast to the Xiongnu), were vanquished by the Xiongnu from these territories around 130 BCE. The Yuezi then traveled further west to the Amu Darya (Greek: Oxus)

River that served as something of a landmark for Alexander and his successors. There the Greeks had established Bactria, and nearby was the culturally Iranian Sogdiana. The Yuezhi settled in the area, eventually becoming the basis for the Kushan empire, which was to be a partially Hellenized center of intercultural congress with its longtime Chinese trading partners as well as India. The travels of the Han representative Zhang Qian took him to the new Yuezhi (soon to be Kushan) stronghold near the Amu Darya just as it was being settled, where he discovered these developments. Qian's comments suggest emerging knowledge of the Parthians (Anxi) and communities possibly as far west as the Hellenistic stronghold of Antioch (Liu 2010:8).

The rise of the Kushan empire starting c. 100 CE in what is today Pakistani territory resulted in further integration of Central Asian sources. Xinru Liu's analysis is revealing: "The Kushans brought with them the beliefs and social structures forged from centuries living on the steppe, and they mixed many of those customs in with the sedentary life of Hellenistic Bactria" (2010:43). An example of the multiculturalism at the center of Kushan life is found in their use of "both Greek letters and the Kharoshthi script (an evolution of the Aramaic script that the Persians had brought to India) to write the various Sanskrit dialects" (Liu 2010:46). In this context, music in Bactria and the wider Kushan territory would have combined steppe influences with legacies from Greece, Persia, and India along with indirect influence from Han China. Earlier and from the other direction, Lawergren (2009) presents pictorial evidence of Achaemenid influence on the *qin* and Chinese and Central Asian harps of various kinds, suggesting that such influence was "facilitated by horse-riders traveling along the east-west expanse of the Eurasian steppes." Among these would have been the Yuezhi that became the Kushans.

Influenced by the Northern Indian cultures with which they interacted deeply after crossing the Hindu Kush mountains sometime in the middle of the first century CE, Kushans adopted Indian religions—but none more strongly than Buddhism. They also embraced the Hellenistic tendency to allow many religions to mix freely, including the Greek pantheon of gods (which may have seemed in concert with that of Hinduism) along with ancestor worship retained from the steppe and Persian Zoroastrianism. However, Buddhism held a special place in this intercultural world, as the sites of religious monuments testify, and in this the Kushans were similar to the earlier Mauryan (Indian) ruler Ashoka (r. 269–232 BCE). The Kushan king Kasnishka (c. 100 CE) "like Ashoka, converted to Buddhism, built monasteries, and supported sculptors and musicians from all over Asia" (Kishore and Ganpati 2003:40). In the Gandhara region (what is now the area around Peshawar, Afghanistan), the rise of Buddhism and associated arts reflected the dynamism of the Hellenistic sweep wedded with Indian and Chinese influences (Wood 2002:39–42). A stupa unearthed in the nearby Swat region features Kushans dressed in a mix of Roman and Central Asian garb playing Greek and Asian musical instruments. Some of the figures look more Mediterranean, while others are more Indic and wear less clothing (Liu 2010:46–50) (Figure 3.2).

Figure 3.2 Kushan (Gandharan) musicians.
Source: Adapted/arranged from photos by Dan Diffendale. Used by permission.

In order to discuss music in this context more thoroughly, a set of distinctions needs to be made between two schools within Buddhism, Theraveda and Mahayana. Both strains laid claim to the original intent of the Buddha, though perhaps the former more literally and the latter more figuratively and interpretively. The Theraveda perspective more explicitly and firmly rejected sensuality, including music, while Mahayana Buddhism evolved towards more freedom in this regard, starting with celebration of the Buddha's life. Lawergren points out that it was the coming of Mahayana Buddhism out of Gandhara probably around the beginning of the Common Era that spread across the Silk Road over the next 1000 years and released adherents from what was a decidedly negative, moralistic view of music. Siddhartha had enjoyed music and its associated sensuality very much in his early search for meaning in pleasure, but became enlightened precisely by rejecting such pursuits. However, he both pointed those seeking Nirvana towards simplicity and poverty and eschewed extreme asceticism. One source dated within 250 years of the Buddha's traditional time of death mentions that his disciples paid "homage to the remains of the Blessed One with dancing, and hymns, and music, and with garlands and perfumes." Eventually, from the Mahayana perspective, music "became synonymous with the highest joys of Paradise" (Lawergren 1994:228).

Ian Mabbett identifies the notion of "impermanence" in Buddhist thinking as the most directly affective of music, for meditation on impermanence is to be conducted in "quietness and solitude" (1994:9). Moreover, the monastery was an ideal, protected place in which to make such a pursuit, away from the world's distractions. This helps explain the extensive networks of Buddhist monasteries along the Silk Road, where art and music grew out of contemplation. In addition, a focus on the impermanence of things in this world and beyond had profound implications for musical time and the nature of rhythmic cycles, in concert with the effect on these elements of Hindu beliefs and early Indian concepts discussed above, for both systems embraced reincarnation of a kind. Therefore, "it is very likely that early Buddhist music drew heavily on existing Vedic musical practice," that is, from the ritual music of Indian Hinduism (Fletcher 2001:107). Chant accompanied by conch shell "trumpets," bells and gongs, woodblocks and drums, sometimes with flutes and harps, became the associated sound world for this tradition, which remains preserved in Korean and Tibetan musical practices.[4] In that religious context, a significant goal is to help induce a meditative state (see Fletcher 2001:107–112). Moreover, "a fundamental Buddhist concept,…elaborated in Mahayana, is that of the emptiness or voidness of all the contents of our material world; they are like smoke, or a mirage, or a conjuring trick" (Mabbett 1994:19). This too helps explain the nature of traditional Buddhist music, meant to evoke a mysterious otherworldliness (or non-worldliness). To Mabbett, this approach still seeks to facilitate the accession of transcendence, but it is very different from the goal of Christian worship, for example:

> [Because] reality is not to be found among the impermanent things of life in the world…[t]here is no room [in essential Buddhism] for gorgeous displays, for *magnificentia* in the mediaeval Christian sense, for the dedication of devoutly nurtured artistic talents to the glorification of the divine".
>
> (Mabbett 1994:9–10)

Mahayana Buddhism also fit the commercial nature of the Silk Road, and may in part have developed as a result of it. Simple economics made the life of itinerate poverty with only a begging bowl described by the Buddha very difficult to maintain as groups of followers (*sanghas*) developed, grew, and traveled from town to town—the people at their destinations could not afford to feed them. As suggested above, this almost certainly encouraged the development of monasteries near commercial towns, but it also led to changes in attitude, allowing Buddhist adherents a different way to show devotion:

> To bridge the gap between the doctrine of self-denial and the materialism of the time, Mahayana Buddhism introduced a host of new deities. Known as bodhisattvas, these were people who had already merited nirvana, but decided to stay outside its threshold in order to help others to cross the ocean of suffering [in the mahayana (the "great vehicle")].
>
> (Liu 2010:53)

Donations could be made in honor of the Buddha himself, or of any number of bodhisattvas (who might assist the believer at a later time). A kind of symbiosis thus developed along the Silk Road between Buddhist monasteries and the merchants nearby who kept them flourishing with contributions from the wealth they generated, leaving the monks to their religious duties and contemplative arts.

The Guttila-Jātaka story, drawn from a very large collection of folklore about previous incarnations of the Buddha—referred to in the story as the "Bodhisatta"

(= bodhisattva), demonstrating further the complexity of the term—reflects something of this context. The tale reveals that excellence, virtue, and humility are highly valued in both the musical and religious contexts, and reinforces the idea that true music exists in something of an ineffable state that can only be approximated in the physical world:

> Once upon a time, when Brahmadatta was reigning in Benares, the Bodhisatta was born in a musician's family. His name was Master Guttila. When he grew up, he mastered all the branches of music, and under the name of Guttila the Musician he became the chief of his kind in all India...

> [Meanwhile, a certain] Mūsila was a player on the veena[5]...Now the Bodhisatta...taught his pupil [Musila] everything [about veena playing] which he knew himself. This done, he said, "Your knowledge is now perfect."

> Thought Mūsila, "I have now mastered my art. This city of Benares is the chief city in all India. My teacher is old; here therefore must I stay." So he said to his teacher, "Sir, I would serve the king."...The king sent for Mūsila. "I understand that you are ready to compete with your master?" "Yes, your Majesty," was the reply...So the king agreed; and he sent the drum beating round the city with this notice: "Oyez! on the seventh day Guttila the Teacher, and Mūsila the Pupil, will meet at the door of the royal palace, to show their skill. Let the people assemble from the city, and see their skill!"

> First the two played each the same piece. When they played, both the same, the multitude was delighted, and gave abundant applause. Sakka spoke to the Bodhisatta, from his place in the air: "Break one of the strings!" said he. Then the Bodhisatta broke the B-string; and the string, though broken, gave out a sound from its broken end; it seemed like music divine. Mūsila too broke a string; but after that no sound came out of it. His teacher broke the second, and so on to the seventh string: he played upon the body alone, and the sound continued, and filled the town: the multitude in thousands waved and waved their kerchiefs in the air, in thousands they shouted applause...Then the king made a sign to the multitude; up rose the multitude, and cried—"You made a great mistake in matching yourself against your teacher! You know not your measure!" Thus they cried out against Mūsila; and...beat and bruised him to death, and seizing him by the feet, they cast him upon a dustheap. The king in his delight showered gifts upon the Bodhisatta, and so did they of the city...

> Sakka summoned Mātali. "The nymphs of heaven," said he, "desire to look upon Guttila the Musician. Go, seat him in my divine car, and bring him hither." The charioteer went and brought the Bodhisatta... "The maidens of the gods," said [Sakka], "wish to hear your music, Master." [Said Guttila,] "I care for no other recompense but this. Let these daughters of the gods tell me what acts of virtue brought them here; then will I play." Then said the daughters of the gods, "Gladly will we tell you after of the virtues that we have practiced; but first do you play to us, Master."

For the space of a week the Bodhisatta played to them, and his music surpassed the music of heaven. On the seventh day he asked the daughters of the gods of their virtuous lives... So also all those who are written in the story of Guttila-vimāna, thirty-seven daughters of the gods, were asked by the Bodhisatta what each had done to come there, and they too told what they had done in the same way by verses.

On hearing all this, the Bodhisatta exclaimed: "'Tis good for me, in sooth, truly 'tis very good for me, that I came here, and heard by how very small a merit great glory has been attained. Henceforward, when I return to the world of men, I will give all manner of gifts, and perform good deeds".

(adapted from Rouse 1895)

During this period key city centers were established that were to serve as Silk Road destinations, and thus areas of cosmopolitan culture, for more than 1000 years. Starting with Dunhuang, as noted earlier, some of these originally grew out of oases that the Han had cultivated through agricultural technology as efficient military outposts once they realized that merchants making the long trek with desired goods needed safe way stations (Liu 2010:10–11). Three major centers circling the Taklimakan Desert (around the Tarim Basin) which formed the most important oases on the Silk Road coming directly out of China were Kucha, Kashgar, and Khotan. Each was well connected to Sogdiana and Bactria and a key part of the Silk Road trading network. Research on the origins of Khotan raises intriguing questions about how far and how early both Hellenistic and Indo-Iranian influence traveled towards China. The Han had from earliest times imported Jade from Khotan through the Yuezhi (Liu 2010:3). Khotan appears to have been founded by Mauryans sometime during the third century BCE, possibly from Taxila, which had been visited by Alexander and his retinue; records show that the Khotans spoke the Eastern Iranian language Saka, of the Scythians, which is closely related to the Sogdian found in the neighboring Greco-Bactrian region (Hill 1988; Stein 1907). Kashgar was important as the point, coming from the west, at which the Road split into northern and southern routes to avoid the worst of the desert, with the northern path leading to Kucha. All three of these cities became Buddhist centers, but Kucha later emerged as a place of special musical renown, as will be discussed further later in this chapter.

Other ancient inter/transcultural oasis cities that became part of the Silk Road developed much further west, at first outside of the direct Chinese sphere. One example is Samarkand, which served as the Sogdian capital prior to Alexander and flourished through the Hellenistic era under the Kushans. Samarkand later fell to the Sassanid (Persian) empire, where it became a center for Manichaeism and served as a major hub for the Sogdian merchants who dominated trade along the Silk Road from about 200 BCE to 900 CE (Wood 2002:65).

Goods and services of every kind, including musical entertainment, passed along these trade routes, allowing styles, instruments, and performance techniques to mingle freely. For example, the Han court acquired jugglers or acrobats, almost certainly accompanied by music, as tribute from Parthia. These performers displayed their talents in the public square of the Han capital, Chang'an, and probably also in Roman provinces (Wood 2002:53).

Rome looking east

Meanwhile, as Rome began to look east, it saw the terrain differently in some respects—but, as it was for the Central Asian tribes, Rome's appetite for Chinese silk was the strongest factor in the development and maintenance of the emerging Road. For its part, Han China was eager to profit from the situation as well as to receive luxury goods from the Mediterranean and Africa through these same trade routes. Silk became part of the fashion and entertainment industry for the wealthy in Rome, often associated with parties and accompanying music. One Roman mosaic from c. 100–300 CE shows a man playing the Greek aulos while a woman in sheer silk dances (Wood 2002:30).

While the Xiongnu challenged the Han at the eastern end of the Road, the Parthian empire (247 BCE–224 CE) posed the biggest threat to Roman expansion and prosperity in the west. The Silk Road city of Palmyra in what is today the Syrian desert, already a center of trade for 2000 years before the rise of Rome but Hellenized under the Seleucids, became a locus for the dynamic tensions between Rome and the Parthians. At the same time, this created a rich milieu in which varying levels and types of inter/transculturality intermingled. Evidence that a great deal of Han Chinese silk reached Palmyra has been discovered, along with Indian cotton textiles, reinforcing its position as the western Silk Road gateway to Rome (Liu 2010:28, 30). It was thus economically highly strategic to the Romans, while Parthian territory around the turn of the millennium extended westward all the way to the eastern doorstep of Palmyra.

> The rise of Palmyra to a position of dominance was, to a great extent, the result of competition and compromise between the Roman and Parthian empires, the two powerhouses in the central part of Eurasia…Because the caravan trade was in the common interest of both empires, Palmyra profited by trading with both the Parthians and the Romans.
>
> (Liu 2010:28)

Situated geographically in the center of this dynamic, Palmyran music—like its art and architecture—would have combined some of the oldest musical sensibilities in the world from the Mesopotamian—Aegean commercial crossroads (such as the Hurrian hymns[6] from the coastal city of Ugarit, near ancient Phoenician territory) with Hellenistic practices, while sounds of Parthian musical elements inspired by ancient Persia and those of Asian cultures further east, delivered by Silk Road caravans, filled its borders.

Rome looked both west and east during the two centuries leading to the first millennium, for it was busy extending, consolidating, and defending a wide variety of its territories. As Rome made the transition from republic to empire during the century following, a tendency not to interfere with the non-bureaucratic aspects of conquered cultures further enhanced its cosmopolitan interest in and contributions to the developing trade routes. Some Romans experienced the frontiers between lingering Hellenistic culture and pre-Islamic Arabic musical sensibilities in the form of the more cultured qiyan (singing slave girls) phenomenon that continued into the Islamic period, as well as the less sophisticated traveling songs of the Bedouins (see Touma 1996:1–4). Meanwhile, the maritime Red Sea/Indian Ocean trade route between Rome, the Arabs, the East African coast, and India brought yet another intercultural context to Rome that was different from that of China and the heart of Central Asia due to simple geography. At the same time, it was a sort of alternative Silk "Road," for many of the same goods, services, and cultural inputs flowed across it, though in different contexts. J.H.K. Nketia (1974:3, 9–12), incorporating commentary from Farmer and Sachs, notes that the effect of Arab traders and settlers on the music of coastal East Africa (and to some extent further inland) was profound as a result, and that the effect went the other direction as well. Peter van der Merwe (1989:12–13, 30) goes further, suggesting that an "Afro-Arab [singing] style" developed that has persisted into the twenty-first century as an important and consistent part of global popular culture (see also Chapters 8 and 9).

The coming of Christianity out of Roman territories (in what is today Syria) at the turn of the millennium was to have a profound impact on the human musical story, as will be discussed further in Chapter 4 in the context of Western European contributions. At its inception, however, music for Christian worship largely imitated the temple music of the Jewish culture out of which it arose, a circumstance that itself reflected ancient inter/transcultural sensibilities (see Chapter 2). In particular, the chanting of Hebrew Old Testament psalms syllabically according to speech rhythms, with some melismas at key structural points, was almost certainly continued by early Christians.[7] These chants tend to use subsets of diatonic collections[8] and recurring melodic motifs as building blocks. In that sense they are "modal" in their focus on intervals and motifs rather than strictly linear scales (Fletcher 2001:136–137, Sachs 1943:82–83), not unlike aspects of Indian raga. In fact, Sachs suggests tuning outside of 12-EDO and puts Jewish music within a broader practice of non-Western "modality" (1943:81, 83) that continued into the practice of Arab/Islamic music as part of the next pivotal convergence of global music history (see Chapter 4). All of this was inherited by early Christians and carried forward for some time by Christian practice in Byzantium (Fletcher 2001:137).

Phase II: The Road evolves, c. 200–900 CE

"The markets and products of the Han, Kushan, Parthian, and Roman empires may have created the Silk Road, but the trade and the cultural exchanges that resulted did not reach full maturity and splendor until after these empires had collapsed. Beginning in the early third century [CE], they were in decline" (Liu 2010:62). By 500 CE, any remnants of stability at either end of the Silk Road had vanished.

This situation created conditions in which the Central Asian regions would develop further as cultural centers in themselves rather than merely places to pass through. "Nearer the center of the Old World Web...this was a time of cultural efflorescence; consequently, these regions influenced others (including China and backward Europe) by exporting manufactures, skills, and knowledge just as civilized centers had always done" (McNeill and McNeill 2003:84). Key cities such as Merv, Bukhara, Tashkent, and Samarkand thus flourished even more, while various religious strains and their associated musics and other arts flowed across the Silk Road. Writing about his travels to and from India in the *Buddhist Records of the Western World* (646 CE), the Chinese Buddhist monk Xuanzang noted that the "skill [of the inhabitants of Samarkand] in the arts and trades exceeds that of other countries" (quoted in Whitfield 1999:27).

During this second phase of the Silk Road, as the Persian Sassanids (r. 224–651 CE) overcame the Kushans and the Parthians, a Golden Age of pre-Islamic Persian music commenced, epitomized by the court musician Bārbad (fl. 590–628 CE). Likely born in the Silk Road town of Merv, Bārbad is credited with organizing the elements that became the basis of modern Iranian musical practice. Indeed, Jean During suggests that Old World modal/melodic material created and codified by Bārbad—i.e., "modal" in the sense described just above—"is the oldest Middle-Eastern system of which some traces still exist" (1991a:39). During also relays the following incident that demonstrates both the perilousness and the power of a top court musician like Bārbad:

> At the Sasanian court, bards (gosans) had to sing the court chronicle and to improvise occasional verses. Khosrow Parviz, the Sasanian king, had vowed that he would slay the one who brought him the bad news of the death of his favorite horse, Shabdiz. When the horse died, no one dared inform the king. Bārbad, the great minstrel of his court improvised a chant containing allusions to this event. "The king suddenly understood the message and cried out: 'Shabdiz is dead.' It's the King himself who announced it, said Bārbad",
> (1991b:154)

thereby likely saving his own skin.

Fletcher suggests that Persian art music coming out of this period also reflected a broad textural principle of Old World monophony—the close heterophonic imitation of vocal melody by an instrumentalist—found in a variety of cultures, including Indian, Southeast Asian, and Japanese musics (2001:15). Based on this distribution, it is not difficult to speculate that musicians traveling along the Silk Road embraced the same textural practice.

While this move on the part of the Sassanids to regain their earlier Persian heritage might be seen as having diluted the inter/transculturality of the territories to Rome's east, it was important to the next pivotal convergence that these Persian elements resurfaced and became part of the development of Islamic musical practice. On the eastern end of the Road, Chinese influences on Central Asia and vice versa continued apace as the result of the Sassanid consolidation since, as the Parthians had done, the Sassanid court sent its best Persian musicians and entertainers to Chang'an, and both empires took an active interest in maintaining the viability of the Silk Road for mutual benefit.

Meanwhile, Roman security within its capital city began to erode under military and economic pressures from all directions, ultimately resulting in a retreat to its eastern territory by the emperor Constantine in 330 CE and the dissipation of the western portion of the empire by 476 CE. Constantine's decision to essentially make Christianity Rome's state-sponsored religion and to move the capital city to Byzantium was fully consolidated by Theodosius I in 380, leaving western Roman territories to a new fate over the coming centuries.

Founded as a key trading city by the Greeks c. 667 BCE, Byzantium was briefly under Achaemanid control, but was re-Hellenized during the Peloponnesian War and remained so after the death of Alexander. It was essentially Romanized after 168 BCE. Renamed Constantinople in honor of the Emperor, the great city had a profound effect on the development of music in the empire and, consequently, in both Western and Eastern Europe:

> By the fourth century, many distinct forms of Eastern (Greek) and Western (Latin) rites emerged... Common to them all was the primacy of the word over music; for the Church Fathers needed to distinguish Christianity from current mystery cults. Although at first, sung, improvised prayer was encouraged, chromatic modes, and instruments, were forbidden; and the rhythmic style of Hellenistic popular music appears not to have influenced early Christian music.
>
> (Fletcher 2001:132)

Musical development continued apace in the new center of the empire, in the form of Byzantine chant for Christian worship—including the emergence of the eight diatonic pitch modes of the Octoechos, to be discussed again in Chapter 4— but also through instrumental music technologies. For example, small pneumatic organs are depicted on the obelisk of Theodosius, "looking like gigantic pan-pipes," though Egon Wellesz, citing pagan association, argues that these were not used in Christian worship and that organs remained proscribed (or strongly discouraged) in the Eastern Orthodox Church for many centuries hence (1961:104, 107).

Just as important musically in this context was the further spread of Greco-Roman, Jewish-influenced Christianity both west of Rome and east of Byzantium. For example,

> Rome [had] unified North Africa by defeating [ancient Phoenician] Carthage and Hellenistic Egypt and by subduing Berber tribes... Many North Africans contributed to Roman culture and to the development and dissemination of Christianity. Indeed, North Africa's provinces converted to Christianity well before those in Western Europe.
>
> (Naylor 2015:35)

This brought early Christian ritual music in contact with North Africa's ancient and highly intercultural context, a situation that would profoundly influence the next pivotal convergence of global music history in al-Andalus (see Chapter 4). However, early Christian leaders in North Africa had a complex view of music and its relationship to religious life. Prominent figures such as Clement of Alexandria (c. 150–215 CE) and Tertullian of Carthage (c. 155–240 CE) vehemently denounced Christian association with contemporary Greco-Roman music in the theater and at private parties, along with the influences of Asia and even of Jewish music, while at the same time seeing music as legitimate within a Classical tradition that was redeemable in new Christian contexts. Wellesz puts it well by saying that "we already find in [St. John] Chrysostom's homilies [(c. 349–407 CE)] the distinction, which was made later by St. Augustine between *musica luxuriantis*, creating *luxuriosa aurium voluptas*, and *musica sapientis*; a distinction of great importance for the development of the art of music in the Middle Ages" (1961:82, referring to Augustine's *Christian Doctrine* IV.7.19, written between 397 and 426 CE). In this way "sensuous, voluptuous, luxurious" music and "wise" music could be separated both conceptually and practically rather than eliminating music altogether from Christian life.

Again, this perspective led the early Christian community, even in highly intercultural North Africa, to seek a music that was set apart from the general Eurasian milieu. Some of the resulting distinctives will be discussed further in Chapter 4 as part of the development of Western European music. However, it is important to note the extant evidence continues to point to a variety of Christian chant styles during this period. The differences between Eastern and Western flavors of Christian music continued to grow, but the process was far more complex than is often acknowledged and many forms of early Christian chant had common Old World roots. Perhaps one helpful distinction to be made in this regard is between the *sound* of the music and its *associations* with unsavory topics. It is a controversy that continues to this day in the Christian community.

At least one early Christian music could not escape African influence, as demonstrated by ongoing practices in Ethiopia of music preserved from the ancient African Christian kingdom of Axum, which converted from a Semitic polytheism to Christianity during the fourth century CE. This heavily intercultural area just above the Horn on the upper East African coast was a key part of the Red Sea/Indian Ocean maritime trading route mentioned earlier, situated deeply within the sphere of both Alexandrian and pre-Islamic Arab influence. The associated musical tradition of Zema chant was established during the sixth century by Saint Yared. It is built entirely around world pentatonic modes and subsets, albeit with highly microtonal tunings and even chromatic ornamentation in practice (Shelemay et al., 1993:100–102), rather different from the expanded Hellenistic modality of other early Christian chants. While the vocalization of the chant itself flows freely through time, rhythmic divisions that change speeds and configurations of even/uneven groupings are beaten out on a wooden floor with a long wooden pole called a *maqwamiya*. Margarita Esipova (n.d.) suggests that this musical trait was shared by Nestorian Christians in their worship along the Silk Road. Fletcher points out that Ethiopian Christians have been recorded singing worship music from Syrian Antioch, "probably the oldest Christian chant of which we have evidence" (2001:179), while Nestorians launched their first missionary journeys eastward from the Syrian city of Edessa (which also had a strong Hellenistic history), near Antioch, and brought with them the Syriac language script which deeply influenced the written forms of Central Asian languages, most importantly Sogdian. They also likely continued the Old World modalities of Syrian-Byzantine chant. These correspondences are not insignificant because Nestorian Christianity originated in Constantinople but was declared heretical and was therefore driven further eastward, first into Persian territory (where the dominant Zoroastrians often persecuted followers) and then all the way to India, China, and Japan over the period of the seventh through ninth centuries CE. Nestorianism therefore represented a more explicitly culturally adaptable Christian practice as it traveled from West to East, apparently reflecting if not tying together musical elements across the Afro-Eurasian Old World. Taken together, this suggests a musical diversity to match the cultural diversity of early Christianity, though the dominant strains clearly survived in the Eastern (Greek) Orthodox and Western Roman (Latin) traditions.

Religion and its musical associations along the Silk Road continued to reinforce inter/transcultural sensibilities more generally. For example, arising out of Persia during the third century CE, Manichaeism took the Road by storm for a period of several centuries. That the early North African thinker Augustine of Hippo (354–430) was a Manichee before he famously converted to Christianity demonstrates the geographical and philosophical influence Manichaeism had at the time. Perhaps not surprisingly, the promise of heaven as a place of reward and refuge from the difficulties of life was a key feature of religions along the Silk Road—and in these heavenly realms was delightful, edifying music. Manichaeism deliberately attempted to integrate Zoroastrianism, Hinduism, Buddhism, and Christianity among other religions into a cosmic meta-narrative about the struggle between Light and Darkness. Gunnar Mikkelsen notes that in thus seeking to convey what life in a heavenly "Land of Light" might look like, medieval Chinese Manicheans turned in at least one instance for inspiration in writing devotional hymns to descriptions of a Mahayana Buddhist paradise offered by the bodhisattvas. In such a world,

> pure and gentle breezes blow among the trees and nets and produce enchanting music and marvellous sounds of the Law which spread to all the buddha-lands in the ten directions of the universe;…the breezes move jewelled bells hanging around the nets and the trees emit the sounds of the Law and spread sweet perfumes;…heavenly music is played by countless gods in countless jewelled pavilions;…ten thousand varieties of music consisting of the sounds of the Law are constantly heard.
>
> (Mikkelsen 2009:203–204)

In another example, Ter Ellingson points out that after c. 500 CE the rise of Tantric Buddhism from India encouraged adherents across the Buddhist world even more strongly than before to attain heightened states of consciousness and reflection of divine beings—towards which music and dance were essential techniques (1980:435). Ellingson shows how rhythmic syllables of chanted mantras from the *Sarvadurgati* Tantric text, appearing no later than the eighth century CE and corresponding to hand drum pattern elements, were intended to induce such states, and how these were in turn part of a larger tradition of chanting/drumming globally, where "drum beats represent vocal utterances, rather than the utterances representing the beats," (1980:432) especially in Indian and African traditions.

Even Joseph Needham (1900–1995), noted advocate of prioritizing Chinese cultural and scientific achievements, admitted that "Indian music came through Kucha to China just before the Sui period [581–618 CE] and had a great vogue there in the hands of exponents such as Tshao Miao-Ta of Brahminical origin" (1954:213–214). By the time the T'ang dynasty was consolidated in China (618–907 CE), some Central Asian cultures had musical styles that came to be in demand towards the East, while towards the West the newly consolidated Sassanid (Persian) and Byzantine Empires continued to develop artistically along the lines of their ancient multicultural roots, though in very different religious directions. Each would in time come to inform and be informed by their respective spheres to some degree—Byzantium in Christian Europe and Persia in the Muslim West and Central Asia—and thus both would ultimately have an influence on North Africa and into Iberia (Chapter 4).

The ancient oasis town of Dunhuang became both a Buddhist center and something of a gateway to China from the west leading up to and during the T'ang era. In his three-part essay on "Dance at Dunhuang," Joseph Houseal (2015a, 2015b, 2016) explores ways in which dance intersected with Buddhist spirituality in a deeply intercultural fashion, as demonstrated by depictions in the nearby Mogao Caves. For example, *feitian* or "sky spirits" fly in dance poses that are not found in Indian Buddhist depictions, suggesting that feitian are of Central Asian rather than Indian origin, perhaps inspired further by gymnastic poses from Daoist thought that were being practiced simultaneously in the Chinese courts. Some feitian also hold instruments in these depictions. They occupy space between the earthly and heavenly realms, suggesting that dance and music, at least in some Buddhist contexts, were seen as spiritual and not merely sensual or diverting. Houseal also discusses how the Sogdian Whirl reflected both the energetic aesthetic of Buddhist dance sensibilities and the social sophistication of the T'ang court in a decidedly inter/transcultural milieu.

Further west and north of Dunhuang, the Tarim Basin city of Kucha was for some time the most populous oasis and the best known for its music from c. 500–900 CE. Among the imports from Kucha was a four-stringed lute with a bent neck that eventually became the very popular Chinese pipa. A wall painting from the Kizil caves about 40 miles from Kucha, dated c. 600–800 CE, shows this instrument being played by a Buddhist feitian (Figure 3.3).

Figure 3.3 Feitian playing early pipa, Kizil cave wall painting.

Source: Freer Gallery of Art and Arthur M. Sackler Gallery, Smithsonian Institution, Washington, D.C.: Gift of Arthur M. Sackler, S1987.265. Used by permission.

A Kuchean pipa player with the Indian name Sujiva arrived c. 568–578 CE in Chang'an with Central Asian (Turkic) princess Ashina upon her marriage to Emperor Wu of the Northern Zhou. Sujiva demonstrated seven pitch modes in ancient Indian musical terms. These modes were new to the T'ang in that they resulted from starting the heptatonic (diatonic) collection on any one of the seven pitches (Picken 2000:205ff.). T'ang poet Po Chu-yi (Bai Juyi, 772–846 CE) captured some of the powerful ethos surrounding Chinese adoption of the pipa in his "Song of the Pipa Player," which is itself in the *yuefu* tradition discussed earlier in this chapter.

Eliot Weinberger paints a vivid picture of the intercultural musical spectacles flowing from Central Asia into T'ang Chang'an:

> All things foreign were the rage…Courtesans sang songs with titles like "Watching the Moon in Brahman Land," playing melodies on foreign

instruments adapted from Indian, Turkish, Korean, and Persian tunes. Entertainment was provided by dancers from Tashkent or the Sogdian "twirling girls".

(2009:117)

One of these "Brahman" (Iranian-Indian-Kuchean) tunes became especially famous because of its association with Nishnag Yuyi ("Rainbow Garment"), a dance piece involving a skirt of colored feathers that legend associates with the T'ang emperor Xuanzong (685–762): the emperor is said to have appropriated the tune and recast it for his purposes. Po Chu-yi refers to this dance and melody in his poem "Song of Lasting Regret" (see Mair 2000:273). Though nowhere presented in notation by its proper name, John Thompson (2013) has speculated that the tune may have been preserved in some form in the Shen Qi Mi Pu collection of qin songs (1425 CE) as Guanghan You ("Wandering in a Lunar Place") or Qingdu Yin ("Heavenly Capitol Melody"). If so, the fact that it is structurally in world pentatonic mode three, a common configuration for Chinese melodies, would raise interesting questions about just what the Central Asian influence might have been: Rhythmic? Performance technique and style? Connections to Indian pentatonicism? Perhaps all of these. Rowell (2000:152–153) suggests an interesting possibility regarding the latter, in that, for example, early South Indian modes included the five configurations of world pentatonic, but these were understood to be subsets of diatonic collections rather than pre-cursors to them. This makes plausible the idea that a tune from a "Western" town like Kucha could have fit comfortably within a Sino-Indian diatonic-pentatonic world with which a musician like Sujiva would have been conversant.

Susan Whitfield, in her extraordinary reconstruction of the life and times of a Kuchean professional musician and courtesan named Larishka who lived c. 839–890CE, provides a detailed and personalized look at the impact of Kuchean music along the Silk Road (1999:138–154). Summing up the situation, Whitfield notes that

Kuchean music was famed along the Silk Road, from Samarkand to Chang'an...Skill on the small Kuchean drum, which rested on a stand, became *de riguer* among emperors and noblemen in China. One of its practitioners was the eighth-century Chinese Tang dynasty emperor Xuanzong who...housed thirty thousand musicians and dancers in the imperial palace, many of them from Kucha or playing in a Kuchean style...Kuchean dancers were as renowned as their fellow musicians for their skill and were sent by the Kuchean court to Samarkand and Chang'an as representatives of the best of its culture. Kuchean dance was not unlike Indian dance,...but it also adapted dance forms from other places, such as the famous Sogdian 'whirling' dance, performed by both men and women. Music, song and dance were Silk Road commodities, bought and sold like silver and jade.

(1999:139–140)

Whitfield's telling of the story of Larishka gives further context to this general picture, particularly regarding the place of women as musician-courtesans. The sites of Larishka's life and career ranged from Kucha to Dunhuang to Chang'an and back to Kucha again. She played both as a soloist and in mixed instrumental ensembles. These orchestras sometimes accompanied theatrical pieces that originated in India, hearkening back to a focus on the relationship between drama and music in the *Natyasastra*, but were adapted culturally as they moved into Central Asia, China, and other parts of East Asia. Indeed, Kuchean musicians sang in Sanskrit among many languages.

Larishka's talents as a musician were acknowledged by way of her participation in the large professional musical retinues of military and political leaders, but she was also often expected to be available for sexual favors. Within that understanding, she was provided a modicum of luxury in her living and social arrangements. As part of these bands of high-profile servants, Larishka found herself more than once caught in the middle of warring factions, and changed hands as a prized possession. On one such occasion, she and her handmaiden ended up in Dunhuang, where, the records indicate, her musical talents were appreciated more primarily and she was allowed to attend Buddhist worship services. Perhaps she also served as a model for a painting in one of the nearby caves, which would likely have resembled the example reproduced in Figure 3.3.

Larishka offered prayers to the bodhisattva Avalokitesvara, who embodies compassion, to remain in this more settled, happier life. Instead, she was sold away to the socially polite equivalent of a "madam" in Chang'an, and began her life anew as courtesan in the capital city for nearly 20 years. While Larishka was by this point getting too old to be desired primarily as a sexualized companion, and thus was "rented out" more for her musical abilities, the pressures from her male customers could not be avoided. Eventually, as her ability to earn top fees decreased, Larishka spent more time in her madam's house, training the younger girls. However, in what would prove to be the waning years of the T'ang dynasty, "Kuchean music was no longer so popular in China: like so much else imported from the Silk Road, it had become unfashionable as the Chinese sought to rediscover and promote home-grown traditions in a time of political disintegration" (Whitfield 1999:149–150).

Fleeing a particularly bloody military encounter, Larishka found her way back to her hometown of Kucha in 881 CE, some 26 years after departing it. There she "was often called upon to play Kuchean songs by the older residents who preferred the traditional music" (Whitfield 1999:153), but the militaristic culture of the local Uighurs promoted a more brash music that drowned out the refined sensibilities of the T'ang court, which itself would be defunct within 25 years.

Yet Kuchean music was not to die out entirely in world music history. Picken and Noël Nickson (2000) have demonstrated how various Kuchean (and by extension Persian and Indian) musical materials acquired by the T'ang court were eventually preserved in evolved forms in the *togaku* repertoire of Japanese *gagaku*, in four ways: (1) with regard to the modality (in the expanded Old World sense highlighted in this chapter); (2) in the form of the instruments and performance techniques that produced these pitch/motivic collections; (3) as secular enter-tainment music "inalienably associated with" dances and suites, sometimes "approaching symphonic proportions" (2000:ix); and (4) in the use of rhythmic organization at both the micro and macro levels closely related to Indian and Indonesian musics (themselves connected to each other and to China and Japan; see Picken, et al., 2000:263–285); all of which further solidifies connections to the known inter/transcultural practices of Kucha. Through the commonalities of Buddhism as well as proximity to China and Japan, musicians from the develop-ing culture of what would be an independent Korea also played a significant role in this process (Picken and Nickson 2000:x, 1). Gagaku reached its first peak of popularity in the Japanese court during the tenth century CE (just after the fall of the T'ang), but declined with the rise of Samurai culture in the early fourteenth century. It was revived starting in the seventeenth century and remains an impor-tant preserved tradition to the present. Though much transformed, it may be the closest thing we have to Silk Road music still extant.

Another key Silk Road destination, Bukhara, regularly hosted Buddhists, Nestorians, Manicheans, Zoroastrians—and not least, Jews who may have emi-grated there prior to or during the Achaemenid Persian era. Sachs notes that Jewish cantillation in Bukhara remained remarkably similar to that of the Sephardim in North Africa (1943:79–80). However, it is important to note that both of these areas were influenced by Muslim cantillation of the Quran very early on, which may account for some of the confluence.

Sogdians continued to dominate the trade routes in the fifth through the eighth centuries CE, but with the emergence of the Persian Sassanids, more Sogdians adopted Zoroastrianism and Manichaeism, which in turn came to be reflected in the art of their towns along the Silk Road. Liu describes a wealthy eighth-cen-tury household in the Sogdian city of Panjikent (still a provincial capital in mod-ern Tajikistan), in which murals depict Zoroastrian, Buddhist, and even ancient Mesopotamian religious elements, noting that "these fragmented murals…pre-serve the last glimpse of the cosmopolitan life in the oasis towns and of the eclectic religious attitude of the Sogdian trading communities before the Islamic conquest" (2010:72).

Along with the full flowering of Chang'an on the Eastern end of the Silk Road during this period, the advent of Islam and the establishment of Baghdad (near the previous Sassanid capital of Ctesiphon and the more ancient site of Babylon) as a Muslim capital after 792 CE encouraged Silk Road travel further into West Asia, including the previously Roman-Judean city of Damascus, after which its path continued towards Tyre (ancient Phoenician territory), Antioch, and Byzantium as in the past, the new key destinations for goods and ideas at the Western end. Each of these centers contributed further to the musical milieu flowing back and forth across the corridor.

Later (c. 1275–1300 CE), Marco Polo traveled through Central Asia and docu-mented for European posterity much of what had developed, at a time when the Silk Road was waning under the Mongols. Indeed, a great deal of the scholarship on the Silk Road has focused on the additional development of its interculturality well past the tenth century CE, even into the fifteenth. Peter Frankopan (2015) goes so far as to suggest, not without merit, that the most important aspects of world history as a whole can be understood as centered along the Silk Road (or rather "Roads," as he notes). For the purposes of a global music history, however, these later developments were overshadowed in terms of impact by the coming of Islam and a subsequent shifting of new musical/cultural energies further westward.

Notes

1 Also later known as the Huns.
2 Traditionally, the implement was identified as a small sword, a whip or a goad, but later scholarship presents a compelling case for a musical/signaling horn; see Duchesne-Guillemin 1980 and Lawergren 2009.
3 These are situated in gestures of the hands and fingers; the term comes from the Sanskrit for that context, and the *talam* are small cymbals used to mark the elements of the cycle (Rowell 1979:100; Fletcher 2001:255).
4 The Japanese Zen Buddhist shakuhachi tradition is also heir to this sound world. Meanwhile, Theraveda traditions remain most vibrant in Sri Lanka and other parts of Southeast Asia, where remnants of Hinduism also survive, particularly in Bali.
5 The seven-stringed veena referred to here was an arched harp rather different from the modern Indian veena; Lawergren notes that "the first representations of arched harps appeared in the third millennium B.C. in Mesopotamia and Egypt" (1994:229, note 17).
6 For interesting details, see Duchesne-Guillemin 1984 and West 1994.
7 Egon Wellesz (1961:34–36) provides helpful details. This view is not without controversy, however; see, e.g., Hiley 1997:55.
8 Though Sachs (1943:81) is strictly correct that Jewish melodies are not pentatonic per se, many of his notated examples can be heard as largely stemming from subsets of world pentatonic mode two (sometimes called "minor pentatonic") with a few additional diatonic ornamental tones.

References

Duchesne-Guillemin, Jacques. 1980. "Cor de Yima et trompette d'Isrāëïl: De la cosmogonie mazdéenne à l'eschatologie musulmane." *Comptes rendus des séances de l'Académie des inscriptions et belles-lettres* 123/3: 539–549.

Duchesne-Guillemin, Marcelle. 1984. "A Hurrian Musical Score from Ugarit: The Discovery of Mesopotamian Music." *Sources from the Ancient Near East* 22:67–94.

During, Jean. 1991a. "Historical Survey." In During, Jean, Zia Mirabdolbaghi, and Dariush Savfat, *The Art of Persian Music*, Washington, D.C: Mage Publishers, 31–56.

During, Jean. 1991b. "Poetry and Music." In During, Jean, Zia Mirabdolbaghi, and Dariush Savfat, *The Art of Persian Music*, Washington, D.C: Mage Publishers, 153–166.

Comotti, Giovanni (trans. Munson, Rosaria). 1979 [1991]. *Music in Greek and Roman Culture*. Baltimore, Maryland: Johns Hopkins University Press.

Ellingson, Ter. 1980. "Ancient Indian Drum Syllables and Bu Ston's Sham Pa Ta Ritual." *Ethnomusicology* 243: 431–452.

Esipova, Margarita. n.d. "Confessional Sources of Ancient Japanese Musical Instruments." Accessed 6-10-2017 at http://ru-jp.org/yaponovedy_yesipova_01e.htm.

Farhat, Hormoz. 1990. *The Dastgāh Concept in Persian Music*. Cambridge: Cambridge University Press.

Fletcher, Peter. 2001. *World Musics in Context*. New York: Oxford University Press.

Frankopan, Peter. 2015. *The Silk Roads: A New History of the World*. New York: Knopf.

Hiley, David. 1997. "Writings on Western Plainchant in the 1980s and 1990s." *Acta Musicologica* 691: 53–93.

Hill, John. 1988. "Notes on the Dating of Khotanese History." *Indo-Iranian Journal* 313: 179–190.

Houseal, Joseph. 2015a. "Dance at Dunhuang: Part One." (Buddhistdoor Global). Accessed 5-23-2017 at https://www.buddhistdoor.net/features/dance-at-dunhuang-part-one.

Houseal, Joseph. 2015b. "Dance at Dunhuang: Part Two—The Case for the *Feitian*." (Buddhistdoor Global). Accessed 5-23-2017 at https://www.buddhistdoor.net/features/dance-at-dunhuang-part-two-the-case-for-the-feitian.

Houseal, Joseph. 2016. "Dance at Dunhuang: Part Three—The Sogdian Whirl." (Buddhistdoor Global). Accessed 5-23-2017 at https://www.buddhistdoor.net/features/dance-at-dunhuang-part-three-the-sogdian-whirl.

Jairazbhoy, N.A. 1975. "An Interpretation of the 22 Śrutis." *Asian Music* 61/2: 38–59.

Keller, Johanna. 2007. "Yo-Yo Ma's Edge Effect." *Chronicle of Higher Ed (The Chronicle Review)* 5329: B10.

Knechtges, David, and Taiping Chang (eds.). 2010. *Ancient and Early Medieval Chinese Literature: A Reference Guide, Part One*. Boston: Brill.

Kishore, Prem, and Anuradha Ganpati. 2003. *India: An Illustrated History*. New York: Hippocrene Books.

Lawergren, Bo. 1994. "Buddha as a Musician: An Illustration of a Jataka Story." *Artibus Asiae* 543/4: 226–240.

Lawergren, Bo. 2009. "Music History. I. Pre-Islamic Iran." *Encyclopædia Iranica* (online edition). Accessed 5-19-2016 at http://www.iranicaonline.org/articles/music-history-i-pre-islamic-iran.

Liu, Xinru. 2010. *The Silk Road in World History*. New York: Oxford University Press.

Mabbett, Ian. 1994. "Buddhism and Music." *Asian Music* 25 1/2: 9–28.

Mair, Victor (ed.). 2000. *The Shorter Columbia Anthology of Traditional Chinese Literature*. New York: Columbia University Press.

Mair, Victor. 2008. "The Synesthesia of Sinitic Esthetics and Its Indic Resonances." *Chinese Literature: Essays, Articles, Reviews (CLEAR)* 30: 103–116.

McClain, Ernest. 1979. "Chinese Cyclic Tunings in Late Antiquity." *Ethnomusicology* 232: 205–224.

McNeill, J.R., and William McNeill. 2003. *The Human Web*. New York: W.W. Norton.

Mikkelsen, Gunnar. 2009. "Sukhavati and the Light-World: Pure-Land Elements in the Chinese Manichaean *Eulogy of the Light-World*." In BeDhun, Jason (ed.), *New Light on Manichaeism: Papers from the Sixth International Conference on Manichaeism*, Boston: Brill, 201–212.

Naylor, Phillip. 2015. *North Africa: A History from Antiquity to the Present* (Revised ed.). Austin: University of Texas Press.

Needham, Joseph. 1954. *Science and Civilisation in China, Volume 1: Introductory Orientations*. Cambridge: Cambridge University Press.

Nketia, J.H.K. 1974. *The Music of Africa*. New York: W.W. Norton.

Picken, Laurence. 1955. "The Origin of the Short Lute." *The Galpin Society Journal* 8: 32–42.

Picken, Laurence. 2000. "Modal Note-Sets and Related Matters in Ancient China; in Ancient and Modern India and Persia; in Ancient Greece." In Picken, Laurence, and Noël Nickson (eds.), *Music from the Tang Court–7*, New York: Cambridge University Press, 185–251.

Picken, Laurence, Nicholas Gray, and Robert Walker. 2000. "Parallels in the Organization of Music in Time in Indonesia, Ancient India and Ancient China." In Picken, Laurence, and Noël Nickson (eds.), *Music from the Tang Court–7*, New York: Cambridge University Press, 263–285.

Picken, Laurence, and Noël Nickson (eds.). 2000. *Music from the Tang Court–7*. New York: Cambridge University Press.

Ropp, Paul. 2010. *China in World History*. New York: Oxford University Press.

Rowell, Louis. 1979. "The Subconscious Language of Musical Time." *Music Theory Spectrum* 1: 96–106.

Rowell, Louis. 2000. "Scale and Mode in the Music of the Early Tamils of South India." *Music Theory Spectrum* 222: 135–156.

Sachs, Curt. 1943 [2008]. *The Rise of Music in the Ancient World*. New York: W.W. Norton. [Reprinted: Mineola, New York: Dover.]

Shelemay, Kay, Peter Jeffery, and Ingrid Monson. 1993. "Oral and Written Transmission in Ethiopian Christian Chant." *Early Music History* 12: 55–117.

Stein, M.A. 1907. *Ancient Khotan*. Oxford: Clarendon Press.

Thompson, John. 2013. Notes on "Wandering in a Lunar Palace." Accessed 6-24-2017 at http://www.silkqin.com/02qnpu/07sqmp/sq18ghy.htm.

Touma, Habib (trans. Schwartz, L.). 1996. *The Music of the Arabs*. Portland, Oregon: Amadeus Press.

van der Merwe, Peter. 1989. *Origins of the Popular Style: The Antecedents of Twentieth-Century Popular Music*. New York: Oxford University Press.

Wang, Yuhwen. 2004. "The Ethical Power of Music: Ancient Greek and Chinese Thoughts." *The Journal of Aesthetic Education* 381: 89–104.

Wang, Yumei. 2012. *Songs that Touch Our Soul—A Comparative Study of Folk Songs in Two Chinese Classics: Shijing and Han Yuefu*. (unpublished master's. thesis). Toronto, Canada: University of Toronto.

Weinberger, Eliot. 2009. *Oranges and Peanuts for Sale*. New York: New Directions Publishing.

Wellesz, Egon. 1961. *A History of Byzantine Music and Hymnography* (2nd ed.). London: Oxford University Press.

West, M.L. 1994. "The Babylonian Musical Notation and the Hurrian Melodic Texts." *Music and Letters* 752: 161– 179.

Whitfield, Susan. 1999. *Life Along the Silk Road*. Berkeley, California: University of California Press.

Wood, Frances. 2002. *The Silk Road: Two Thousand Years in the Heart of Asia*. Berkeley, California: University of California Press.

4   The second pivotal convergence

Al-Andalus, Byzantium, and the European coming of age c. 700–1500 CE[1]

Figure 4.1 Map of key locations, second pivotal convergence.

The plaza of Purchena [in Granada] was ready for the dances, with many carpets spread; all the important people were seated round about with Ibn Humeya on a dais; and lute and timbrel in place.

Then Ibn Humeya ordered that the Moorish [Morisco: Muslim converted to Christian] maidens should come out alone to dance, and there were many who danced gracefully. Last came the lovely Luna, a native of Purchena... [She] carried a rich scarf or veil made of fine silk of many colors, embroidered in Tunis, and tipped with pure gold of great price.

Then Ibn Humeya commanded that the musicians should play and sing... Gironcillo, born in Granada and remembering the flowery days of his youth passed there, took the lute and... sang so charmingly in Castilian that everyone fell in love with his playing and singing.

Next Ibn Humeya asked the most beautiful Moorish maidens to sing. These were unable to play on the lute; so a tambourine was brought for one, while another played the timbrels in the Moorish fashion. They sang a ballad and then a song

called tangia. Then, while many lovely and well-attired Moorish maidens were assembled, the beautiful Luna was importuned to sing in Arabic.
—Seventeenth-century account of Gines Perez de Hita (possibly fictional; quoted in Ribera 1929:146–147)

Figure 4.2 Thirteenth-century Arab and Spanish musicians.

Source: Public domain: Reproduction from *Cantigas de Santa Maria* El Escorial manuscript, in Ribera 1922.

Even as the Silk Road continued through the second phase of its trajectory well into the fifteenth century CE (after which it was eclipsed as a nexus of economic development by the exploration of the Americas), Islam arose as a cultural force beginning c. 632 CE and served over many centuries to connect much of the inter-culturality of the Old World to the rise of Europe and, indirectly, the New World.

Despite deep ambivalence about the nature and role of music in religious life, the Arab culture in which Islam was embedded rapidly emerged as a vehicle for both synthesis and advancement in the musical arts. Arabs were full participants in the continuing Silk Road networks, while the close proximity of the Arabian peninsula to the East African coast provided opportunities for influence from those musical cultures as well. "Free to adopt anything from…other cultures that did not contradict Islamic teaching, the Arabs enthusiastically assimilated the aesthetic and spiritual legacies of the Greeks, Romans, Persians, Egyptians, Assyrians, and Babylonians, ultimately merging them into something new and unique" (Touma 1996:5), and, by extension, resituating the artistic legacy of the Silk Road in yet another complex cultural and religious context. As Peter Fletcher puts it, "Islamic art music was essentially a synthesis of Greek and Persian traditions. If its theorizing derived from Hellenic Alexandria, its musical practice was based on that of Persia...[Moreover,] many Persian instruments had their origins in ancient Mesopotamia" (2001:213). Yet this is something of an oversimplification, since Islamic culture took these musical legacies of West and Central Asia in new directions both artistically and geographically. In addition, during the period of approximately 700–1500 CE, the impact of Islam on global music history stood in complex relationship with another Old World, Silk Road connector: the further flowering of Byzantium and its influence on the rise of the West.

What the Arabs called *al-Andalus*—parts of the Iberian peninsula and the areas of North Africa directly south—served as a locus of and a conduit for the conditions that spawned a new era. It both arose from and created a broader, continuing set of ancient intercultural connections spanning from West Africa to West Asia. These conditions were established early on and followed by additional intercultural waves brought by the Arabs and Byzantines from further east and, with the fall of Rome in Iberia, by Germanic Visigoths. In all this, the stage was set for an era of military conflict between Christians, Muslims, and African Berbers during the period considered in this chapter, certainly, but that very circumstance created opportunities for ongoing intercultural exchange. Byzantium reinforced Christian legacies and brought its brand of Asian cultural connections directly to the region during the sixth and seventh centuries. The indigenous Berbers, meanwhile, both forged alliances with and provided resistance to various actors at different times. Not inconsequential were the contributions of Jews who settled in the Iberian peninsula and North Africa throughout the period under consideration, bringing ancient Semitic traditions with them even as they negotiated these challenging contexts. In the midst of significant religious-political tensions across a number of centuries, an astounding series of artistic and other cultural synergies nevertheless arose and flourished.[2]

To summarize: *The second pivotal transcultural convergence in global music history with which this chapter is concerned was essentially driven by a westward movement of energy from a nexus across Central Asia to a nexus across the Eastern Mediterranean, North Africa, and Iberia further into Europe, where a new synthesis emerged.*

"Arab Spain was of enormous importance to Europe, a door to the learning and science of the East...[The] Arab stamp [in Spain] went very deep, as many students of the later, Christian, Spain have pointed out, and can still be observed in language, manners and art" (Roberts 2004:341–342). As Fletcher succinctly illustrates (2001:416–420), Arabic music—and other West and Central Asian traditions it carried with it—in turn influenced European music through Spain, into France, and even the Germanic states, during and after European Christian kingdoms regained these areas from Muslim control. Outside of Spain, participation of leaders such as Richard I ("Lionheart") of England and Phillip II of France in Crusades on Muslim-held territory in Jerusalem and its vicinity was also conducive to "the establishment of a new and distinctive European civilization from a mixture of Judaic, Graeco-Egyptian, and Islamic influences" (Fletcher 2001:414).

There is more agreement about the first part of this thesis than about the last. Amnon Shiloah sums up the former carefully but clearly by stating that "in the decades following the Muslim conquest [of 710], the different components of the heteroclite Iberian society were, in one way or another, active in the process of crystallizing a social and cultural symbiosis, within the framework of which music occupied a prominent place," where heteroclite Iberian society included "Hispano-Christians who converted to Islam, a strong element of Berbers, a significant number of Negroes and freed slaves from Eastern and Western Europe…, those who refused to convert, namely, the Christians, who qualified as Mozarabs, and the Jews" (1991:14–15). Meanwhile, the direct and indirect effects of Byzantine Christianity on the music of early Western Christianity was profound. The later flowering of a Norman-Arab-Byzantine culture between c. 1050 and 1250 on the island of Sicily, built upon still older Greco-Phoenician roots, was another manifestation of this inter/transcultural milieu; a combination of Arab and Byzantine artistic and architectural techniques is featured throughout the Cappella Palatina in Palermo, for example. Limited but tantalizing evidence has also been found of material in Sicilian Christian chant from the ancient city of Acre (currently in North Israel near the Syrian border), known for East–West interaction over many centuries (Hiley 1981:8), most likely a result of Crusader activity.

However, the latter part of the proffered thesis—that this situation had an essential impact on the development of Western European music more broadly, and specifically through Afro-Arabic influence in al-Andalus—remains far more controversial. It has had no stronger nor more articulate advocate than Henry George Farmer (1930, e.g.), who spent a large part of his career demonstrating extensive evidence of Arab musical influence on medieval Iberia and into France, Italy, Germany, and beyond.[3] The subject of significant criticism, Farmer's analysis retains its essential value despite suffering both from some rhetorical excess that unnecessarily weakened the impact of its arguments and, in fact, from too small a vision: Farmer failed to see that the fascinating story he illuminated was ultimately best understood in a larger, longer-term, and more broadly global context. The issue is not really one of precisely who should be credited with originating what we now call Western music. It is rather a question of how the Andalusian (and, for that matter, the Western) musical story fits into the flow of global musical history, about musical directions that emerged from the extraordinary fusions of indigenous (North) African, Iberian Gothic Christian, and Arabic Muslim musical inputs—including, again, the revival of key elements from Greek music theory via the Arabs—and how much global influence these trajectories subsequently wielded.[4]

The purpose of this chapter is to examine and reframe these trajectories and outcomes, acknowledging that Western Europe developed at least two musical characteristics that were essentially distinct from the general milieu and its Old World roots, but which at the same time can plausibly be seen as intertwined with the intercultural complexities of both the area and the era. Moreover, what the West in turn bequeathed to the New World musically (and then eventually back to the global community) was just as important as its own continuing identity.[5]

A large portion of traditional music history has focused on the rise of the West, and there is no need to reproduce that vast corpus of work here. Indeed, the sheer volume of study is far too great even for meaningful reference, and the variety of views is substantial. However, because they were so consequential to the third pivotal convergence in the Americas, it is crucial to a global music history to identify the distinctive musical contributions that ultimately emerged from Western Europe. These can be summarized as true polyphony and a closely related focus on vertical harmony within a chromatic concept of tonality (developed from earlier modality), using what came to be known as "major" and "minor" scales in 12 chromatic "keys" and concomitantly distinctive pitch ordering functions as the seventeenth century commenced.[6] The streams leading to those results, and the general nature of Western music, however, were multivariate. They did not arise in a vacuum and they could not escape congress with Eastern inputs.

Adoption of the view that Western music should be seen primarily in the midst of an Old World/New World/Global continuum will not, of course, be without controversy. Western European music history and theory have dominated the field for many centuries: on one hand they have been seen as something of a human culmination while on the other there have been an increasing number of voices who aim to contextualize Western music as part of an exploitative imperialist paradigm by which its host cultures are now often framed.[7] But since one of the key aims of this book is to reconsider the place of each musical culture in a coherent global musical story, the reasons for why Western music came to have such a strong voice in that story—both in Europe and then in a transformatively integrative way in the Americas and beyond—are not as important as the fact that it did indeed have such influence. This is no less so than any number of other correspondences between cultural inconveniences and musical developments that have been seen or suggested herein.

Even from the most traditional perspectives, temporarily putting aside what the Arabs brought from the East to the conversation via al-Andalus, Western Europe as a whole was a product of significant cultural fusion, including inputs from West Asian Judeo-Christian, Germanic, and Greco-Roman sources. From a political view, one can easily take as "the birth of the West" the establishment of the Frankish Germanic ruler Charlemagne c. 800 and the configuration of territories that were eventually to become the Central-Western European nations. A generation earlier, Charles Martel's defeat of the Muslim conquerors at Poitiers-Tours in 732 is typically seen to have prevented Islam from invading nascent Western Europe and changing its course. However, the streams and their interactions leading to the West's *musical* identity were far more complex, and certainly more inter/transcultural, than such a narrative implies. These interactions and confluences can be conveniently grouped into Hellenistic, Christian, and Afro-Asian categories, though with considerable overlap. In this context, there was a very long incubation period for what came to be understood as "Western music."

J.M. Roberts provides a useful general analysis:

> Europe would long be a cultural importer. It took centuries before its architecture could compare with that of the classical past, of Byzantium or the Asian empires, and when it emerged it did so by borrowing the style of Byzantine Italy and the pointed arch of the Arabs. For just as long, no science, no school in the West could match those of Arab Spain or Asia. Nor could Western Christendom produce an effective political unity or theoretical justification of power such as the eastern empire and the caliphates,
>
> (2004:393)

structures conducive to stable economies and societies in which the arts may flourish. To this may be added, by extension, that without elements bequeathed from non-Western cultures, Western music as we know it (and certainly as it has since evolved globally) would not have existed. The debate is over how precisely and how accurately the West may have defined itself against the Silk Road legacies represented and transformed by Byzantium and the Arabs.

Early Arab-Islamic musical contexts

Habib Touma provides a helpful summary of foundational Arab music traditions (1996:1–8), themselves situated in intercultural contexts. The early Islamic capital city of Medina on the Arabian peninsula, originally settled by Jews, already had a robust musical life and quickly became known as a center for training singers, including Persians, Ethiopians, and Africans from further south, a reputation it maintained even after the capital was moved north to Damascus in 661. Singing and poetry were at the heart of Arab-Islamic music from its inception. Two of the most famous singers prior to the establishment of Baghdad as the cultural capital of the Abbasids (c. 762)—who were especially sympathetic to Persian customs—were Tuways (632–710), an influential performer and teacher, and Jamilah (d. 720), who put on elaborate concerts with large ensembles and dancing in her palace at Medina. Flowing out of the pre-Islamic *qiyan* (female courtesan-musician) tradition, singers were accompanied by lutes (*ouds*), flutes (*nays*), frame drums (likely both round and square), rattles, and zithers, all of ancient Afro-Asian origins. Ensembles grew in size as these traditions developed, and sometimes included choirs as well. Another singer, Yunus al-Katib (d. 765), collected musical material and wrote several treatises analyzing the poetry, melodies, and rhythms of Arabic song, works that were preserved into the ninth and tenth centuries as key sources by later scholars, including Abu al-Faraj al-Isfahani. Yunus is immortalized in nights 684 and 685 of the *Thousand and One Nights*, where his singing and musical instruction help bring him into the patronage of Walid ibn Yazid during the latter's very brief term as caliph (Touma 1996:743–744).

Under the famed Harun al-Rashid (c. 765–809) the Persian musical family of al-Mawsili flourished, providing additional connections to ancient pre-Islamic cultures, while Indian mathematics and sciences also came to the Abbasid court of Harun's predecessor al-Mansur (r. 754–775) in the form of Brahmagupta's seventh-century treatise *Brahmasiddhanta*. It is not insignificant that Harun moved his capital further north and west to Raqqa (in modern Syria) in 796, for Raqqa had been established as a Hellenistic city c. 300 BCE during the reign of Seleucus the first, original compatriot of Alexander the Great. Raqqa was well within the orbit of Byzantium as well as the Silk Road city of Palmyra, and thus again of Damascus.

Four prominent West-Central Asian scholars who developed Arabic music theory in ways that sought to harmonize Helleno-Persian and Islamic thought were (1) al-Kindi (died c. 870) of Baghdad; (2) al-Farabi (d. 950), who also flourished primarily in Baghdad but was born in Central Asia (near modern Otrar, Kazakhstan) and died in Aleppo, Syria (Ehrenkreutz 1980) having had meaningful visits to Damascus and Egypt; (3) Ibn Sina (Latin: Avicenna, d. 1037), who was born and raised in the Silk Road town of Bukhara before travelling to Baghdad and eventually further west; and (4) Safi ad-Din al-Urmawi (d. 1294), whose *Kitab al-Adwar* has rightly been called "the most influential of all Arabic treatises on music" (Wright 1995:455), since it consists of a codification of foundational modes and rhythmic cycles along with their relationships for composition and performance.

Meanwhile, the Umayyad Caliphate inherited the long intercultural history of the Iberian peninsula and the adjacent areas of North Africa to the south when it established al-Andalus during the period of c. 670–721 CE. A number of relevant musical stories from this milieu appear in al-Isfahani's massive *Kitab al-aghani* (*Book of Songs*, mid-tenth century), a major source of information that connects the musical histories of Baghdad and al-Andalus.

The North African transcultural context was complex from earliest times, and has remained so; Phillip Naylor rightly calls it "one of those rare regions of the world that serves as an axis of cultures and civilizations" (2015:1). For the purposes of a global music history, it has been convenient to separate Egypt from the rest of North Africa prior to the coming of Islam, but Egypt's legacies as both one of the earliest centers of civilization and later as a Hellenistic Roman state merged with those of the Arabs as they swept westward across North Africa into the eighth century. Coptic Christianity in Egypt and its influence in other parts of the region must also be considered. In all these ways, Egypt played an important role in the reformed transcultural corridor that arose in the Mediterranean, North Africa, and into Europe through the end of the fifteenth century as the remnants of the Roman Empire were themselves being transformed.

Byzantium and many cultures even more ancient had already left a mark on North Africa and Iberia long before the Arabs arrived. For example, as first noted in Chapters 2 and 3, the Phoenicians and their successors had brought West Asian features from Tyre and Sidon both prior to and after the rise of the Silk Road, establishing flourishing sites in what are today Tunisia, Morocco, Algeria, and into Spain (Naylor 2015:25). They were some of the first non-Africans of record to intermingle substantially with the indigenous populations of North Africa, collectively known historically as the Berbers (from the Greek for "barbarians"). This effectively connected North Africa very early on to the legacies of the Nile-Indus-Aegean corridor and later to the western end of the Silk Road. From their capital civilization of Carthage, the Phoenicians "sought trade with [the Berbers], especially metals—gold, silver, copper and tin...[and] accumulated great wealth while serving as middlemen between the Berbers and Mediterranean clients. In turn the Berbers also participated in trans-Saharan trade" as part of a larger common West African trade network with North African communities from earliest times (Naylor 2015:26; see also 3, 24, 47).

In this context, elements of sub-Saharan African culture on the western coast exerted influence on the region; the surviving traditional musics and other arts of North Africa as well as the hybrids established later retain elements that are clearly tied to West African sensibilities. The traditional Moroccan Ahouache dance (an original Tamazight language term) reflects strong indigenous elements in the form of short, repetitive phrases in world pentatonic pitch structure and rhythms that resemble those still found in sub-Saharan West Africa, though some later Arabic influence appears to remain—for example, prominent use of a version of the nay flute. The round hand drums (*bandir*) used in the region are ubiquitous from earliest times, and may be African or Asian in origin. Morocco also features Gnawa music of West-Central African origin, utilizing short, repetitive phrases in African "blue-note" tunings and call and response techniques, as well as the *gimbri*, a long-necked bass lute that is very similar to the Amazigh (Berber) *loutar*. Farmer (1928) refers to Ibn Batutta's fourteenth-century mention of the gimbri (*gunbri*) as originating from Mali. Theodore Grame provides the following field description of a mid-twentieth-century Shluh (Berber) performance in Morocco:

> There are two standing musicians, dressed in the white robes of the Shluh. Each of them plays a small lute (the gunbris)...[which] are held in a fashion almost identical with the way in which their ancestors, the lutes of ancient Egypt, were carried. The performers sing a short, unvaried melody antiphonally; the tune as sung does not vary from stanza to stanza, though the heterophonic instrumental parts do. The music possesses little in the way of microtonal inflection...[In some instances the ensemble was augmented by] a performer who sat on the ground striking with two metal rods on circular piece of steel (naqus). Frequently this individual maintained a lengthy cross-rhythm against the prevailing one...The ensemble...is quite unlike an "African" ensemble since it lacks any membranophones; it is, however, equally unlike an Arabic one, and for the same reason. The heterophony of the musicians seems Arabic and the antiphonal singing African, as does the lack of chromaticism...Actually, the Shluh performance reminds us in many ways of the ancient Egyptian performance, as far as we can discuss it from iconographical evidence.
>
> (1970:84–85)

Edith Gerson-Kiwi (1967:17ff.) discusses similarities between Berber and Middle Eastern music that might in part be the result of intercultural contact with Jews who migrated to the Atlas Mountain region during the era of Phoenician colonization, noting that this may account for chromatic inflections around otherwise pentatonic structures in that region. Contemporary popular bands such as Tinariwen, in the Tuareg tradition from Saharan Mali, demonstrate the continuing globalization of the region, retaining Berber elements while embracing Arabic elements such as the singing style, incorporating American rock-pop influence with modern acoustic and electric guitars, and integrating the West African *djembe* (goblet hand drum), for example.

It is also interesting to note that very early in Muslim history, a perspective arose that eventually came to be called Sufism, seeking the attainment of a more mystical spiritual experience with God rather than mere legalism. Though the movement began as an ascetic one, the most liberal forms of Sufism were not unlike Mahayana Buddhism and even Hinduism in their attraction to the arts as a means of worship, to poetry, music, and dance (*sama* in Sufism) as vehicles to the heart of the divine and religious ecstasy. In some cases, this applied even to erotic love poetry as reflective of the love of God. The extent to which a follower of Islam accepts the value and legitimacy of sama is essentially the extent to which he embraces music as a religious element. Singing, music, and dance very often form part of the Sufi *dhikr*, in which the devotee rhythmically repeats the name of God or other expressions about aspects of divinity, alone or in groups. It is perhaps not surprising that, given a long and strong tradition in the arts, many Persian Muslims adopted Sufi perspectives. The famed Persian Sufi mystic Abu Hamid al-Ghazli (c. 1058–1111), for example, urged adherents to

> Know that hearts and consciences are treasuries of secrets and mines of jewels. Wrapped within them lie their jewels just as fire is enveloped in iron and stone, and hidden like water is concealed under dust and loam. There is no way of extracting such hidden things save by the flint and steel of audition to poetry and music (sama), and there is no entrance to the heart save by the ante chamber of the ears. So musical tones, measured and pleasing, bring forth what is in it and make evident its beauties and defects.
>
> (quoted in Lewisohn 1997:1)

Perhaps the most musically famous Sufis are the Turkish Mevlevi order, followers of the twelfth-century Persian mystic Rumi, who are known as the Whirling Dervishes due to the spinning dance dhikr they perform as part of their sama ceremonies.

Eventually, India and North Africa also emerged as centers of Sufi Muslim activity. Full acceptance of Sufi perspectives embracing sama came later to al-Andalus, reaching a peak in the eleventh to thirteenth centuries, where its most famous advocates were Ibn Barrajan and Ibn Arabi. The spread of Andalusian musical style and repertoire during this period was significantly enhanced by the activities of Sufi brotherhoods (Reynolds 2015:259; Fletcher 2001:210).

Today the bandir frame drum common to both North Africa and West Asia is frequently played by Sufi musicians as part of the dhikr (Touma 1996:136).

By c. 770 the Abbasids and the Umayyads had effectively created parallel centers of Islamic power and culture in Baghdad and Cordoba respectively. Touma suggests that by c. 800 the full flowering of medieval music in both these regions was underway and would continue until the thirteenth century (1996:9–11). A.J. Racy (1992) notes that this dually interactive atmosphere contributed substantially to a predilection toward musical synthesis in the larger Islamic world, setting the stage for yet later developments in turn. The tensions between the two Caliphates were to play a role in Islamic relations with Europe in ways that had a relevant effect on cultural exchange. In the midst of that, the music of al-Andalus, born of its particular intercultural context, would become something unique.

Networks of medieval musical streams

Ultimately, the West succeeded in substituting harmony for melodic ornamentation as a chief expressive device, which separated it from its predecessors. Harmony in turn proved to be essential to distinguishing polyphony and its full affective powers from other complex textures such as heterophony. Yet even polyphony and harmony had rudimentary precedents in and influences from what the Arabs and Byzantines contributed to the broader Mediterranean sphere to which Western Europe was connected.

Unfortunately, the European musical story is too often framed around some sort of pure ancient Greek heritage, which seeks to cast Arabo-Byzantine Mediterranean inputs in a lesser light despite the fact that the Hellenistic legacy was common to them all. The traditional view may be summarized as follows: The Roman philosopher Boethius (c. 480–524 CE), confidant to the Ostrogothic ruler Theodoric, helped reconnect the West with original Greek music theory (see Boethius's *De Musica Institutione*, for example), which in turn informed the *Musica enchiriadis* (c. 895) and *Scolica enchiriadis* in which early principles of true polyphony, called organum, were first elucidated. Composers of the Notre Dame School in Paris, most notably Perotin (c. 1200) expanded organum considerably further into three and even four rhythmically independent parts. Throughout the fourteenth, fifteenth, and sixteenth centuries, composers such as Guillame de Machaut (c. 1300–77), Guillaume Dufay (1397–1474), and Josquin des Prez (c. 1450–1521) developed polyphony within older modal frameworks. Western ideas on rhythm, which were soon to move away from the more complex rhythms in previous musics and toward concepts that allowed a focus on harmony to prevail, received early explication in treatises such as the *Ars cantus mensurabilis* (c. 1260) by Franco of Cologne and the *Ars nova notandi* (1322) attributed to the composer Phillipe de Vitry. Major-minor tonality and associated harmonic principles were clarified over the course of the seventeenth century. Jean-Philippe Rameau (1683–1764, roughly a contemporary of J.S. Bach, 1685–1750, whose music expanded greatly on the resources of tonality) first attempted to explain these principles in his *Treatise on Harmony* of 1722. The rise of this tonal system and its associated aesthetic priorities was to spur the reimagining of everything from singing style to musical instrument design.

This narrative contains many elements of truth, warranting a return to its key aspects in due course. Nevertheless, it is far too narrow to fully frame what happened musically in "the West"—which from a global perspective should really be redefined as "West of the Gulf of Oman"—from c. 700–1500. Nor does it contextualize what in turn flowed even further west across the Atlantic in the subsequent era. In reality, Hellenistic, Christian, and Afro-Asian cultures and musics intermingled in a network of medieval streams during this period as Western Europe emerged, and it is ultimately this legacy that set the subsequent course of global music history.

In that light, the importance of Byzantium cannot be overstated. As Roberts notes,

> The Byzantine inheritance was not only imperial [i.e., Roman] and Christian. It also owed debts to Asia. These were not merely a matter of direct contacts with alien civilizations symbolized by the arrival of Chinese merchandise along the Silk Road, but also of the complex cultural inheritance of the Hellenistic East.
>
> (2004:350)

Under Justinian (r. 527–565 CE) and his dynastic successors, Byzantine influence spread more forcefully across North Africa, especially Carthage, and into Southern Spain. Their relations with indigenous North Africans were complex, and theological controversies in Alexandria kept tensions high between Christians in Egypt and the Byzantine Church in Constantinople, weakening imperial authority but also reinforcing diversity.[8]

Even the role of the Frankish Carolingians centuries later should be seen in a more complex light in this context, outside of the purely military-political. From his court at Aachen, Charlemagne clearly supported the development of the arts and learning in the form of the classical trivium and quadrivium—"Every monastery and every abbey [must] have its school, in which boys may be taught the Psalms, the system of musical notation, singing, arithmetic, and grammar" (from the *Capitulary* of 789, as quoted in Lewis 2008:295)—and did not resist intercultural contact in that context. Charlemagne seems to have inherited this spirit from his royal ancestors, for his immediate predecessor Pepin III famously received a musical organ from Constantinople[9] and there was contemporaneous exchange between Harun al Rashid's court and that of the Franks as Western Europe was beginning to emerge. Too often less emphasized than the victory of Charles Martel at Poitiers-Tours is the fact that the Carolingian court subsequently sought and partially achieved something of an alliance with the Abbasid court in Baghdad, from the mid-eighth to the early ninth centuries, precisely as a strategic gambit against the Ummayad center of power in al-Andalus. It thereby maintained a conduit for artistic and intellectual influences from Eastern culture generally.

At first glance, Arab-Afro-Asian influence on the early development of the music of the West is probably most clearly seen in the areas of (1) instruments; (2) rhythm (including early rhythmic elements of polyphony); (3) the relationship between poetry, rhythm, and musical process; and (4) a reinforcement of implications of Greek music theory with regard to pitch. As a result, it would not be wholly unfounded to assume that these musical streams affected popular/secular Western music more directly than they did sacred (Christian) music.

Indeed, both Western Christian and Islamic Arabic cultures have tended to distinguish religious from non-religious music. Even today, in stark contrast to Sufi perspectives, many conservative Muslims regard music strictly as a form of secular entertainment with which religion may never be sullied. The Quran is "recited" rather than "sung," for example, even though such cantillation displays as much musical sophistication and virtuosity as any religious chant. The Arabic word *musiqa* is directly borrowed from Greek, and generally refers to music as a theoretical subject, whereas *ghina*, meaning "song" is the most common classic word for actual musical activity, in combination with *tarab*, the emotional joy of musical experience. Yet none of these words is applied to cantillation of the Quran, which proceeds from a set of rules called *tajwid*. Here the differences with Christian chant are clear, for the words of the Bible, especially the Psalms, were freely sung and understood as music at the outset. Still, the West has at many points had at least a philosophical sacred-secular divide that extended not only to words and associations but also to actual musical style. In early Western-Christian musical development, this distinction centers largely on the role of rhythm—both its sensual power but also its associations with non-Christian cultures—and the use of instruments, neither of which convey the propositional meaning of words as singing does.

However, it is impossible to entirely disentangle the sacred-secular threads, since they were not absolutely cordoned off from one another. The West had monasteries, courts, and cathedrals in which intellectually sophisticated music was developing, but, as across the Silk Road, these were part of economic networks that included the whole populace. At the same time, notated chant was not for mass congregational singing, but rather for professional clergy, just as use of the written Bible was typically restricted to professional recitation and commentary to a largely illiterate public of worshipers. Awareness of these aspects of early Christian life, tied up in the development of monastic and university communities where literacy and musical education were included, is critical to understanding the questions around medieval musical complexity and simplicity. The aspirational architecture of cathedrals and churches, which reinforced the purity of low-ratio intervals (2:1 octave and 3:2 fifth especially), drove developments toward musical simplicity and eventually harmony: one could not understand the sung words as well otherwise. At the same time, popular "folk" music included instruments and dancing situated around entertainment and rhythmic vitality. The tensions arising from this context have continued to play out in Christian-Western culture in the form of more or less anti-intellectual and anti-artistic bents. Some of these tensions have been mitigated since the eighteenth century by the European

Enlightenment, but controversies surrounding levels of acceptability of popular ("low culture") vs. academic ("high culture") styles as musically (or spiritually) "legitimate" remain unresolved.[10]

Old World monophonic/monodic legacies and Christian chant

Because both sacred and secular music in the Mediterranean-European region arose from an ancient monophonic/monodic tradition that had largely developed further East, consideration of how that process might have unfolded is in order. Western European music was to diverge more significantly from this system throughout the period of 700–1900 CE (less so in Eastern Europe), but that divergence was not straightforwardly linear, and in fact elements of the two legacies would eventually be reunited in the musics of the twentieth century and beyond.

What Touma calls the "maqam phenomenon" (1996:38–45) was an influential contribution of the Arabs, one that eventually spread back through Central Asia and remains vibrant to this day as a contrast to Western tonality, especially in that the latter developed more toward harmony than (often microtonally) ornamented melody.[11] Nevertheless, the following comment by Curt Sachs is essential to understanding not only how this phenomenon emerged from within the broader milieu of antiquity, but also why the Arabs held Greek music theory in such high regard and passed it along to Western Europe:

> 'Melody,' in the Orient, has always meant one of those flexible patterns that the Arabs finally classified as *maqamat* and the Hindu as *ragas*, which imposed upon the [musician] their specific genera, scales, pitches, accents, tempos and moods, but granted him full personal freedom for their elaboration...Ethos was among the qualities of maqamat as it pertained to ragas and [Greek] harmoniai, though perhaps to a lesser degree.
>
> (Sachs 1943:83, 285)

From this coalesced was what might for historical purposes be called the "maqam/harmoniai/raga complex" (implied further in Sachs 1943:249–250, 285–286). Western modality/tonality, understood broadly, emerged later. Yet all these systems are actually modalities of a kind rather than strictly linear scales per se, with conventions that revolve around dynamic acoustic principles of tension and release common to a larger master pitch set (see Hijleh 2012:59–108). The intercourse of manifestations of these dynamics within and across musical cultures was important to the increasingly globalized result that coalesced into the twentieth century and beyond.[12] For one thing, the maqam/harmoniai/raga complex included intervals (both theoretical and performed) outside of diatonic or even chromatic tuning that, though theoretically rejected by the West for many centuries, re-emerged in twentieth-century globalized musics in various forms. On the other hand, certain psycho-physical-ethical implications of pitch modalities inherited from the Greeks through the Arabs and Byzantium were clearly a part of Western musical thinking as it developed within the Christian church tradition.

It is not much more of a stretch to see the Hindu, Buddhist, Daoist, and even Confucian legacies as generally of a piece with this same idea—reflecting another qualified human musical universal.

The two most distinctive Western musical elements (polyphony and tonal harmony) were ultimately interdependent, but it is important to acknowledge that, historically, they did not start out that way. Polyphony developed within an older modal system that retained ties to monophonic/monodic traditions, long before tonal harmony was settled in the West. From this perspective, the "birth of Western music" as a truly distinctive style should probably be placed no earlier than sometime between c. 1200, with the florid organum of the Notre Dame School in Paris as the first true polyphony, and c. 1350 with the rise of harmonic and rhythmic language that began to emerge in the work of Machaut and others to more carefully guide that polyphony. This perspective will be taken up further in a subsequent section of the chapter, but the temptation to reach all the way back to the consolidation of Gregorian chant during the eighth and ninth centuries CE or even earlier for this purpose should be resisted. Rather, in a global music history, Western plainchant was yet another manifestation of the long, strong, and complex monophonic/monodic tradition of the Afro-Eurasian Old World that can be seen in the various forms of Christian chant—including the Byzantine, Ambrosian (Milanese), Gallican-Frankish (before adaptation to the Roman/Gregorian), Old Roman, and Mozarabic (Visigothic/Spanish) practices that seem to have more clearly carried ancient Asian elements with them.

It is therefore useful at this juncture to consider some of the details of Christian chant in terms of musical style—ornamentation, modality, rhythm, and other elements affecting complexity and clarity prior to, during, and after Western European consolidation of its chant repertoire. Early Christians wanted their ritual music to be different, holy, set apart from what they considered to be pagan Hellenistic music. Early Christian chant was therefore likely stylistically less Hellenistic in some respects than it was broadly Asian. At the same time, its melodic system came to be understood as built on the same Greek mathematical roots as its counterpart in Arabic monophony.

Christian music was not "Western" at its inception—indeed, it could not be. Peter Jeffery has demonstrated that the various streams of early Christian chant likely had common roots in the practices of Jerusalem, a cosmopolitan city in which, for example, use of "Greek, Syriac, …Georgian, Armenian…and Arabic" for Christian worship rather than Latin exclusively appears to have been the norm (1994:4). Accompanying these languages would almost certainly have come more complex melodic ornamentation and tuning practices from their respective cultural traditions. Meanwhile, "the liturgical and musical influence of Jerusalem on Constantinople…is known to have been considerable" (Jeffery 1992:172) and, conversely, Jerusalem was fully in the sphere of Byzantium during the fourth through the early seventh centuries before falling to Muslim conquerors in c. 638, where it remained under Arab cultural influence until the First Crusade in 1099. Thus, there was an established flow in both directions—and Arabic artistic culture in Jerusalem mirrored that of Baghdad and al-Andalus (though not at the same heights) during these crucial centuries in which Christian chant was developing. The same Umayyad caliph who had authorized the crossing of the Strait of Gibraltar to take Iberia in 711, al-Walid I, had just built two of the first major artistic expressions of Islam in the form of the al-Aqsa Mosque in Jerusalem and what became known as the Umayyad Mosque in Damascus. Damascus had for some time been a Silk Road destination, and al-Walid's Mosque there reflected at least an effort at "inter-cultural translation" between Arabic and Byzantine visual cultures (Flood 2001:12). More likely, it was a broadly deliberate attempt to "consciously engage the extant [regional-historical] artistic traditions in an exchange that resulted in an original art form[,]...to selectively endow the Umayyads' rising culture with historical continuity [and] territorial rootedness," situating the new Islamic empire in a line of cultures it was absorbing (Rabbat 2003:80–81). This context makes quite plausible the notion that an inter/transcultural artistic milieu pervaded from Jerusalem to al-Andalus, conducive to a commensurate effect on musical elements in the Mediterranean and across the developing West, one of which was Christian chant.

In the end, Western Europe opted for simplification and clarification of rhythm, ornamentation, and modality in order to focus on the effect of harmonically driven polyphony—and this tendency emerged even in the developments that led to the ninth-century Frankish modifications to chant under Charlemagne and his Northumbrian (English) intellectual aide Alcuin that came to be labeled "Gregorian."

> The forms of Western chant were developed in the West, even if they were sometimes stimulated from the Orient...It has become evident that the [Gregorian] neumes are of Carolingian origin. They were developed in France in the ninth century, possibly under Byzantine influence, in the course of the adaptation and theoretical appropriation of the chant repertory by the Franks.
> (Hucke 1980:439, 445)

The Franks clearly wanted to suppress the more "oriental" (they thought of it as "Roman") style that remained evident to them. Kenneth Levy also suggests this simplification was to aid in Frankish learning, which Charlemagne also seems to have done with the Byzantine music (2000:98–99).

However, the highly simplified (and now ubiquitously copied) style of interpreting Gregorian chant that was developed into the early twentieth century by the monks at Solesmes Abbey in France has been disputed as being an accurate representation of what was intended by Gregorian notation. Marcel Peres, founder of Ensemble Organum, for example, notes that even "in the Gregorian neumatic notations, a lot of signs can be performed as ornaments or even formulas" (quoted in Sherman 1997:31–32). Meanwhile, Lance Brunner delivers a compelling analysis on that matter:

> Florid ornaments, spirited performance, virtuoso singing—all in evidence in medieval documents, even though their exact nature remains elusive—are

outside the aesthetic framework within which the modern restoration of chant was carried out. Moreover, a number of scholars have speculated that early medieval chant was not as securely diatonic as it appears in later manuscripts with staff notation, and that many of the puzzling symbols, especially those associated with ornamental neumes, involved micro-tonal inflections. Such interpretations, alien to Western musical training and conditioning, could never have been considered seriously by the monastic scholars who helped create and shape the old Solesmes style, a style in which the guiding principle was, as Heinrich Besseler put it, 'to smooth over as much as possible all the rough edges with a soft legato.'...When the frame of reference is expanded to include a wider range of possibilities,...bolder interpretations of the orna-ments, involving mordents and microtones, are very convincing.

(1982:324)

Wili Apel (1958) presents both documentary and analytical evidence reinforcing these perspectives. Christian chant in Western Europe (emerging from Roman Gaul and Hispania) prior to c. 750 derived stylistically from Jerusalem and Byzantium and presumably carried West Asian elements (Jewish or other) with it, and at least some chanting in the second, third, and fourth centuries was sty-listically elaborate. Already there was also likely impetus toward simplification/ clarification, both to set it apart from "pagan" Hellenistic music and to ensure the words were understood (Apel 1958:37–40). However, even into the ninth to tenth centuries, after Frankish efforts at simplification had been underway for some time, there is notational evidence of complex ornamentation, including micro-tonal elements (Apel 1958:108–118). These would not be structural, as with Arabic music, but they still likely derived from Eastern roots.

Reasonably, much stock has been placed in the interpretation of Western chant notation as it developed over the centuries. In fact, however, these neumistic nota-tions cannot be relied upon to tell the whole story; rather, how the notation is understood to have actually been used becomes critically essential. Specifically, it is not clear whether chant notation was meant to capture even the most fundamen-tal stylistic performance nuances or not. Certainly, music notation developed very slowly from out of a robust history of oral traditions. Indeed, Shai Burstyn (1989) points out that East–West musical confluences may simply have been a conse-quence of shared orality, rather than any deliberate decision: as the West moved toward literacy and concomitant musical notation, it moved away from its focus on oral tradition, especially in formal sacred music—and thus the transitional evi-dence remains clearest in the secular music that was notated. Leo Treitler (1984) expands and applies this analysis of orality vs. literacy regarding early chant nota-tion, which in turn would have implications for its performance practice.

Thus, the question of what chant notation captured and what it did not is crucial to interpretation. There is no question that chant was an oral tradition for many centuries, even after it began to be notated. If the notation is to be seen as some-thing more like modern lead sheet notation, intended to remind the performer of an oral repertoire rather than to specify every detail (see, e.g., Hucke 1980:448ff.), then it is reasonable to assume that performance practice could have mirrored the multicultural Mediterranean world in many instances. In Frankland it may very well have been influenced by nearby Iberia. Indeed, it may have been just such a situation that drove the Franks toward an attempt to simplify.

Although caution should be exercised in drawing historical conclusions from recent performance practice, Byzantine–Greek Orthodox chant singing may offer considerable illumination for understanding ancient Byzantine chant. Burstyn (1989) suggests that the study of shared orality among medieval cultures East and West might benefit from observance of living traditions, of which this is one of the oldest and most venerable.

Having studied living Byzantine chant with "Stilianos Floikos, the youngest—and possibly the last" living chanter of a particular "millennium-old tradition at the Patriarchal church of Constantinople, in Istanbul, Turkey," Alexander Khalil discovered that

> when chanting a written line [Stilianos] perceives multiple layers of remembered melody, together with people and events associated with them. By chanting with and against these melodies he creates resonances. These resonances create for him an environment of constant recontextualization, imbuing his every act with multiple meanings while bringing him into dialogue with…the past.
>
> (2009:xxi–xxii)

Included in this study are statistical observations of performance ornamentation that is not explicitly marked in the musical notation (2009:110–126). Among the findings were that the execution of unmarked ornaments was remarkably consistent, and that the performer perceived and experienced them as gestures rather than as strings of individual notes and rhythms. This reinforces two ideas: that oral tradition can successfully coexist with notation, and that such a context is conducive to gestural thinking and organization learned outside of strict notation—which ideas were surely passed along in the development of early Western notation as well. Even more intriguing, while the performer did not feel he had agency over variations in ornaments, he did understand that he had considerable freedom over even more fundamental surface details—though the composition remained fully recognizable (2009:127ff.).

In a similar vein, Markos Skoulios provides a fascinating and detailed analysis of the intersections between Greek-Orthodox ("Byzantine") notation, tradition and contemporary performance practice, demonstrating that its rootedness in orality leaves the chanter free "to interpret a composition in his/her own personal taste, modifying phrases, time and even the intervallic and modal physiognomy of a piece" (2012:15). The confluence of Greek and Byzantine cultures meant that, from earliest times, Pythagorean mathematical principles were at the heart of pitch and interval content, allowing for a wider variety of tuning, including the microtunings still on display in practice. Indeed, this reinforces the notion developed in this study that early Christian chant, and especially the Byzantine style that survives in the Greek-Orthodox practice of today, operated for some time within a larger system of Old World modal thinking: "The old form of Octoechos [(the eight Byzantine pitch modes)] was an original descendant of the ancient hierarchical and symmetrical closed-ended modal systems tradition of the great civilizations that flourished in the area between Eastern Mediterranean, Central Asia and the Indian subcontinent," though the modern Octoechos is less strictly within this same tradition (Skoulios 2012:24). Apel notes that Byzantium "exercised considerable influence on Western thought during the eighth century," and that the Western "system of eight [chant] modes has an exact counterpart in Byzantine theory, where it is known as the octoechos" (1958:134–135).

Richard Barrett (2010) sums up the debate well, referencing key participants on both sides such as John Finley, Alexander Lingas, H.J.W. Tillyard, and Timothy McGee. Barrett notes that "the 'Orientalizing' of the Byzantine chant repertoire…assumes the supremacy of Western scholarship and, ultimately, culture over that of scholars and singers who are native to the region and to the repertoire" (2010:186). By "orientalizing," Barrett essentially means an impetus to impose Western European musical interpretations on Byzantine Christian music because to do otherwise would be to admit defeat to the Arab-Turkish culture of Byzantium's conquerors, "a typically Orientalist narrative of decline" (181).

Inter/transcultural Andalusian Iberia and the European convergence

This strongly suggests a general atmosphere in which intercultural influence across the region was not uncommon, even as passionate political and religious differences were being emphasized—differences that were felt to be existentially vital, and nowhere more so than on the borders of al-Andalus and proto-Europe, in Northern Iberia, Catalonia, and into Franconia. Nevertheless, these borders were far more culturally porous than has typically been portrayed.

Andalusian Iberia was at the center of the various streams and their convergences. It is important to recall that Spain—Hispania—was a key Roman province from 218 BCE, long before the Visigoths arrived, until well into the fifth century CE and therefore strongly Hellenized. "Its provinces contained the empire's most Latinate populations outside of Italy. Emperors Trajan, Hadrian, and Marcus Aurelius were natives of Hispania…[and] Cordoba was the birthplace of the philosopher Seneca" (Lewis 2008:109). This was no cultural backwater: post-Roman Seville, for example, benefited from the revered classical scholar Isidore (c. 560–636 CE) as its most famous Christian archbishop, and the Visigoths retained a "complicated affinity for the culture of the Greeks" (Lewis 2008:113). At the same time, Hispania's fundamental interculturality flourished after the departure of the Romans: by the end of the seventh century only about 400,000 true Visigoths ruled over some five million "Hispano-Romans, Jews, and Greeks, along with Galicians, Basques, and Celts" (Lewis 2008:111). Most of the South-Southeastern coastal region (along with appreciable chunks of coastal North Africa) was also under Byzantine rule from c. 550–625.

Through the seventh century the advancing Arabs came to something of a tentative equilibrium with the North African Berbers, who in turn assisted with the invasion (and eventual government) of southern Iberia as the eighth century commenced. Yet another new era of inter/transculturality thus developed in the region as the eighth century progressed into the ninth, and began exerting influence (or pressure, depending on one's perspective) ever northward towards proto-Europe.

Among the many key musical figures of this period in al-Andalus under the great patron of the arts Abd al-Rahman II (792–852) was the performer and teacher Abu al-Hasan "Ali Ibn Nafi," known as Ziryab (c. 789–857), a pupil of Ishaq al-Mawsili (whose father had studied within the instructional lineage of Yunus) and allegedly so nicknamed because his dark skin and beautiful singing voice invited comparison to the blackbird ("ziryab" in colloquial Arabic). Though most likely born near Baghdad, Ziryab was of a lower social class (apparently from a non-Arab family who converted to Islam) and may even have been a slave of East African origin; such would raise further interesting questions about the influence of sub-Saharan African music on Andalusian music since Arabs had much congress with both East and West Africa over many centuries in the form of the slave trade. If the musical results of African slaves later in the New World are any indication, it is not unreasonable to assume that the Arab-African slave trade would have produced a similarly profound effect. Indeed, much comment is made in primary texts about the place of the female *qiyan* (higher class singer-courtesan-slaves) and *jawari* (of lower or more general slave class) in Arab cultures,[13] as indicated in this passage from Ibn Hayyan's (c. 987–1076) *Kitab al-Muqtabis* (The Book of Quotations) describing the Cordoban court of Abd al-Rahman II in which Ziryab flourished:

> The Emir Abd al-Rahman ibn al-Hakam was a great admirer of singing. He was enamored of listening to it and placed it above all his other pleasures. He patronized singers who competed in it, and had a predilection for the best of them. He sought out the most skilful among them by inquiring after those of the highest rank [in this craft] and he directed his generosity exclusively to [his singers] with liberal gifts, extensive accommodations, and constant support. He offered them all that his palace and his private orchestra (*sitara*) contained in the way of skilful female singers (*qiyan*) and excellent singing slave women (*jawari*). He selected the best among them [to send] to the male singers he had taken into his service so that these latter could be their guides in this art, transmitting through them [the female singers] their artistry, in search of ever greater gratification in listening [to music], always guided by the pursuit of excellence.

(quoted in Reynolds 2008:158)

Dwight Reynolds provides a description by al-Maqqari (seventeenth-century Moroccan) of a particularly accomplished female singer from early ninth-century al-Andalus, professionally named Qalam:

She was of Andalusian origin, a Christian, from among the Basque captives. As a young girl she was taken East and ended up in Medina…and there she learned the art of singing and mastered it. She was refined, clever, possessed a beautiful hand in calligraphy, was a reciter of poetry, a memoriser of historical accounts, and was knowledgeable in all genres of literature and etiquette.

(2015:250)

Though Reynolds (2008) makes clear that Ziryab was not likely the mythical musical-cultural demi-god portrayed by later authors, sources from the time of Ziryab's life do paint him as a consummate artist who brought sophisticated musical ideas from Baghdad to al-Andalus and remained at the center of the Cordoban court as these were transformed into a new Andalusian phenomenon. This court was home to Jews and Visigothic Christians as well as Berber Muslims and others who brought deep North African connections with them. Such conditions suggest that what emerged in the time of Ziryab and following would have been influenced by multiple cultural streams and thus would have been different from strictly classical Arabic culture. In short, the music that arose in al-Andalus was not simply transplanted from the Muslim Middle East. Reynolds' comment that "in Arabic, the term 'Andalusian music'—*al-musiqa al-andalusiyya*—is understood to mean not that all of it comes from medieval al-Andalus, but rather that it is composed within the genres, themes and style first established there" (2015:247–248) simply reinforces the evolutionary roots of the music that emerged from the transculturality of the region. Caroline Wendt summarizes a few interesting, interrelated distinctions in this regard:

Ziryab and his followers' concern with the cosmic and ethical qualities of music outlasted that of their Near Eastern counterparts, who, influenced by Greek theorists, became more occupied with modal analysis, an area of less concern in Andalusia…[The Andalusian] tradition thus evolved in more popular directions, with greater emphasis on composed orchestral and choral forms, and less on the solo improvisation favored in the Eastern courts.

(2000:191)

This disposition may help account for some of the ways that Iberian music developed differently from that in other parts of Europe in the ensuing centuries, and in turn for some of the particularities exported with it to the New World.

Ahmad al-Tifashi (c. 1184–1253), in his *Pleasure to the Ears, On the Art of Music*, hints later at the direction this state of affairs took by noting that "as for the people of Ifriqyi [i.e., North Africa, and specifically modern Tunisia], their method of singing combines the method of the people of the Maghrib and the people of the East, for it is faster than the style of the people of Andalus and has more notes than the style of the people of the East," stating further that the famed Andalusian Muslim intellectual Ibn Bajja (d. 1138) "combined the songs of the Christians with those of the East, thereby inventing a style found only in

Andalus" (quoted in Liu and Monroe 1989:36, 42). Ibn Bajja (Latin: Avempace) also influenced the Cordoban Ibn Rushd (Latin: Averroes; d. 1198 in Morocco), whose commentary on Aristotle's *De Anima* directly addresses a theory of sound (and by extension, of music).

The living tradition perhaps most closely reflecting this particular synthesis is the Andalusi nuba or nawba of Morocco, Algeria, Tunisia, and Libya. Touma notes that the legacies of Ziryab thrive therein: "In Tunisia can be found the old style of early Seville; in Algeria, that of Cordoba; and in Morocco, that of Granada and Valencia" (1996:69). Using two similar poetic forms known as *muwashshah* and *zajal*—each of which reflects Berber, Jewish, and Christian influences interacting with Arabic classical forms (Reynolds 2015:252)—the vocal sections of the nuba are accompanied and augmented by an instrumental ensemble consisting of the oud, *rebab* (bowed chordophone), nay, *qanun* (box zither) and *darabuka* (goblet drum)—all of which have very ancient Old World heritages as noted throughout this study. Manuel Ferreira succinctly states that

> Moorish-Andalusian (or Ibero-Arab) music is not just, or even mainly, Arab music per se. It is a hybrid Western tradition which evolved independently from oriental trends from the ninth century onwards and reached its highest level of integration of Western and oriental elements in the twelfth century. The originality of Andalusian music, when compared with other Western medieval traditions, is to be sought primarily in the aspects of form and rhythm. Form represents the Peninsular indigenous element; rhythm the Arab one.
>
> $(2000:8)^{14}$

Meanwhile, Christian Iberian musical traditions arose both prior to and simultaneously with the those of the Arabs and Berbers in the region. The Western Goths who settled into Hispania, during their migrations from what are today Scandinavian regions, came into contact with and were converted to Christianity on the eastern outskirts of Rome, in Thrace (modern Bulgaria) near Byzantium, sometime during the mid-to-late third and mid-fourth centuries. In so doing, they embraced the same fervent Christianity that Rome had bequeathed to North Africa and Iberia in the later centuries of its Empire. The Gothic leader Wulfila (Ulfila) is known to have been ordained in Constantinople in the 340s (Herrin 2007:37), and there is evidence of Gothic connection to Cappadocian Christianity (Schwarcz 1999:454). Thus, early Gothic Christian practices were almost certainly Eastern-Byzantine, which they would have brought to the full establishment of their kingdom in Western Europe—proto-France and then Spain—as Visigoths within the subsequent two to three centuries. Certainly there was a flourishing Visigothic Christian musical tradition in centers such as Seville, Toledo, and Saragossa long before the Arabs arrived, which centers were also influenced by Byzantine culture and from points possibly further east (Anglés 1940:495–499).

The Visigothic chant that became established in Iberia in the sixth and seventh centuries would already have been rooted in Afro-Asian Old World monophony, and thus very likely shared ornamental and other stylistic characteristics with early Byzantine chant and its Eastern precedents. As a result, the later Mozarabic version of the chant in Iberia may have expanded on or at least retained some of these features longer than other European forms. Anglés hints that some Spanish folk song and European Christian chant might have had in common the use of non-Western ornamentation in performance (1964:55). Christian chant further north did not even begin moving firmly toward being something recognizably proto-Western in the musical sense until sometime in the ninth century. Simultaneously, "in the ninth century, Cordova became a center of liturgical musical culture, and there, in the midst of the Andalusian califate, famous men did much for the chant" (Anglés 1940:499). That the music developed there incorporated popular styles, and later posed a threat to the consolidation and standardization of the Roman authorities, is important (Anglés 1940:501–2). Even in the midst of Frankish-Roman chant consolidation, Iberian Christian music retained its distinctives; these would not be fully suppressed until the end of the eleventh century, beginning with the recapture of Toledo by Christian forces in 1085.

As such, the artistic products of Iberian Mozarabs who adopted Arabic cultural traits while retaining their Christian faith illustrate important elements of the Andalusian convergence. One extraordinary example of Mozarabic creativity is the *Antifonario Visigótico Mozárabe* (Visigothic-Mozarabic Antiphonal) in Leon Cathedral, thought to be an eleventh-century copy of a seventh-century Visigothic manuscript, but clearly illuminated in the Andalusi Mozarabic style and acknowledged as a source of Andalusian Mozarabic music notation (alas, largely undecipherable as of this writing). Since all early chant notations, and certainly Visigothic-Mozarabic neumes, are merely outlines of basic pitches or pitch contours and how they align with texts, what is most important is how the chants would actually have been realized contemporaneously. The notation undoubtedly lacks key surface details that were added in performance. Therefore, what can be gleaned about the general artistic milieu of al-Andalus, through visual art and literature, for example, is highly relevant. Krysta Black (2012) shows how the Leon Bible of 960, also known as the Visigothic-Mozarabic Bible, not only includes clearly intercultural designs in its illuminations, but in fact features elements directly from Persian Sassanid and early Islamic (Umayyad) art. Jacques Guilmain (1960) echoes this general point about Mozarabic manuscripts, but goes on to suggest that interlace patterns in sample North Iberian manuscripts very similar to those in the Visigothic-Mozarabic Antiphonal—dating no more than 100 years prior to the latter—reflect both Byzantine influence and that of Carolingian art. The implication is that this represents clear intercultural intention across borders on the part of the artists. Certainly the manuscripts analyzed by Guilman include the Andalusian elements noted above. That the interpretation of the Mozarabic musical notation would reflect this same openness to relevant interculturalities seems likely.

Another prime example of influential intellectual-artistic flow between al-Andalus and the West can be pieced together in the tenth-century person of Gerbert of Aurillac (c. 940–1003), later Pope Sylvester II. Charlemagne's son

Louis recaptured Barcelona in the Catalonian region in 801, inheriting much further north an area that had been intercultural for centuries and which was representative of the sorts of border areas in which intercultural artistic and intellectual influence would flow between al-Andalus and proto-Europe. Mozarabic artistic-architectural influence can be seen, for example, at the Church of Saint Quirze de Pedret near Barcelona. From 967 to 970, Gerbert studied the classical quadrivium at the monastery in Vic (and/or possibly Ripoll), near Barcelona, and very likely even as far south as Cordoba itself (Lewis 2008:328–329; Zuccato 2005[15]). His commentaries on Boethius's *De Musica Institutione* in correspondence (Otisk 2015) and evidence of his use of the monochord and the measurement of organ pipes in pedagogical contexts (Flusche 1995) reveal an understanding of music deeply informed by concepts with which Arab theorists such as al-Kindi would have been very familiar and on which they were articulate. Marco Zuccato (2005) convincingly demonstrates the role of Gerbert in transmitting general scientific knowledge from al-Andalus to France, and given Gerbert's deep involvement with music, it is highly probable that Arabic musical insights were likewise involved. Otto I (descendant of Charlemagne) employed Gerbert in Rome to teach his son, Otto II, who sought stronger alliance between Byzantium and the West through dynastic intermarriage. Gerbert then taught at the Cathedral school at Reims from 972—where the pivotal Western European composer Guillaume de Machaut (c. 1300–1377) later studied and eventually worked. Anne Robertson (2002:35–7) presents evidence showing that Machaut's education and network likely also included meaningful contact in Rome with Phillip de Vitry, attributed author of the pivotal *Ars nova* (c. 1300).

Diplomatic relations between al-Andalus, the court of Otto I, Constantinople, and Jerusalem proceeded in the tenth century in the person of Racemundo, Mozarabic bishop of Elvira and ambassador of the Cordoban caliph Abd al-Rahman III. These relations can be seen from a European perspective as crucial to an Ottonian Renaissance, perhaps even a continuation of the general Carolingian Renaissance that Charlemagne and Alcuin presided over two centuries earlier. The circle may then be completed by viewing the twelfth-century renaissance (beginning c. 1070), which ushered in the full flowering of European Gothic, as arising from continuation of such interculturality. Referring to a siege of the Muslim-controlled town of Barbastro along the northeastern Spanish border in 1064, Lewis notes that

> The Christian knights were entranced by the lyrics of the *qiyan* (singing girls)…[An] intermediary sent to bargain for the release of a dead commander's daughter found [the captor] enjoying the daughter's lute-playing. The Norman dismissed the ransom money and, as the historian Ibn Hayyan reported, grandly declared that her singing was worth all the world's gold.
>
> (2008:354)

Barbastro was reclaimed the following year, but "history remembers that Duke William VIII of Aquitaine, [the one] who delighted in the company of [that] lute-playing *qiyan*, was father to William IX, founder of France's wandering troubadours" (2008:355). The "lute" in question would of course have been an Arabic oud.

Considering these borderland convergences, the possibly interrelated developments of rhythmic features across sacred and secular medieval music are especially intriguing. Comparing samples from the *Codex Calixtinus* and Paris Bibliotheque Nationale MS lat. 1139, Theodore Karp (1967) has theorized that the rhythmic modes of the Notre Dame School were a continuation of work already in progress at the Cathedral Santiago de Compostela in northwest Spain and the abbey of St. Martial at Limoges in central France. Karp goes on to speculate that these developments were not unrelated to the rhythmic development of secular monophony in France as well. Elizabeth Aubrey notes that, for example, "at least two trouveres, Adam de la Halle and Jehannot de Lescurel, composed both monophony and polyphony, using the same type of poetry for each. The lines between monophony and polyphony thus were quite blurred" (2000:135). If accurate, this draws a plausible musical line from intercultural al-Andalus to Paris and other parts of France, for although Santiago was firmly in the Christian Kingdom of Leon at the height of the Caliphate of Cordoba, c. 1000, its region of Galicia did not completely escape Muslim-Berber occupation/influence earlier on. Just as compelling, though, there is evidence that Andalusi immigrants (some with Arabic names) traveled from as far away as Cordoba to settle at the famed Mozarabic sites of San Miguel de Escalada in Leon and San Salvador de Celanova in Galicia (both located on the pilgrim routes to Santiago de Compostela) during the ninth and tenth centuries (Hitchcock 2008:60ff.). Taken together, such examples demonstrate that intercultural artistic influences transcended political boundaries, as they do today.

Likewise, it is interesting to consider possible relationships between the rhythmic modes that emerged in Paris as the twelfth century gave way to the thirteenth (discussed, for example, in Riemann 1962:153ff.) and Arabic rhythmic modes that had been established previously, possibly as early as the seventh or eighth century (Farmer 1930:58). Both systems were derived from poetic language rhythms that combine long and short syllables. The most common Western rhythmic modal patterns were:

- long-short (trochee) and short-long (iamb), in both of which the long is twice the length of the short (e.g., quarter-eighth for troche and eighth-quarter for iamb in modern notation)
- long-short-short (dactyl), in which the first long is three times the length of the first short, but the second short is twice as the first (e.g., dotted quarter-eighth-quarter in modern notation)

These note-length relationships were understood to reflect generally "perfect" divisions into subgroups of three, while duple divisions and groupings were considered "imperfect," since they did not reflect Trinitarian Christian doctrine. Sachs (1943:287) further suggests that since the Arabic rhythmic modes (*iqa'at*) were credited to Tuways, a Persian, they may be the point of connection between Indian and Arabic rhythmic theory.

By way of comparison and contrast, it is helpful to consider the medieval Arabic system of poetic meters created by combinations of short-long (*watid*) and long (*sabab*) units into feet and then into metrical patterns. The watid in its basic form is equivalent to an iamb while the watid can also be inverted (reversed) to create the equivalent of a trochee (long-short). On the other hand, watids and sababs are often combined into asymmetrical groupings of threes and twos, as in the most important Arabic meter, *tawil*: short–long long/short–long long long/ (repeated), or 3+2+3+2+2. In one variant the first portion of the meter can be can be short-long-short, which consolidates the features of watid and inverse watid into one figure. Another difference is that the sababs and watids can be subdivided, which, when translated to musical rhythm, creates faster note values within the basic pattern. Any of these divisions may be silent, unaccented, or accented. The Arabic system is thus conducive to what would eventually in the West be called "syncopation" (superimposition of uneven patterns over a steady beat), which feature does not seem to be inherent in the Western medieval rhythmic modes. In his late thirteenth-century *Kitab al-Adwar*, Safi ad-Din al-Urmawi puts forward several Arabic rhythmic cycles in detail, two of the most ubiquitous of which are the *thaqil thani* of 3+3+2 and *thaqil awwal* of 3+3+4+2+4 (Wright 1995:472–473). In each of these, a rest constitutes the last item of each subgroup, emphasizing the sense of syncopation. Meanwhile, the Western medieval rhythmic modes tend to lope along in what sounds like modern 6/8 meter, though Hugo Riemann insists that duple divisions and patterns—codified "imperfections"—emerged first from instrumental music and later made their way into vocal music (1962:186–187).

Thus, the two systems seem to have underlying conceptual similarities while creating a different world of common surface results. The Arabic system appears to have had much greater variety and complexity earlier, and the realm of instrumental music may have been the area in which the sensibilities mixed most readily. While composition and performance probably diverged at times from the theoretical rhythmic modes, and likely included combinations across them, it is far more likely that Afro-Arab-Asian influences—which may also have survived in remnants of Hellenistic ritual and entertainment rhythms—explain the observable discrepancies within and between various early Western musics. Alexander Ringer concludes:

> Considering the veil of obscurity that shrouds the origins of the Gothic rhythmic modes, it seems rather peculiar that scholars should have turned to the poetic meters of St. Augustine as a likely source while completely ignoring the far more plausible impact of the Arabic modes which governed the music played originally on the many instruments that so beguiled Europe at that very moment.

> (1966:81)

Farmer goes much further, suggesting that Arabic, Persian, and medieval European rhythm all had the same bases (1930:58).

This may also be one of the keys to understanding the rhythmic nature of Spanish folk music both in its continental home and in the New World. The correspondences between Arabic poetic-rhythmic theory and practice and that of early European music (or even juxtapositions/superimpositions of the two systems) would be mutually reinforcing of Andalusian–European convergence, since both appear to derive from similar philosophical roots. Such considerations form the core of the arguments in favor of Arab-European synthesis in Andalusian music. Israel Katz, in his discussion of the traditional folk music of Spain (1974), cannot deny a significant role for Arabic influence despite some measure of skeptical caution, echoing the analysis of Robert Stevenson (1960:23). By way of specific example, the aggregate work of scholars such as Ramon Pidal (cited in Stevenson 1960:18), Isabel Pope (1940), and Manuel Ferreira (e.g., 2004, 2015a) has demonstrated that the Arabic zajal, the French virelai, and the Spanish folk-song form known as the *villancico*—which appeared in Europe chronologically in that order—are very closely related, raising the question of which genre influenced which and when, but in any case confirming a strong likelihood of cross-pollination.

Stevenson provides a useful summary analysis of the issues surrounding music in Islamic Spain (1960:17–31), and goes on to discuss the subsequent development of music in Spain as a European center, noting for example that "Salamanca University [est. 1243], though not as ancient as the Universities of Paris and Oxford…,was nevertheless the first medieval university with a chair of music," that the holder of this chair was paid well and that it was likely the idea of Alfonso X (1960:47), whose most significant contribution to global music history is discussed in the next section.[16] Among the takeaways of Stevenson's and I. Katz's analyses is that folk tunes remained a vibrant source within Spanish musical cultures, and Anglés further suggests that certain ploughing and tilling songs of "some regions of Spain" perhaps best constitute "a remembrance of the song of primitive people of oriental origin who have passed through our peninsula" (1964:55). Medieval rhythmic remnants in *Hoy comamos*, an especially rousing late fifteenth-century villancico, will be considered later in this chapter.

The Cantigas de Santa Maria

Meanwhile, a clear example of the transcultural musical synthesis in, around, and through al-Andalus within the realm of monophony can be found in a Christian musical collection from the reign of king Alfonso X, 1221–1284 CE (who Anglés calls "the lover of music and friend of troubadours," 1940:523), titled the *Cantigas de Santa Maria*. That this work emerged from a region of Iberia that had remained essentially Christian only makes more compelling the Arab-Andalusian musical-poetic influence it displays. The scholarship of Manuel Ferreira over the last two decades (2000, 2004, 2015a, 2015b) makes highly plausible the thesis that the Cantigas is in fact an inter/transcultural creation arising from the complexities of the European-Andalusian context noted above. Ferreira's route of inquiry runs through the Arab-Andalusian muwashshah and zajal[17] poetic forms in relation to the European rondeau and virelai, as well as the fact that some notational features of the Cantigas pre-date the same features in Parisian sources.[18]

It is also worth emphasizing that we have in the Cantigas the first substantially transcultural musical work in decipherable notation, in the form of four manuscripts: two at El Escorial in San Lorenzo (near modern Madrid), one at Madrid's National Library, and one in Florence, Italy. Three of these are visually illustrated/illuminated in ways that provide helpful interpretive context. In particular, one from El Escorial includes miniatures in color showing musicians playing instruments in combination that demonstrate considerable integration of East–West sources. The second version from El Escorial and the one from Florence include revealing narrative material as well.

The El Escorial manuscript depicting Afro-Asian and proto-European instruments has been the subject of considerable commentary (e.g., Rosario Alvarez, who notes that the diversity therein could represent "Byzantium, Central Asia, India, the Near East, North Africa, Sicily, the British Isles and Continental Europe," 1987:88). The illumination for Cantiga 120 is quite striking in that it shows two musicians playing identical long-necked chordophones that appear similar to the Persian tanbur, dutar, or setar, one musician in Arabic garb and the other dressed as a medieval European (Figure 4.2). Another, for Cantiga 170, shows two Europeans playing an Arabic rebab (European rebec) and an oud, respectively. This is but one of many examples of these two instruments in the collection, the former of which is the ancestor of the violin and the latter of which became the lute, both at the center of European musical development. In the illumination for Cantiga 300, a European man plays the medieval Spanish *albogon*, a long horn derived from the Arabic *al-buq* which is also the ancestor of the Basque *alboka*. A woman in the same illustration appears to be playing an unusually shaped goblet drum held over her shoulder that looks suspiciously like an Arabic darabuka.

Three examples from the Cantigas, transcribed here into modern notation from original mensural manuscripts, show possible Arabic rhythmic influence in addition to the formal poetical-musical elements. Ferreira (2000) explores the detailed bases on which such rhythmic and periodic relationships may be demonstrated, providing much of the context for the analyses that follow. Meanwhile, it is important to note that the Cantigas pitch material appears to be entirely modal in the ways that have come to be associated with early Western ecclesial and vernacular traditions. One might speculate that some of the pitches were performed with tunings that reflect Arabic maqam. While there is no direct evidence of that, it is useful to recall that maqams proper are performed to this day with some variety of microtonal tuning in actual performance, just as in jazz the micro-tunings are understood to be appropriate even though they are not usually notated. It might also be that un-notated ornaments were part of the contemporary performance tradition. The performances that Thomas Binkley and others have put forward, for example, include the expected lengthy improvisatory introductions featuring the oud that bring these ornamental and maqam-like perspectives to bear on the musical sensibility, in the tradition of the Andalusian nubah in which the muwashshah and zajal were and are the key song forms (see, e.g., Touma 1996:70 and Davis 2004:8).

The appearance of the following rhythm at the very beginning of Cantiga 1 (repeated later in a different pitch sequence) suggests the Arabic drum pattern known as *maqsum*, which seems to be derived from the core of Urmawi's thaqil thani of 3+3+2, and explains why many modern performances can be heard using that rhythm in a drummed accompaniment. The example below shows the opening notes of Cantiga 1, followed by the maqsum drum pattern:

Ex. 4.1 Cantiga 1 rhythmic pattern; maqsum drum pattern.

This 3+3+2 pattern in particular is also ubiquitous in African music, and later in that of Latin America; indeed, it has become one of the most common globalized patterns observable as of the twenty-first century. Ferreira (2000:11–13) makes the general point that the syncopations created by the superimpositions of uneven groups over even meters/patterns would not be expected from the conventions of Western rhythmic modes in mensural notation, the latter of which would typically have maintained pre-determined groupings of three throughout (as previously discussed).

Analysis of the likely rhythmic underpinnings in Cantiga 92 is a more complex endeavor. In the example below, groups of two are denoted by slurs while groups of three are indicated with brackets, with two possible interpretations:

Ex. 4.2 Cantiga 92 rhythmic pattern.

Ferreira (2000:11–13) suggests that in the analysis on top of the staff, this cycle can be seen as a double variant on what al-Farabi calls the "heavy Ramal." Here again, the interplay of grouping of twos and threes produces a level of dynamism that Ferreira calls "syncopation" which could be extended to "hemiola," as in Cantiga 166 below.

A particular form of hemiola called *sesquialtera*—regrouped alternating patterns of twos and threes, each grouping occupying the same amount of time, such as featured in the song "America" from Leonard Bernstein's Broadway musical *West Side Story* (see Hijleh 2012:31 for additional analysis)—was well established in Iberia by the sixteenth century. Yet the origins of the phenomenon are far less clear. Stanford (1972) discusses how the sesquialtera rhythm in Spanish music was likely introduced by the Arabs, and Cantiga 166 provides one particularly clear instance demonstrating that it might already have emerged by the end of the thirteenth century. In the following excerpt two interpretations of the groupings are shown as before, one above the music and the other below:

Ex. 4.3 Cantiga 166 excerpt.

Modern performers seem to choose between these two options somewhat equally, but the sesquialtera interpretation (above the staff) is worth noting because it became a staple of Iberian and then Latin American music (see Chapter 5). Another instance of sesquialtera can be found in Cantiga 330 (not shown here). Generally, the 3:2 durational relationship at various hierarchical levels—both simultaneously and consecutively—is also an important part of West African rhythmic structures. It is possible that the intermingling of both North African and sub-Saharan rhythms with Arabic music reinforced this dynamic sensibility by the late thirteenth century. Certainly it seems to have been so a few centuries later in the New World, indicating a possible continuation of these precedents.

Western European music comes of age

If Western European music was born sometime between 1200 and 1350 then its distinctives first coalesced more clearly sometime between 1450 and 1550. During the seventeenth century, its synergies emerged as a pivotal force in global music history. Meanwhile, it was being continuously exported to the New World throughout later stages of its maturation.

The early stages of a transition from florid organum to the polyphonic techniques that were eventually to be fully integrated with tonal harmony was underway in Paris just as the *Cantigas de Santa Maria* were being composed in Northern Iberia. As noted, coordinated polyphony and a more clearly delineated system of tonal harmony came to define the most important differences between Western European music and its predecessors. And yet, Paris was not isolated in witnessing these developments. The following statement by Anglés, based on considerable extant evidence, is astonishing in light of the traditional Parisian view: "We are firmly convinced that polyphonic music was cultivated in the Cathedral of Toledo contemporaneously with the school of Notre Dame de Paris" (1940:523). If so, it is likely that such developments were underway previously, for in general Spain seems to have been as well connected to overall musical developments as any European center was during these periods. Even after coming under Christian rule again in 1085, Toledo had remained one of the most vibrant cities for the consideration and dissemination of Arabic knowledge—and it was the Alfonso X's city of birth.

The *Cantigas*, though displaying Marian devotion, were courtly and popular rather than formally "sacred" music, yet the rhythmic content they display and their possible correspondences with Arabic patterns are clearly in the same universe as the rhythmic modes with which organum was composed and which continued to influence fourteenth-century secular music. On one hand, earlier forms of organum featuring both parallel and variable intervals without rhythmic independence, such as examples that occur in the *Musica enchiriadis*, may be precursors to the harmonic thinking that came to distinguish Western music from the monophonic/monodic tradition. On the other hand, Farmer (1930:102–112, 329–347) suggests tantalizing evidence that what amounts to proto-organum (and thus proto-harmony of a kind) is referred to by al-Kindi at about the same time as the *Musica enchiriadis*, and more explicitly a little later by Ibn Sina (d. 1037) in his *Kitab al-shifa*, references that occur amid discussion of oud technique. Farmer is quite explicit that "Ibn Sina unmistakably describes the performance of the *simultaneous consonances* of the fourth, fifth and octave, and the passage does not occur in the theoretical part of his treatise, but in the practical" (1930:112, emphasis added). This is precisely the sensibility we see prevailing into the thirteenth century in Europe.

The move from ever more complex monophony to more of a harmonic focus drove rhythm in Western music toward simplification (or perhaps more precisely, clarification) of a kind. In the end, the melodic and harmonic were wedded in the West in the form of carefully worked out "homophonic" textures, though these and other textures may be better understood as falling within a more complex continuum (see Hijleh 2012:133–153). However, in the interim, polyphony stood in tension with this direction, since independence of simultaneous rhythms is necessary for true, perceivable polyphony. Polyphony added (or retained) rhythmic complexity, a continuing legacy of Old World monophony now multiplied to more than one melodic line.

In a seminal article, Ringer frames both the questions and the evidence for the emergence of polyphony from the medieval milieu outlined in this chapter. Ringer notes that what he calls an "evolutionistic atmosphere in which the first serious investigations of medieval music were carried out" (1966:76) led to biased conflations around the various stages of polyphonic development that would not admit non-Western influence at any point. Once these are disentangled, it is easier to see how certain rhythmic-textural features from Afro-Asian music that grew out of monophony nevertheless contributed to true polyphony.[19] The ancient practices of parallel motion in octaves, fourths, and fifths, and droning, are prime examples, since the former shows up in the earliest stages of Western polyphony in the form of parallel organum and the latter as late as the Notre Dame School in the way that cantus firmus notes are hyper-extended while the florid upper voices unfold against it. Droning also leads to the polyphonic concept of oblique motion generally. Meanwhile, heterophony, a key feature growing out of monophony across many regions, cultures, and eras, hints at the technique of canonic imitation, which is an extension of rotas ("rounds") such as the famous *Sumer is Icumen in* from the mid-thirteenth century. When one views the questions through the lens of how repetition and imitation are managed, correspondences between non-West and proto-West become clearer. Isorhythm, for example, is a carefully controlled management of cyclic melodic repetition in which established pitch and rhythmic patterns match up in different ways throughout the music, something that is just as foundational to how many West African musical textures are created. Ringer wonders whether it is more than a coincidence that the rhythmic patterns of isorhythms came to be called *taleas* (Latin: "cuttings") in the fourteenth century in the same general time that Arabs in al-Andalus and elsewhere would have been familiar with the *talas* (origin: "gestures of the hands") of Indian rhythm (1966:81). Hocket, another semi-polyphonic textural feature typically mentioned as arising from this era, remains common in African, Indonesian, and Arabic music (see, e.g., McPhee 1949:272; Touma 1996:113; Nketia 1962[20]), suggesting it predates medieval European use.

Yet another important question surrounds the level of influence popular music likely had on the sophisticated "art music" emerging from cathedral-universities during the thirteenth and fourteenth centuries. Such a conduit makes even more plausible the idea that Afro-Arab influence crept into the latter. In that context, the role of instruments in the development of both tone and texture, including singing style and vocal compositions, became even more important. And thus, once again, consideration of the relationship between likely performance practice and extant notation comes to the fore. As discussed previously, early notation almost certainly did not capture many stylistic performance nuances.

A succinct history and analysis of issues surrounding the evolution toward an "Arabic style of performing [European] medieval music" has been provided by John Haines, who accurately credits scholar-performer Thomas Binkley with reinvigorating "an orientalism of early music performance practice already established by the 1950s" that had "been imagined by nineteenth-century music historians" (2001:376). Haines also suggests that Andalusian practice was only one input into what he calls Binkley's eclectic "Southern style." Meanwhile, Kirsten Yri (2010) does an outstanding job of reviewing and defending Binkley's approach to medieval European music as being deeply informed by Arab-Andalusian music. Yri's efficient analysis of the literature and the issues reveals a powerful bias against acknowledging the reality of the Arab-European musical nexus from the eighth through the sixteenth centuries. Likewise, Maria Menocal (1981), in discussing the analysis of Roger Boase, demonstrates that while there were complexities and the transfer was not direct from south to north, the medieval troubadour tradition of southern France was very likely deeply influenced by the poetic conventions of courtly love from al-Anadalus; from this it may be surmised that the musical conventions followed suit. Indeed, one of the most convincing things about Boase's analysis and his ultimate conclusion, as Menocal points out, is its comparatively thorough and even-handed review of the many possible theories of origin for the concept of courtly love. Menocal also argues that this view is too often dismissed out of hand by Romance scholars. Her explication (1985) of the frequently rejected etymological relationship between the Arabic word *taraba* (one meaning of which is to entertain through singing, but also to convey emotional meaning in music), the Provencal word *trobar* (modern French *trouvere*, "to find"), and its meaning for "troubadour," is especially convincing. This is one important basis on which many musicians continue to perform the songs of troubadour Bernart de Ventadorn (c. 1135–90?) with some of the rhythmic and textural characteristics of the Hispano-Arabic style. Bernart was one of the most influential figures in the genre, and, though anchored in France, his travels to England in the path of Eleanor of Aquitaine and the Plantagenet court would have spread these sensibilities even farther north.

Fletcher (2001:420) mentions the Arabic *taqsim* and its freely improvisatory nature within a maqam/mode as a model represented in performance of medieval monophony. Many modern performers seem to agree, using the style as introductory to the rhythmically notated sections of songs. Ringer (1966:81–82) extends this thinking even to different sections within organa. Meanwhile, Timothy McGee (1998), based on analysis of neumes and other comparative data, posits that the singing style of medieval music across Europe was similar to that of Western and Central Asia, bequeathed to it by Eastern Rome. Ringer (1966:82) affirms the likelihood of this same influence on vocal style emanating from Arab sources. Peter van der Merwe's identification of an Afro-Arab singing style that made its way to the Americas also dates from this era (1989:12–13, 30), a continuation from Silk Road precedents. Another prominent performer of medieval music, Jordi Savall (1992), has discussed the nuances inherent in making these performance decisions based on knowledge of both living traditions in Spain and of the known contexts from which the music originally emerged, including Arab influences. Performance style would certainly have affected musical development at some fundamental level.

In short, the soil out of which truly "Western" music arose remained inter/ transculturally complex for many centuries into the process. At the same time, there is considerable consensus that its distinctive outlines became clearer as the thirteenth century gave way to the fourteenth. Contemporary theoretical treatises on the European continent—such as the *Ars cantus mensurabilis* (c. 1260) attributed to Franco of Cologne, the *Ars Musice* of Johannes de Grocheio (c. 1270s), the *Tractatus de Musica* (c. 1300) of Jerome (Hieronymus) of Moravia, and the *Ars nova notandi* (1322) attributed to the composer Phillipe de Vitry—offer some insight into the perspectives swirling around Europe at the time. Their discussions around rhythm tend to be viewed as most important (see, e.g., Apel 1961:310–367)—especially the move away from triple rhythm as a basis to an unbiased mixture of duple and triple structures—at a time in which Arabic rhythm was likely exerting influence, and was already far more advanced in how its duple and triple structures were integrated.

Since an important aim here is to identify those elements that helped to more clearly define coordinated counterpoint and harmony, it is useful to concentrate on the evolution of consonance and dissonance between simultaneous pitches as well as the level of rhythmic complexity within which these pitch relationships would have been perceivable. In particular, the move from understanding octaves and fifths (and the inversion of the fifth, the fourth) as the most perfect consonances to admitting major and minor thirds as legitimate and even desirable consonances was essential to this process, since the harmony in question was to be triadic harmony built on thirds. Sachs (1943:295–311) puts forward the theory that the source of triadic harmony in Europe was an ancient emphasis on melodic major and minor thirds rather than octaves and fifths in a number of what he calls "primitive" cultures. Riemann (1962:xxff.) asserts that polyphony too arose from a context of thirds in certain Germanic folks musics, first from Scandinavia and then, through migration, to Scotland. Riemann also points out that discussion of admitting thirds as consonances took some time: though Jerome of Moravia makes mention of them as no longer strictly dissonant, consensus on their consonance did not coalesce until the end of the fifteenth century (1962:92–94). Gilbert Reaney confirms a similar analysis while looking at fourteenth-century developments (1953:130–132). Yet Riemann also presents evidence that the notion of deliberate attention to "harmonic principles" was emerging as the thirteenth century proceeded into the fourteenth, and that this coincided with the development of a rhythmic system capable of true polyphonic-harmonic coordination (1962:115–116).

Three Franco-Flemish composers

It is likely no coincidence that additional key developments during the fourteenth to sixteenth centuries emerged from Franco-Flemish regions that connected Iberia to the rest of Europe, as these areas had absorbed much from al-Andalus. Further consideration of three composers from this region mentioned earlier is instructive, because their music represents a discernible process of evolution in coordinated polyphonic and harmonic language flowing from within the West: Guillaume de Machaut (c. 1300–77),[21] Guillaume Dufay (1397–1474), and Josquin des Prez (c. 1450–1521).

To better understand the seismic shift in Western musical style represented across the work of these three composers, it is essential to understand the move away from what was considered the mathematically perfect to something that came to be considered more aurally pleasing in Europe, a result of the rise of "humanism" as the fourteenth century progressed into the fifteenth and beyond. From a Christian worldview, this entailed a shift toward understanding natural human capacity and perspective as a good creation of God rather than as a sinful impediment to God's perfection. From a non-religious perspective, it simply meant that humanity could find the resources within itself, including the use of technology especially, for bettering life. Thus Western art of many kinds came to reflect an appreciation of "natural" human qualities, including the appearance of the body and a preference for aural "euphony" that was experiential rather than theoretical.[22] As a result, many self-imposed religious fetters were removed from Western musical development and there was movement toward a new concept of aural beauty that involved coordinated triadic harmonic built on thirds, to which counterpoint (and thus to some degree rhythmic complexity) was to be subordinated.

Perusing the isorhythmic motets of Machaut, such as the oft-cited and per-formed *Quant en moy*, one is struck by the level of rhythmic complexity, but also by the mixture of harmonic consonance and dissonance that unfolds. Alice Clark (2004) provides an interesting survey of perspectives on listening to motets in Machaut's time, suggesting that the mind and the ear were both expected to be involved and that Machaut himself went to some technical lengths to make the musical processes within his motets comprehensible to the listener.[23] Reference has already been made to Machaut's connection to the cathedral at Reims, to which Gerbert of Aurillac had brought Arabic musical knowledge some centuries earlier.

Drawing on the fourteenth-century treatise *Quicumque voluerit duos contra-puncti* as well as the work of Sarah Fuller (1986), Jared Hartt demonstrates that Machaut followed the general principle in three-voice writing that "compos-ing a sonority that contains a perfect and an imperfect interval brings a sweet sound to the ear, as long as no dissonance occurs between the upper two voices" (2010:187). Each sonority occurs structurally/metrically in relation to the *tenor* (not taking the faster melodic ornamental pitches into account), thereby illuminat-ing clear steps toward the mixture of perfect and imperfect intervals at the heart of Western harmony. Machaut also uses occasional deliberate discords at important structural moments to create a higher level of harmonic tension that is subse-quently released to consonance of different degrees of "perfection." Harmonic rules are understood to be in concord with melodic-contrapuntal voice-leading principles already established, though by no means are there "functional" chord progressions in this music of the type understood from the seventeenth century onward (Reaney 1953:133). Specific accidentals outside the mode (*musica ficta*) were used to smooth harmonic intervals, in part by reducing the level of interval-lic imperfection leading to perfect consonances (1953:135). Much of this sensibil-ity was to continue into the era of functional tonal harmony.

Quant en moy, and most of Machaut's other motets, likely date from the 1350s or 60s (Reaney 1967:95). Nearly a century later, Dufay's *Nuper Rosarum Flores* moves a number of steps further in the directions hinted at by Machaut. The work was written for the 1436 consecration of a new dome by the architect-engineer-artist Filippo Brunelleschi for the cathedral in Florence. Stanley Boorman (1974) and Howard Brown (1974), both writing on the 500th anniversary of Dufay's death, trace his work, especially *Nuper Rosarum Flores*, as representative of how humanistic perspectives manifested themselves in music, in some ways in parallel with visual art and architecture: the attention to proportion and form; the coordi-nation of pitch and rhythm so as to emphasize (smoother) shapes of melodic lines; Dufay's embrace of English influence in the use of more thirds melodically and harmonically[24]; and the ways in which the use of isorhythm is evolving away from strict technique and towards freer and more aurally expressive results. Brown summarizes that

> [Dufay's] method of writing melodies in free prose rhythms was taken up and refined over the next hundred or so years. His techniques for underpin-ning the structure of a composition by carefully planned networks of tonal

cadences were imitated and eventually led the way to full-blown sixteenth-century tonality. His chaste regulation of dissonance gave to music a characteristic sound widely adopted throughout the period. In some of his later works the hierarchical, layered texture of the Middle Ages began to be modified in favour of a homogeneous sound that later composers came to prefer. Above all, his music is distinguished for its formal clarity.

(1974:233)

Meanwhile, Thomas Brothers traces the dissipation of isorhythmic technique from Dufay to Josquin, noting that

Isorhythmic technique, as practiced in the French motet from Philippe de Vitry through Du Fay, had three essential components—a repeated pattern of pitches [*color*], a repeated pattern of rhythms [*talea*], and some kind of transformative process…In the last phase of its history, isorhythmic technique had been simplified to the point where color and talea were coextensive; transformation was achieved by leading successive [repetitions] through changes in mensuration or by strict diminution.

(1991:3)

Brothers goes on to demonstrate that Josquin was "less concerned with rhythmic diversity within a phrase, using an even smaller variety of rhythmic values" (1991:38). In short, complex isorhythm gave way to more aural clarity in the form of imitative development of identifiable melodic-rhythmic units, in which rhythmic diversity was reduced. This allowed the listener to focus on the effect of straightforward contrapuntal development while also enjoying harmonic focus. That transition likely led theorist Johannes Tinctoris (c. 1435–1511) to famously exclaim that the works of Dufay and the succeeding generation "are redolent of such sweetness that in my opinion they are to be judged most worthy not only for men and demigods, but even for the immortal gods" (quoted in Wegman 2003:173). The "sweetness" has much to do with harmonic, rhythmic, and melodic clarification and coordination.

Josquin's motet *Ave Maria Virgo serena* epitomizes the results of this process. Each section commences with clear imitation between the four voice parts, arranged to emphasize consonant intervallic and chordal sequences. These give way in alteration to passages in which duos, trios, and quartets of the voice parts are simultaneously nearly homorhythmic—hints of a chorale style that was to continue to emerge.

Even a secular entertainment piece such as Josquin's *El Grillo* (The Cricket) emphasizes clarity of text, harmony, and motivic material: any real counterpoint is absent and the voices are simply chanting harmonies in identical rhythms throughout. That it is an Italian *frotolla* (a precursor to the Renaissance madrigal and chanson) with some obscure Hispanic textual touches[25] by a Franco-Flemish composer indicates something of Josquin's pan-European experience and mastery. The Spanish villancico of the same period also bears many correspondences with the frottola, and not only as lighter secular fare. Indeed, Edward Lowinsky comments that "in the advance of tonality in European music, both frottola and villancico take a place of honor" (1962:14).

Still, harmony by the time of Josquin was not yet "tonal" in the classical Western sense. It remained modal in a way not entirely divorced conceptually from the Old World modality of the Silk Road and the earliest Christian music, since it continued to operate around linear formulas, though now focused on arrangement of consonances and dissonances so as to create a series of chordal directions as well. John Caldwell has argued in this historical context that the harmony of modality and of tonality belong to the same universe, that "tonality" means "the processes by which the pitch elements of music are brought into relation with one another and provide it with its meaningfulness," and that "the study of harmonic tonality is really the study of the conventions which have made it possible for harmony to act as an independent force which can either confirm or contradict the implications of melody" (1984:2–3). Further,

> the significance of chords is that they symbolize and to a certain extent replace the melodic functions from which they ultimately derive…[;]in the context of the existing theory and practice of counterpoint, triadic harmony freed chordal progressions from purely contrapuntal restraints and to a certain extent equated vertical combinations of notes with the boundaries of the species of fourth and fifth which for fifteenth-century theorists represented the crystallization of melodic idioms.
>
> (1984:8–9)

In a similar way, Bonnie Blackburn (1987:225–226) frames this coalescence as the emergence of "harmonic composition." Blackburn notes that for the fifteenth-century theorist Giovanni Spataro (c. 1458–1541), "harmony is a process of consonance and dissonance…[in which] chords must move in a logical progression, with dissonances resolving into consonances…Harmony is a principle, not a system of chordal analysis, and it can exist in music that is contrapuntally or chordally conceived." But she also demonstrates that Spataro understood harmony to be a distinctive element, something other than strictly a product of linear motion, and certainly more than a series of consonances. Western harmony is in fact a carefully ordered progression of both consonances and dissonances, an idea that the famed theorist Gioseffo Zarlino (1517–1590) affirmed in the subsequent generation (Blackburn 1987:228–230). From this perspective, whether the scale from which chordal relationships are formed is "modal" or "tonal" does not actually determine whether the harmony is functional or not. This is a key clarification going forward in global music history, as various approaches to harmony within modality and tonality have continued to operate.

Blackburn sums up the issues:

> As soon as composers began writing harmonically, whatever may have been conceived initially as a contrapuntal pair was now subject to alteration on

harmonic grounds…As soon as pervading imitation became the norm it was necessary to work with more than two voices at the same time. The history of the growing ability to integrate the texture of multiple voices while preserving good harmony is a fascinating one…One can see the struggle with the alto in the full-voice sections of Josquin's *Ave Maria … virgo serena*.

(1987:277)

As harmony came to be the driving element in Western music, some voices in four-part textures tended to become less contrapuntally important. Eventually, the relationship between bass and soprano, the outer voices that are heard most clearly, became more important. The understanding of coordination between the horizontal and the vertical also emerged as conceptually more and more clear as the sixteenth century progressed to into the seventeenth. And as further developments in use of "ficta" (chromatic alterations) within scales proceeded, many based in part on previous linear precedents, these also created the harmonic implications that defined the Western "Common Practice" harmony (c. 1600–1900) that has been so well documented and taught.

Even in these contexts, Arab scholarly influence continued in Europe into the fifteenth century and beyond, not least in Spain:

> The late XV-century scholar Bartolome Ramis de Pareja is a leading case: a theorist born in Andalusia, publishes a treatise in Italy taking up the Aristoxenian idea of the 'well-tuned' thirds, probably borrowed from the Arabian milieu; this occurred seventy-six years earlier than Zarlinian ideas, to say nothing of Ramis' whole pragmatic and demythicizing attitude towards Boethius and Guido *auctoritates* carrying again to Arabian music theory, [the treatise in question being Ramis' *Musica Practica* of 1482 in Bologna], among the first treatises we know to have been printed. This little treatise aroused bitter controversy which whirled around Ramis, his pupil Giovanni Spataro and two outstanding Renaissance theoreticians, Franchino Gaffurio and Nicolas Burzio.
>
> (Leoni 1996:169)

Stevenson (1960:57–58) indirectly demonstrates that Ramis's ideas on altered temperament/tuning to achieve more distributed consonances pre-date similar thoughts of Zarlino by some 75 years. Stefano Leoni discusses at length the general point that the Andalusian Ramis thus reflects an orientation very different from the European mainstream of the time:

> It is Ramis' practical attitude that amazes and brings us back to the same attitude in Arab and Mozarab surroundings. Arab (and Arab-Andalusian) musical theory results are connected to needs closely linking musical practice and theory; meanwhile the first-hand and deep study of Greek theory (as of Aristoxenus) can have directed Arab and Mozarab scholars, or scholars formed and cultured in the Arabic ambience, as Ramis was, towards

more original and interesting solutions in comparison with the basically inelastic...survey of Western theorists.

(1996:170)

Leoni is in effect claiming that the musical humanism of the fifteenth century and beyond owed a great deal to Arabic musical precedents. Seen in the light that the Arabs contributed much to the sensuousness of courtly love poetry in Europe some centuries earlier, this claim makes considerable sense.

Tonal harmony, and particularly the later development of the piano, eventually brought with it a controversy that has not been entirely resolved in the meantime: the standardization of twelve-tone equal temperament/tuning within a perfect octave (conveniently abbreviated hereafter as 12-EDO), which allowed harmonies to be presented on a single instrument in any of 12 major or minor keys.[26] J.M. Barbour details the emergence of 12-EDO in the West, identifying the Spanish organist and University of Salamanca music professor Francisco Salinas (1513–1590) as the first to precisely describe it (in *De musica libri septem*, 1577) while noting that "the history of equal temperament...is chiefly the history of its adoption upon keyboard instruments" (1951:6). The fixed pitch of keyboards logically requires such a system unless the intention is to play in tune in only a small number of keys or to have a multitude of separately tuned keyboards and strings incorporated into a single instrument. The tension between Western keyboard harmony in 12-EDO and the acoustic colors of non-Western tunings and performance practices in later eras spurred much creativity as musicians attempted to synergistically reconcile the attributes of both for expressive musical effect. Because singers and players of non-fixed tuning instruments constantly adjust their intonation to any number of subjective factors, as even fifteenth-century theorists understood,[27] the variances across cultures merely continued the same tension, though perhaps at higher or lower levels in individual instances.

A generation later, Marin Mersenne (French, 1588–1648), in his *Harmonie Universelle* (Paris, 1636–37), based a great deal of harmonic analysis on his initial perceptions of the overtone series for a fundamental pitch arrived at through experiments with stretched strings.[28] This reinforced the major triad—with its mix of major and minor thirds as well as a perfect octave and perfect fifth—as the basis for harmony. Indeed, Mersenne's considerations seem to lead him to very nearly declaring the reduction that was to constitute the major-minor tonal system in Western music: he recognized that "certain modes have more resemblance with some than with others" (Gruber 1970:61ff.), and, as such, they can be characterized as essentially major or minor based on the third from the tonic.

Interestingly, both Mersenne and Vincenzo Galilei criticized polyphony and advocated a return to the monophony of the Greeks—indeed, this is where the focused meaning of the term "monody" came into use. Galilei, as one of the Florentine Camerata, is widely credited with significant involvement in moving Western music back toward solo singing in the form of what came to be called "opera." Yet the accompaniment of vocal melody was now to be reinforced by harmony, itself implied by linear principles.

Early exportation of European music to the New World

Spain, France, and England were the three countries that were to have the most important European musical influences in the New World. In general, though each county's folk music had characteristics that likely contributed to musical developments in their respective colonies (especially Spain due to its unique inter/transcultural history), European music in this era was rather pan-European.

The "Hundred Years' War" (1337–1453) continued to ensure the cultural commerce between England and France that had preceded it for many centuries as the two empires remained intertwined. Interestingly, in practice, English music seems to have migrated earlier toward freer use of thirds as harmonically consonant. The English round *Sumer is Icumen in* (late thirteenth or early fourteenth century) is striking not only because of the resulting polyphonic texture but also because the use of thirds in the tune creates thirds in the resulting harmonic scheme. Tinctoris rightly pointed to the work of the English composer John Dunstable (c. 1390–1453) as leading the way toward further embrace of thirds and triadic harmony, which influenced the Franco-Flemish developments noted above. By the mid-sixteenth century, England had effectively separated itself ecclesiastically from the continent, and the seventeenth century saw the rise of an English style in the realm of art music, both sacred and secular. It was this continuing style that English pilgrims brought to North America soon thereafter, along with a well-developed style of English folk music (see Chapter 6).

Europe was just beginning to come into its own musically as Christopher Columbus set sail for what he thought was Asia in 1492, the same year in which Spain completed its expulsion of the Muslims from Iberia and initiated a new global age of European empires. Not long before (1453), Byzantium had come fully under Ottoman rule, and Arabic musical legacies flourished ever more brightly into parts of Eastern Europe and North Africa. The profoundly musical city of Venice, the home of Zarlino and the locale where Italian opera first burst forth as an art form for a wider public, was right on the Ottoman doorstep, and cultural exchange was vibrant (Howard 2007). European music continued to develop in some of the ways suggested in this chapter even as it was being exported over the next 500 years to the Americas—and Spain was the most direct conduit.

> The Romance and villancico were major influences in Latin American popular music, and it was through them that many features of Spanish folk music—some embodying African and Asian traits—were transplanted to the New World. Such features included alternation between major and minor thirds, use of sharpened fourths and unresolved sevenths, and a proclivity for melodies in parallel thirds [in addition to sesquialtera].
>
> (Fletcher 2001:492)

In that context, it is useful to consider the work of Juan del Encina (1468–1530), a well-known Spanish composer and dramatist at the time of Columbus, for much of his music synthesizes the developments in European harmony with Spanish folk rhythms and poetry. A good example of this is Encina's villancico *Hoy comamos*. "Originally written for a Mardi Gras playlet, this…song takes for its theme: Eat, drink, and be merry, for tomorrow we die; and the music marvelously catches the dramatic mood" (Stevenson 1960:255). The work appears in the Cancionero de Palacio collection (1474–1516), and thus corresponds directly to the era of Columbus's explorations. Two centuries after the *Cantigas de Santa Maria, Hoy comamos* retains the feature of rhythmic groupings of twos and threes superimposed ambiguously over a duple meter. Meanwhile, harmony is coalescing as more of a driving force than any appreciable counterpoint:

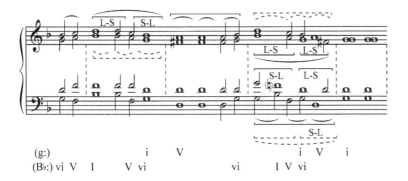

Ex. 4.4 Distilled harmonic rhythm excerpt, *Hoy comamos.*

As shown in the rhythmic grouping analysis of this excerpt (adapted from the original manuscript notation), a type of sesquialtera is evident, as well as the short-long and long-short medieval modes, sometimes simultaneously. These interactions are especially complex at the cadence point, as expected. The proto-tonal harmony takes advantage of dominant-tonic relationships in both the minor and the relative major "modes," providing clear functionality, though not yet entirely as in the later Common Practice; the open fifths on the final tonic chord are ancient reminders of that. *Hoy comamos* is typically performed at a brisk tempo, emphasizing its rhythmic vitality. As expected for the period, both voices and instruments are often used in various combinations for its performance: from *a cappella* vocal ensembles, to a soloist with lute or *vihuela* accompaniment, to mixed chamber orchestras with choirs. Charlotte Stern describes it as "reminiscent of the raucous tavern songs of the medieval Goliardic poets,…inspired by folk traditions…In keeping with peasant tradition, Encina's carol was probably accompanied by a traditional shepherds' dance, either a line or circle dance similar to the English hornpipe and characterized by strenuous leaping" (1965:189–190). It is a carefully crafted piece that seems to capture the spirit and promise of the time while remaining connected to venerable Iberian traditions. Associated with Encina's dramatic work as it is, *Hoy comamos* even reminds one somewhat of certain pieces from Claudio Monteverdi's early operas.

Meanwhile, Spanish vocal composers of the next generation, including Cristóbal de Morales (c. 1500–1553), Francisco Guerrero (c. 1528–1599), and Thomas Luis de Victoria (c. 1548–1611, an example of whose work is featured in Chapter 5) continued to absorb, integrate, and transmit across the Atlantic the harmonic styles and formal innovations coalescing across Europe in both sacred and secular music—Victoria and Morales representing Italian sensibilities and Guerrero, an Andalusian, something more of the Spanish homeland.

Opera, organs, and orchestras

A word must be also said about the further development of the organ, early European opera, and the expansion of instrumental ensembles through the seventeenth and eighteenth centuries, for these profoundly influenced the Latin American musical synthesis in the New World.

Organs and collections of other instruments were a very important part of cultural exports coming from Iberia to the Americas, largely because they were used in Christian worship. The styles of Spanish cathedral music quickly became part of the New World landscape. This music, though it differed modestly from some other European sacred styles of the time due to Spain's self-imposed religiously conservative isolation during the seventeenth century, nevertheless carried with it the developing attributes of harmony tempered by more vestiges of older polyphonic thinking than elsewhere.

In 1638, the cathedral in Quito, Ecuador reported acquisition of a 600-pipe organ while "by 1622 the Jesuit church in Buenos Aires [Argentina] had a primitive organ and a choir of consisting wholly of African slaves" and the Jesuit church of indigenous members in Lima that same year "had two organs, four sets of shawms, two trumpets, many viols and other instruments" (Fletcher 2001:494). The most important organist-theorist-composer of this same time in Spain itself would have been Francisco Correa de Arauxo (1584–1654), who was following in the footsteps of Antonio de Cabezón (1510–1566) and Sebastian Aguilera de Heredia (1561–1627). Arauxo demonstrated a proclivity toward unusual pitch combinations and higher levels of dissonance, including the use of augmented triads and direct chromatic conflicts, as well as more complex rhythmic vitality— perhaps, one might speculate, unconsciously in search of a way to reconnect with the colorful musical past of al-Andalus. Willi Apel has also demonstrated the use of the globally ubiquitous 3+3+2 rhythmic pattern in Spanish organ music of the seventeenth century and other related instances (1960; 1962:177).

European opera gradually replaced church music as the dominant "high-culture" musical influence in Latin America during the eighteenth century. With the Bourbons in possession of the Spanish crown, more direct influence came from France, where opera had rapidly developed in scope under Jean-Baptiste Lully (1632–1687) and his successor Jean-Philippe Rameau (1683–1764), both also influential theorists of harmony. However, Italy, from whence opera had arisen during the seventeenth century, could not be overshadowed, and even Spain contributed its *zarzuela*, a mixed pop-art form that had largely developed from the musical-dramatic outlines forged by Encina and his ilk.[29] In short, cutting-edge genres, techniques, and instruments from throughout Europe were consistently exported to the New World over several hundred years, where they continued to influence the development of the new synthesis underway there from early on. This is important in that the New World did not experience artistic isolation as it evolved, nor did its European inputs remain static. The intercultural convergences, fusions, and transformations of global music history were about to erupt to a level previously unavailable—and therefore previously unseen.

Spotlight: rabab, rebec and the advent of the violin as a global instrument

Bowed chordophones have been perhaps less common than those plucked (culminating in the guitar; see Chapter 5), but no less consequential to global music history. Touma (1996:117) notes that, by virtue of al-Farabi's description from as early as the tenth century, the rebab is the logical precursor of the violin, having been introduced to Europe through al-Andalus. Rebabs are clearly depicted in the illuminations for the *Cantigas de Santa Maria*, for example. The rebab, among a number of similar instruments in the "spike fiddle" family, has actually taken a number of forms in Asian cultures historically, including, for example, in Indonesian gamelan. It is mentioned in several ancient texts, suggesting it was established prior to al-Farabi's reference, perhaps as early as 800 BCE. Jeremy Montagu (2007:161, 163) addresses some of the evidence for these perspectives, and goes on to distinguish the Arab/North African rebab from the Spanish rebab andaluz, the latter of which seems to have spread more widely and influentially to other parts of Europe after the Reconquista. Meanwhile, the boat-shaped rebec, held more vertically on the arm or under the chin and rising to popularity in Medieval and Renaissance Europe, was a further step toward the violin proper. Numerous examples of the rebec are captured in artistic visual depiction, such as in the English Queen Mary Psalter of c. 1320 and the 1509 painting "Virgin among Virgins" by Gerard Davis. The Byzantine lyra and the Medieval French vielle can also be understood as within this lineage, as can the family of European viols that persisted well into the eighteenth century.

The final journey from precursors to the modern Western European violin is less well mapped. David Schoenbaum asserts that "by the end of the twentieth century, there was general agreement that the [modern] violin appeared sometime between Columbus's first voyage in 1492 and the birth of Shakespeare in 1564" (2013:vixxx). As Schoenbaum further demonstrates (2013:xvii–xxvi, e.g.), the violin as we know it came to be one of the world's most global instruments because of its versatility and adaptability to many acoustic and ensemble contexts. For example, another version of the spike-fiddle, the kamanjah, was replaced in Arab ensembles by the violin during the twentieth century (Touma 1996:116). Moreover, according to Schoenbaum, "by the mid-nineteenth century, local players had introduced the violin to south Indian Carnatic music," and in 1998 noted Hindustani violinist V.G. Jog "acknowledged regretfully that his violin bore much of the responsibility of driving the viol-like saringhi[30] into near extinction" (2013:xxiii).

This transformation and transfer leading to the modern violin, along with that of oud to lute and guitar, epitomized the emergence of an Afro-Arabo-Hispanic-American nexus into the subsequent era of global music history.

Notes

1 Shai Burstyn (1989) provides an astute, well-documented and compelling analysis of both the promise and the challenges of key elements of the general thesis proposed in this chapter.

2 Incidentally, there is no need to hold that al-Andalus was a medieval "paradise" for all the peoples living there in order to acknowledge that it was conducive to the historical musical developments suggested in this chapter. See also "A Word on Creativity and Injustice," Chapter 1.

3 In something of a contrast to Farmer, Dwight Reynolds argues a distinction between "contact," which he admits is difficult to deny in this context, and "influence," which may be harder to verify, but then actually suggests that influence is too constricting a concept: "the various relationships that existed from the early medieval period up to the seventeenth century between Arabo-Andalusian music and more northerly musical traditions were far too complex to be narratized as a straightforward history of 'influence' (or lack thereof), and...even the term *hybridization*, becoming more and more common in medieval Iberian studies, falls short of capturing the multidimensional nature of those relationships" (2009:237). At best this leaves unanswered the key question of how any style that can be shown to contain identifiable elements from different musics came to be something other than any of its presumed sources. Perhaps at the heart of this reticence is the now often-expressed ethnomusicological concern that somehow some culture is being exploited and eventually destroyed because its indigenous musical expression is being transformed by intercultural exchange, especially when one of the cultures involved is able to exert more power of one kind or another. In the particular case of al-Andalus, power shifted back and forth between Arab Muslim and Spanish Christian cultures during the periods in question, and yet there seems to be little evidence that this shifting corresponded with musical fusion moving one direction or another stylistically in any given moment—which conclusion is precisely in keeping with Reynolds's larger point. If Arabic musical culture was entirely superior, why did it not prevail unaffected in spite of political loss? Or, alternatively, why did so much of it remain identifiably intact, albeit reframed, after political loss? Musical transformation of the kind argued in this book is not based on the vagaries of political power, chance, or systematic determinism, but rather on the endlessly creative disposition of the human musical spirit, which transcends such restrictive particularities in favor of adopting and integrating that which fascinates it—thereby always discovering something new.

4 Among Spanish musicologists of the same generation, Higinio Anglés joined Farmer in theorizing about the role of Iberia in European musical developments from the sixth to the fourteenth centuries, noting that little is known about even the more famous sources and figures said to be influential during this period in the West (1940:517–518)—and thereby implying we should not exercise a double standard in considering them. Julian Ribera, another Spaniard one generation earlier, also promoted an "Arabist" thesis of Spanish music, concluding that "the music of the Andalusian Moors had possessed vitality enough to filter into Christian Spain and there become an important element in Christian Spanish folk-music" (1929:4); Ribera's theories too were widely criticized on musicological grounds in succeeding generations, but the line of inquiry has been subsequently revived in various forms, as noted herein.

5 Ted Gioia (2011:5–6) offers a compelling thesis on this point: That the key musical aspects leading to American jazz began in al-Andalus almost exactly a millennium

before the founding of New Orleans in the United States in 1718, from whence it would emerge in full. See also Chapter 6.

6 Hewett (2015:20–21) goes some way toward making this context clear, especially with regard to polyphony.

7 See, e.g., Taylor 2007; Bellman 2011.

8 Byzantium also effectively brought the Slavic peoples into the Christian European realm, which development was to be crucial to the globalization of Western art music into the twentieth and twenty-first centuries; for example, the emergence of the Rus— eventually Russians—as a culture developed through Byzantine influence had long-term implications for the West (see Chapter 7).

9 See Williams 1993:139–149 for interesting details.

10 van der Merwe (1989:15–20) addresses some of the complexities of this issue as global popular music continued its development.

11 See the many sections on Central and West Asian maqam/maqom/makam in Church (2015), where the concept is put forward as a consolidating musical force across the heart of the modern Afro-Eurasian world. Shiloah (1981) provides additional details regarding the complexities by which this maqam system evolved further, particularly after the thirteenth century, demonstrating its divergence even from the modalities of Andalusian music. This in turn reinforces the notion that Western tonality diverged from the maqam phenomenon and emerged as a distinctive element. Even so, some of the ancient Pythagorean foundations shared between all the systems (which, again, reflect even more ancient Mesopotamian evidence) cannot be denied.

12 As an example of the convergences implied, consider how raga Mayamalavagowla (which tradition says was introduced by the sixteenth-century Carnatic musician Purandara Dasa) and maqam Hijaz-kar (ostensibly introduced by Iraqi Mulla 'Uthman al-Mawsili near the turn of the twentieth century) represent identical scalar collections—though the way the collection is developed melodically varies by context, reinforcing these as modalities rather than scales.

13 Simone Prince-Eichner (2016) provides additional detail about these groups of women, not all of whom might necessarily have been African, but who were generally situated within the Islamic slave-trade networks that were heavily Africa-oriented. Prince-Eichner points out, for example, how the Western understanding of the term "slave" would not necessarily describe the high social status of a certain kind that many qiyan achieved. This does not take away from the main point, however, of the indirect interculturality likely embedded in the context.

14 Interestingly, Ferreira also maintains that Andalusian melodic modality resisted migration away from original Arabic diatonicism, eschewing microtunings and other ornamental complexities featured in contemporaneous Eastern Mediterranean and West Asian music (2004:132–133). Such a view would resolve a number of concerns from scholars over conflicting evidence of whether these elements had effectively invaded the Western European frontiers. But it would also raise the question of whether diatonic modality was actually an Arab contribution to European development rather than a result of European resistance against Eastern influence.

15 In fact, Zuccato argues that Gerbert probably could only have acquired the knowledge he later demonstrated by travelling in al-Andalus well south of Ripoll and Vic; at the same time, it appears that al-Andalus and Catalonia enjoyed positive cultural commerce during the period in question (2005:752–753).

16 It should be noted, however, that Stevenson, like Higinio Anglés (whom he quotes frequently), is not entirely convinced of the Andalusian musical origins or character of the *Cantigas de Santa Maria*.

17 Farmer (1930:147), echoing others even earlier, came to the same conclusion about the zajal and the Cantigas.

18 Ferreira astutely summarizes the history of views on the Cantigas and defends his particular lines of inquiry in "The Periphery Effaced," concluding that "The discipline

has been keen to incorporate fashionable social issues in its discourse but has failed to address the unfairness of the historical balance within Europe itself. If musicology is to cease in its complicity in effacing the periphery and the corresponding ideological empowerment of the centre, it must acknowledge the contribution of the southern regions, both West and East, in shaping European culture" (2015b:39).

19 Sachs also discusses proto-polyphony in non-Western cultures (1943:48–51, 145–148, 289).

20 The fact that Nketia goes out of his way to distance African hocket from medieval European hocket on the basis of the social situations in which the practices are embedded does not preclude the question of whether or when Europeans may have experienced the technique in the course of intercultural contact.

21 Machaut is included here as "Franco-Flemish," even though he is not normally, because the concordance across these regions from France to the Netherlands was far more robust than is sometimes acknowledged; Paul Lang (1939) has offered a more detailed synopsis on this point.

22 In reality this is a highly complex and subjective concept, since the human ear seems to prefer low-number ratios of intervals, including 2:1 (octave), 3:2 (fifth), 4:3 (fourth, inversion of fifth)—the very bases for medieval ideas of consonance. The introduction of major and minor thirds—in ratios of 5:4 and 6:5 respectively as they occur in the "natural" overtone series that creates a major triad—are a modest extension of the same phenomenon. The psychology of why they may be heard as more "euphonious" than octaves or fifths, and more importantly how much human perception of the broader system of Western tonality emerges from acculturation, remains complex, however (see, e.g., Burns 1999; Shuter-Dyson 1999:633–636).

23 Clark also indirectly makes the point that Machaut is singled out as exceptional for his time and place—a tendency that pervades Western analysis of its own music, where the innovatives rather than the typical creatives are emphasized.

24 Theorist Johannes Tinctoris (c. 1435–1511) rightly pointed to composer John Dunstable (c. 1390–1453) as having led in this development.

25 See McDonald 2009:52.

26 Stock (2013:404) provides an appropriate reminder that 12-tone chromaticism long predates the rise of the West, particularly in China. However, such phenomena unfolded far differently from the systemic harmonic context that arose in the modern West.

27 Including Vincenzo Galilei (1520–1591), an accomplished lutenist who devoted considerable time to the acoustics of stretched strings, thus continuing (whether he knew it or not) an approach to musical discovery used by Arab theorists from many centuries earlier. Where Zarlino continued to rely on purely mathematical modeling, Galilei was among those who took into significant account the human experiences of musicians, thereby reviving elements of Aristoxenian thinking. This turn led also to a further emphasis on the relationships between sound and emotion in music that was to drive a good deal of seventeenth- to nineteenth-century European musical exploration.

28 See, e.g., Gruber 1970; interestingly, *Harmonie Universelle* also includes a diagram of an Indian vina, indicating the rise of exoticism that was already well underway in Europe by the seventeenth century.

29 European operatic singing style is discussed in the spotlight on global singing in Chapter 8.

30 Based on its historical placement, the saringhi itself likely derived from the earlier rebab.

References

Alvarez, Rosario. 1987. "Los Instrumentos Musicales en los Códices Alfonsinos: Su Tipología, su Uso y su Origen. Algunos Problemas Iconográficos." *Revista de Musicologia* 101: 67–104.

Anglès, Higinio. 1940. "Hispanic Musical Culture from the 6th to the 14th Century." *The MusicalQuarterly* 264: 494–528.

Anglès, Higinio. 1964. "Relations of Spanish Folk Song to the Gregorian Chant." *Journal of the International Folk Music Council* 16: 54–56.

Apel, Willi. 1958 [1973]. *Gregorian Chant*. Bloomington, Indiana: Indiana University Press.

Apel, Willi. 1960. "Drei plus Drei plus Zwei = Vier plus Vier." *Acta Musicologica* 321: 29–33.

Apel, Willi. 1961. *The Notation of Polyphonic Music: 900–1600* (5th ed.). Cambridge, Massachusetts: The Mediaeval Academy of America.

Apel, Willi. 1962. "Spanish Organ Music of the Early 17th Century." *Journal of the American Musicological Society* 152: 174–181.

Aubrey, Elizabeth. 2000. "French Monophony." In Duffin, Ross (ed.), *A Performer's Guide to Medieval Music*, Bloomington: Indiana University Press, 134–143.

Barbour, J.M. 1951. *Tuning and Temperament: A Historical Survey*. East Lansing, Michigan: Michigan State College Press.

Barrett, Richard. 2010. "Byzantine Chant, Authenticity, and Identity: Musicological Historiography through the Eyes of Folklore." *Greek Orthodox Theological Review* 551-4: 181–198.

Bellman, Jonathan. 2011. "Musical Voyages and Their Baggage: Orientalism in Music and Critical Musicology." *The Musical Quarterly* 943: 417–438.

Black, Krysta. 2012. "Bible Illustration in Tenth-Century Iberia: Reconsidering the Role of al-Andalus in the León Bible of 960." *Ars Orientalis* 42: 165–175.

Blackburn, Bonnie. 1987. "On Compositional Process in the Fifteenth Century." *Journal of the American Musicological Society* 402: 210–284.

Boorman, Stanley. 1974. "The Early Renaissance and Dufay." *The Musical Times* 115(1577): 560–561, 563–565.

Brothers, Thomas. 1991. "Vestiges of the Isorhythmic Tradition in Mass and Motet, ca. 1450–1475." *Journal of the American Musicological Society* 441: 1–56.

Brown, Howard. 1974. "Guillaume Dufay and the Early Renaissance." *Early Music* 24: 218–233.

Brunner, Lance. 1982. "The Performance of Plainchant: Some Preliminary Observations of the New Era." *Early Music* 103: 316–328.

Burns, Edward. 1999. "Intervals, Scales, and Tuning." In Deutsch, Diana (ed.), *The Psychology of Music* (2nd ed.), New York: Academic Press, 215–264.

Burstyn, Shai. 1989. "The 'Arabian Influence' Thesis Revisited." *Current Musicology* 45–47: 119–146.

Caldwell, John. 1984. "Some Aspects of Tonal Language in Music of the Fifteenth and Sixteenth Centuries." *Proceedings of the Royal Musical Association* 110: 1–24.

Church, Michael (ed.). 2015. *The Other Classical Musics*. Woodbridge, Suffolk: Boydell and Brewer.

Clark, Alice. 2004. "Listening to Machaut's Motets." *The Journal of Musicology* 214: 487–513.

Davis, Ruth. 2004. *Ma'lūf: Reflections on the Arab Andalusian Music of Tunisia*. Lanham, Maryland: Scarecrow Press.

Ehrenkreutz, Stefan. 1980. "Medieval Arabic Music Theory and Contemporary Scholarship." *Arab Studies Quarterly* 23: 249–265.

Farmer, Henry. 1928. "A North African Folk Instrument." *The Journal of the Royal Asiatic Society of Great Britain and Ireland* 1: 24–34.

Farmer, Henry. 1930. *Historical Facts for the Arabian Musical Influence*. London: William Reeves.

Ferreira, Manuel. 2000. "Andalusian Music and the *Cantigas de Santa Maria.*" In Parkinson, Steven (ed.), *Cobras e Som. Papers from a Colloquium on the Text, Music and Manuscripts of the Cantigas de Santa Maria*, Oxford: Legenda, 7–19.

Ferreira, Manuel. 2004. "Rondeau and Virelai: The Music of Andalus and the *Cantigas de Santa Maria.* " *Plainsong and Medieval Music* 132: 127–140.

Ferreira, Manuel. 2015a. "Rhythmic Paradigms in the Cantigas de Santa Maria: French versus Arabic precedent." *Plainsong and Medieval Music* 241: 1–24.

Ferreira, Manuel. 2015b. "The Periphery Effaced: The Musicological Fate of the *Cantigas.*" In Gilbert Stöck, Paulo Ferreira de Castro, and Katrin Stöck (eds.), *Estes Sons, esta Linguagem": Essays on Music, Meaning and Society in Honour of Mário Vieira de Carvalho*, Leipzig: CESEM/Gudrun Schröder-Verlag, 23–39.

Fletcher, Peter. 2001. *World Musics in Context*. New York: Oxford University Press.

Flood, Finbarr. 2001. *The Great Mosque of Damascus: Studies on the Makings of an Umayyad Visual Culture*. Leiden: Brill.

Flusche, Anna. 1995. *Organa Doctorum: Gerbert of Aurillac, Organbuilder?* (unpublished doctoral dissertation). Houston, Texas: Rice University.

Fuller, Sarah. 1986. "On Sonority in Fourteenth-Century Polyphony: Some Preliminary Reflections." *Journal of Music Theory* 30: 35–70.

Gerson-Kiwi, Edith. 1967. "Migrating Patterns of Melody among the Berbers and Jews of the Atlas Mountains." *Journal of the International Folk Music Council* 19: 16–22.

Gioia, Ted. 2011. *The History of Jazz* (2nd ed.). New York: Oxford University Press.

Grame, Theodore. 1970. "Music in the Jma al-Fna of Marrakesh." *The Musical Quarterly* 561: 74–87.

Gruber, Albion. 1970. "Mersenne and Evolving Tonal Theory." *Journal of Music Theory* 141: 36–67.

Guilmain, Jacques. 1960. "Interlace Decoration and the Influence of the North on Mozarabic Illumination." *The Art Bulletin* 423: 211–218.

Haines, John. 2001. "The Arabic Style of Performing Medieval Music." *Early Music* 293: 369–378.

Hartt, Jared. 2010. "Rehearing Machaut's Motets: Taking the Next Step in Understanding Sonority." *Journal of Music Theory* 542: 179–234.

Herrin, Judith. 2007. *Byzantium: The Surprising Life of a Medieval Empire*. Princeton, New Jersey: Princeton University Press.

Hewett, Ivan. 2015. "Europe." In Church, Michael (ed.), *The Other Classical Musics*, Woodbridge, Suffolk: Boydell and Brewer, 216–245.

Hijleh, Mark. 2012. *Towards a Global Music Theory*. Farnham, Surrey: Ashgate.

Hiley, David. 1981. "The Norman Chant Traditions: Normandy, Britain, Sicily." *Proceedings of the Royal Musical Association* 107:1–33.

Hitchcock, Richard. 2008. *Mozarabs in Medieval and Early Modern Spain: Identities and Influences*. New York: Routledge.

Howard, Deborah. 2007. "Cultural Transfer between Venice and the Ottomans in the Fifteenth and Sixteenth Centuries." In Roodenburg, Herman (ed.), *Cultural Exchange in Early Modern Europe: Forging European Identities: 1400–1700, vol. 4*, Cambridge: Cambridge University Press, 138–177.

Hucke, Helmut. 1980. "Toward a New Historical View of Gregorian Chant." *Journal of the American Musicological Society* 333: 437–467.

Jeffery, Peter. 1992. "The Lost Chant Tradition of Early Christian Jerusalem: Some Possible Melodic Survivals in the Byzantine and Latin Chant Repertories." *Early Music History* 11: 151–190.

Jeffery, Peter. 1994. "The Earliest Christian Chant Repertory Recovered: The Georgian Witnesses to Jerusalem Chant." *Journal of the American Musicological Society* 471:1–38.

Karp, Theodore. 1967. "St. Martial and Santiago de Compostela: An Analytical Speculation." *ActaMusicologica* 393/4: 144–160.

Katz, Israel. 1974. "The Traditional Folk Music of Spain: Explorations and Perspectives." *Yearbook of the International Folk Music Council* 6: 64–85.

Khalil, Alexander. 2009. *Echoes of Constantinople: Oral and Written Tradition of the Psaltes of the Ecumenical Patriarchate of Constantinople* (unpublished doctoral dissertation). University of California-San Diego.

Lang, Paul. 1939. "The So-Called Netherlands Schools." *The Musical Quarterly* 251: 48–59.

Leoni, Stefano. 1996. "The Casket of (Music) Rarities: Ars Musica and Musica Practica between Islam and Christianity." *International Review of the Aesthetics and Sociology of Music* 272: 167–183.

Levy, Kenneth. 2000. "A New Look at Old Roman Chant." *Early Music History* 19: 81–104.

Lewis, David. 2008. *God's Crucible: Islam and the Making of Europe, 570–1215*. New York: W.W.Norton.

Lewisohn, Leonard. 1997. "The Sacred Music of Islam: Samā' in the Persian Sufi Tradition." *British Journal of Ethnomusicology* 6: 1–33.

Liu, Benjamin, and James Monroe. 1989. *Ten Hispano-Arabic Strophic Songs in the Modern Oral Tradition: Music and Texts* (University of California Publications in Modern Philology 125). Berkeley: University of California Press.

Lowinsky, Edward. 1962. *Tonality and Atonality in Sixteenth-Century Music*. Los Angeles: University of California Press.

McDonald, Grantley. 2009. "Josquin's Musical Cricket: El Grillo as Humanist Parody." *Acta Musicologica* 811: 39–53.

McGee, Timothy. 1998. *The Sound of Medieval Song: Ornamentation and Vocal Style according to the Treatises*. New York: Oxford University Press.

McPhee, Colin. 1949. "The Five-Tone Gamelan Music of Bali." *The Musical Quarterly* 352: 250–281.

Menocal, Maria. 1981. "Close Encounters in Medieval Provence: Spain's Role in the Birth of Troubadour Poetry." *Hispanic Review* 491: 43–64.

Menocal, Maria. 1985. "Pride and Prejudice in Medieval Studies: European and Oriental." *Hispanic Review* 531: 61–78.

Montagu, Jeremy. 2007. *Origins and Development of Musical Instruments*. Lanham, Maryland: Scarecrow Press.

Naylor, Phillip. 2015. *North Africa: A History from Antiquity to the Present* (Revised edition). Austin: University of Texas Press.

Nketia, J.H.K. 1962. "The Hocket Technique in African Music." *Journal of the International Folk Music Council* 14: 44–52.

Otisk, Marek. 2015. "The Philosophical and Mathematical Context of Two [of] Gerbert's Musical Letters to Constantine." *Gerbertus* 8: 19–38.

Pope, Isabel. 1940. "The Musical Development and Form of the Spanish "Villancico"." *Papers of the American Musicological Society* 1940: 11–22.

Prince-Eichner, Simone. 2016. "Embodying the Empire: Singing Slave Girls in Medieval Islamicate Historiography." *2016 Claremont Colleges Library Undergraduate Research Award*, Paper 2. Accessed 3-21-2018 at http://scholarship.claremont.edu/cclura_2016/2.

Rabbat, Nasser. 2003. "The Dialogic Dimension of Umayyad Art." *RES: Anthropology and Aesthetics* 43: 78–94.

Racy, A.J. 1992. "Music." In Hayes, John R. (ed.), *The Genius of Arab Civilization: Source of Renaissance* (3rd. ed.), New York: NYU Press, 151–171.

Reaney, Gilbert. 1953. "Fourteenth Century Harmony and the Ballades, Rondeaux and Virelais of Guillaume DeMachaut." *Musica Disciplina* 7: 129–146.

Reaney, Gilbert.1967. "Towards a Chronology of Machaut's Musical Works." *Musica Disciplina* 21:87–96.

Reynolds, Dwight. 2008. "Al-Maqqarı's Ziryab: The Making of a Myth." *Middle Eastern Literatures* 11 2: 155–168.

Reynolds, Dwight. 2009. "Music in Medieval Iberia: Contact, Influence and Hybridization." *Medieval Encounters* 15: 236–255.

Reynolds, Dwight. 2015. "North Africa and the Eastern Mediterranean." In Michael Church (ed.), *The Other Classical Musics*, Woodbridge, Suffolk: Boydell and Brewer, 247–69.

Ribera, Julian. 1922. *La Música de las Cantigas. Estudio sobre su Origen y Naturaleza conreproducciones fotográficas del texto y transcripción moderna*. Madrid: Tipografia de la Revistade Archivos.

Ribera, Julian (trans. Hague, Eleanor and Marion Leffingwell). 1929. *Music in Ancient Arabia and Spain*. Stanford, California: Stanford University Press.

Riemann, Hugo (trans. Haggh, R.). 1962. *History of Music Theory Books I and II: Polyphonic Theory to the 16th Century*. Lincoln, Nebraska: University of Nebraska Press.

Ringer, Alexander. 1966. "Eastern Elements in Medieval Polyphony." In Sommerfeldt, John (ed.), *Studies in Medieval Literature II*, Kalamazoo, Michigan: The Medieval Institute, Western Michigan University, 75–83.

Roberts, J. M. 2004. *The New Penguin History of the World* (4th ed.). New York: Penguin.

Robertson, Anne Walters. 2002. *Guillaume de Machaut and Reims: Context and Meaning in his Musical Works*. Cambridge: Cambridge University Press.

Sachs, Curt. 1943 [2008]. *The Rise of Music in the Ancient World*. New York: W.W. Norton. [Reprinted:Mineola, New York: Dover.]

Savall, Jordi. 1992. "Performing Early Spanish Music." *Early Music* 204: 649–653.

Schoenbaum, David. 2013. *The Violin: A Social History of the World's Most Versatile Instrument*. New York: W.W. Norton.

Schwarcz, Andreas. 1999. "Cult and Religion Among the Tervingi and the Visigoths and Their Conversion to Christianity." In Heather, Peter (ed.), *The Visigoths from the Migration Period to the Seventh Century: An Ethnographic Perspective*, Woodbridge, Suffolk: The Boydell Press, 447–472.

Sherman, Bernard. 1997. *Inside Early Music: Conversations with Performers*. New York: Oxford University Press.

Shiloah, Amnon. 1981. "The Arabic Concept of Mode." *Journal of the American Musicological Society* 341: 19–42.

Shiloah, Amnon. 1991. "Round Table IV: The Meeting of Christian, Jewish and Muslim Musical Cultures on the Iberian Peninsula (Before 1492)." *Acta Musicologica* 631: 14–20.

Shuter-Dyson, Rosamund. 1999. "Musical Ability." In Deutsch, Diana (ed.), *The Psychology of Music* (2nd ed.), New York: Academic Press, 627–651.

Skoulios, Markos. 2012. "Modern Theory and Notation of Byzantine Chanting Tradition: A Near-Eastern Musicological Perspective." *Near Eastern Musicology Online* 11:15–34.

Stanford, E.T. 1972. "The Mexican Son." *Yearbook of the International Folk Music Council* 4:66–86.

Stern, Charlotte. 1965. "Juan del Encina's Carnival Eclogues and the Spanish Drama of the Renaissance." *Renaissance Drama* 8: 181–195.

Stevenson, Robert. 1960. *Spanish Music in the Age of Columbus*. The Hague, Netherlands: Martinus Nijhoff.

Stock, Jonathan. 2013. "Four Recurring Themes in Histories of Chinese Music." In Bohlman, Philip (ed.), *The Cambridge History of World Music*, New York: Cambridge University Press, 397–415.

Taylor, Timothy. 2007. *Beyond Exoticism: Western Music and the World*. Durham, North Carolina: Duke University Press.

Touma, Habib (trans. Schwartz, L.). 1996. *The Music of the Arabs*. Portland, Oregon: Amadeus Press.

Treitler, Leo. 1984. "Reading and Singing: On the Genesis of Occidental Music–Writing." *Early Music History* 4: 135–208.

van der Merwe, Peter. 1989. *Origins of the Popular Style: The Antecedents of Twentieth-Century Popular Music*. New York: Oxford University Press.

Wegman, Rob. 2003. "Johannes Tinctoris and the 'New Art'" *Music & Letters* 842: 171–188.

Wendt, Caroline. 2000. "North Africa: An Introduction." In Stone, Ruth (ed.), *The Garland Handbook of African Music*, New York: Garland Publishing, 188–205.

Williams, Peter. 1993. *The Organ in Western Culture: 750–1250*. New York: Cambridge University Press.

Wright, Owen. 1995. "A Preliminary Version of the 'kitāb al-Adwār'." *Bulletin of the School of Oriental and African Studies, University of London* 583: 455–478.

Yri, Kirsten. 2010. "Thomas Binkley and the Studio der Frühen Musik: Challenging 'the Myth of Westernness'" *Early Music* 382: 273–280.

Zuccato, Marco. 2005. "Gerbert of Aurillac and a Tenth-Century Jewish Channel for the Transmission of Arabic Science to the West." *Speculum* 803: 742–763.

Part II

The New World Web, the third pivotal convergence, and the acceleration of fusion, c. 1500–1920 CE

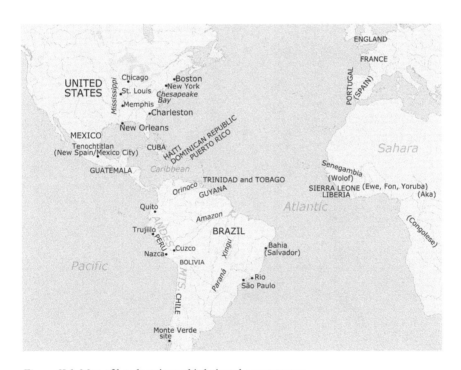

Figure II.1 Map of key locations, third pivotal convergence.

5   A musical Columbian exchange

The New World...offers several advantages as a domain in which the influence of society upon music can be studied...[The] essential acculturative components are known—the continental traditions of [indigenous] America, Europe, and Africa...[A] fresh process of acculturation began, and we can study it through written and other records, in both extent and depth, over a period of 450 years...Perhaps the history of America from 1500–1950 is a fairly normal picture of the earlier phases of grand acculturation processes.

—Charles Seeger (1977:184–185, 192)

A good guitarist will play on one string...God writes on crooked lines.

—Latin American proverbs

The transcultural roots of Latin American music

The development of the distinctives of Western European music was essential to the great transcultural convergence that gave rise to the musics of the Americas, and in turn to the acceleration of fusion and the current global musical web. In what was eventually to be called Latin America—Mexico and points further south—Iberian musical culture reflected the general Western European milieu,[1] but also contributed features of its own that were to profoundly shape musical history in the form of various three-way syntheses that branched into areas of the Americas from Mexico southward, especially a long-developed openness to multicultural artistic endeavors and a Catholic rather than a Protestant orientation to Christianity. Over several hundred years the strong musical characteristics of African slaves interacted with European elements and some distinctive features of indigenous musics in this part of the world to form what became known as Latin American music, parallel to the rise of Latin American culture more broadly (see, e.g., Kupperman 2012, Fletcher 2001:481–532). It is important to reiterate that the Common Practice period of Western European music was itself in significant development during this same time frame, and that the elements of that development continued to flow across the Atlantic.

As suggested earlier, this study need not argue the details of precisely when and how human cultures may have crossed what was then the Beringian continent from Asia into the Americas.[2] Likewise, there remains significant disagreement about which peoples ended up further north or south and in which time frames (see, e.g., Oppenheimer 2004); that too need not be relitigated herein. It will be assumed that these first immigrants to the Americas brought with them the same ancient, qualified-universal musical traits that eventually led to the development of the early human musics to which we have access.[3]

Music in the Americas became important, indeed pivotal, to global music history when the cultural exchanges and syntheses with which this chapter is concerned began. The level and depth of convergence in Latin America (and in the United States) reached an extent not previously seen in global music history, arising from the coalescence of Atlantic culture and the agricultural/technological/political potential of the New World (Kupperman 2012).

There were remnants of global musical influence in the European elements that arrived in the New World from c. 1500, elements such as rhythmic groupings of twos and threes across variable time frames called "hemiola" (one particularly Iberian version of which came to be known as *sesquialtera*[4]) and some freer improvisatory textures that were reflective of Arabic styles long remembered from al-Andalus. Peter Fletcher (2001:491–493) emphasizes that many aspects of Iberian folk music had as much influence in Latin America as art music, noting, for example, that

> about the time the Spanish arrived in the New World, the Gypsies, who are thought to have originated in Rajastan (in North India), were arriving in Spain. They brought with them elements of Indian music and dance. The virtuoso footwork of Indian *Kathak* dance is also thought to have originated in Rajastan, and its influence is clear in the *zapateado* footwork of Spanish flamenco. Flamenco itself did not become standardized until the eighteenth century, but many of the features from which it evolved—hemiola rhythms, hand-clapping, finger-snapping, and *zapateado* footwork—were present in Spain at the time of New World settlement. These features, likewise, were copied in Latin America.
>
> (493)

This facilitated the integrations discussed throughout this chapter. At the same time, Europeans brought with them distinctive modal/tonal harmony and polyphony along with instruments, vocal styles, and other resources developed around euphony, as well as larger ensembles and longer forms: music for Christian worship in Cathedrals, opera, and instrumental music designed for performance halls. Moreover, because the colonists and *conquistadores* believed that Divine Providence had brought them to these shores, they spared no effort in attempting to "civilize" the natives, musically and otherwise. In that context, both indigenous peoples and Africans with musical proclivities living among Europeans in the New World ended up absorbing key European musical conventions, most often voluntarily for the purpose of improving their opportunities for a better life in that context.

The following excerpt from the soprano part of the Spaniard Thomas Luis Victoria's motet *O Magnum Mysterium* (1572) exemplifies not only the pitch modality but also one type of rhythmic complexity coming from Europe through Spain to the New World, there to interact with indigenous and African elements just as complex in their own right.[5] The rhythmic analysis that follows is based on a proper pronunciation of the word, al-le-***lu***-jah. Brackets represent groups of three and slurs groups of two at various hierarchical levels (see Hijleh 2012:17–58 for further details on this system):

Ex. 5.1 Victoria, *O Magnum Mysterium*, melody excerpt.

The peculiar ambiguity of the seventh scale degree (A/A-flat in this instance, as the tonic is B-flat) that characterizes developing Western European tonality is also on display, while the G-natural, resulting in Dorian mode when A-flat is used, is a reminder that a clear distinction between modality and major-minor tonality was not yet in place in sixteenth-century Europe. This same freer modality became a feature in Latin American approaches to pitch as they developed.

Meanwhile, as European polyphony evolved into more harmonically driven styles through the late seventeenth century and beyond, the rhythmic dynamism on display in this motet excerpt gave way to more straightforward metrical settings for harmonic (tonal) clarity. Yet because this music continued to interact with African and native elements in Latin America, its course was altered from that on the European continent.

As early as 1502, music from sub-Saharan (largely Western) Africa arrived in the Iberian American colonies due to the influx of black slave labor for the cultivation of luxury crops such as sugar cane, especially in the Caribbean and the coastal areas of Brazil where the indigenous populations had been decimated or had fled and were unavailable for the necessary high-demand labor. The African musical styles that came with these peoples included emphasis on pattern repetition and subtle variation, socially participatory formal processes such as call and response, pitch collections that feature microtonal elements outside Western 12-EDO, and highly sophisticated layering of interlocking rhythmic patterns that included complex mixed groupings of twos and threes. (The latter, superimposed on the steady, simpler duple and triple meters of European music, would later be called "syncopation.") Both African and indigenous American musicians incorporated arrays of percussion that would have been quite exotic to Europeans, along with vocal styles that seemed more immediately emotional, aggressive, or plaintive and would have been considered far less refined than European bel canto. As with indigenous American musics, the nature of particular African musical characteristics that were important to the synthesis under consideration here will be explored further in context in this chapter. It is also worth reiterating that these sub-Saharan African musics were to have their strongest impact on global music history through American inter/transcultural convergences, however unfortunate the circumstances under which that too often came to be.

Scant direct evidence exists for the musical elements of most indigenous cultures in the Americas prior to the arrival of European colonists; much of the musical story must be imagined in tandem with the larger story, and retroactively reconstructed based on later evidence. As in other ancient cultures considered in this book, organological evidence provides much insight, along with ritual depictions and descriptions. Musically, based both on records and living traditions that survive to date, a wide variety of percussion was featured along with flutes, conch shells, and other trumpets, as well as both tuned and unpitched idiophones, all of which nearly always accompanied singing, dancing, or both. Though evidence strongly suggests the predominance of melodic monophony,[6] accompanying percussion and aerophonic noisemakers intended to creatively reflect nature likely produced much more complex textures. Because indigenous cults revolved around nature-oriented deities and violent blood sacrifice,[7] many soundscapes featured what Europeans would have considered wild animalistic elements that were musically more chaotic but that held deep religious and cultural meaning. Dale Olsen, for example, describes instruments of the Tairona who lived in what is now Colombia as being in the shapes of both humans and a variety of animals (2008:17), while Anthony Seeger confirms a similar conceptual connection between music, animals, and magic/religion among the Amazonian Suyá (2004). Bernal Diaz del Castillo (c. 1492–1585) a soldier in Cortes's group that eventually conquered the Mexica Aztecs, described his encounter with their music this way:

> As we were retreating we heard the sound of trumpets from the great Cue [where stand the idols of Huitzilopochti and Tezcatlipoca], from which its height dominates the whole City, and also a drum, a most dismal sound indeed it was, like an instrument of demons…, and with it many small tambourines and shell trumpets, horns and whistles. At that moment, as we

afterward learnt, they were offering the hearts of ten of our comrades and much blood to the idols that I have mentioned... The Mexicans offered great sacrifice and celebrated festivals every night at their great Cue at Tlatelolco and sounded their cursed drum, trumpets, kettledrums and shells, and uttered yells and howls.

(quoted in Stevenson 1968:13–14)

Ancient civilizations from which indigenous musics arose included: (1) those in Monte Verde (Chile) dating from 11,000 BCE; (2) proto-Caribbean cultures found at the Orinoco River mouth in Venezuela from 5000 BCE before they immigrated across the water to the islands; (3) those along the Peruvian coast such as the Caral (Norte-Chico) from c. 3500 BCE; (4) the Olmecs from c. 1300 BCE and Mayans from c. 600 BCE in Mexico; (5) the Chavin culture in the Andean-Amazonian regions from c. 900 BCE; and (6) later Peruvian coastal groups such as the Nazca and Moche. These were in turn precursors to the Central/South American cultures that European colonists encountered in the form of four main groups: (1) those in the Caribbean nations; (2) the Aztecs in Mexico; (3) the Inca in the Andean regions; and (4) a variety of tribes in the interior (Amazonian and Xingu) such as the Suyá and Kaiapo, as well as those in the larger Tupi group including the Guaraní. Each of these contributed indigenous musical features that had influence on the fusion process, and are discussed in this chapter in the regional and chronological contexts of the intercultural American encounters of which they were a part.

The Caribbean

As it happens, the locus of the first Spanish arrival in the New World was also one of the areas that gave birth to the strongest tri-cultural musical integrations over time. When Columbus and his crew set foot in the Caribbean in 1492, they were greeted by Arawak-Taino natives at war with Island-Carib peoples, both of which likely migrated across the waters from the Orinoco River region of Venezuela, the former sometime after c. 5000 BCE and the latter much later, perhaps c. 1200 CE (Rouse 1992). These were highly musical people, especially in connection with religious ritual (see, e.g., Rouse 1992:15). Evidence of singing and instrumental resources is extant in both domestic contexts and the Taino *areito* ceremony, which included the use of hollow-log idiophones (*mayohuacán*) and maracas featured in other Central/South American musics as well (Averill and Wilcken 2008:127; Davis 2008:143–144). Interestingly, Gage Averill and Lois Wilcken also mention castanets, which are closely associated with Spano-Arabic dance traditions coming out of al-Andalus (and possibly even earlier, with the Phoenicians), as they are illustrated clearly in early *Cantigas de Santa Maria* manuscripts. There may also have been a relationship between castanets and Arabic finger cymbals (Blades 2005:386).

We might get a very faint glimpse into one of the musical styles that early Spanish settlers may have encountered in the form of a Carib shaman's traditional exorcism song, *Ae cho ko noye oh*, from the Guyana coast south of the Orinoco, an excerpt of which is transcribed below (from Stiffler 1982: track 1):

Ex. 5.2 Ae cho ko noye oh excerpt

Stiffler comments that this recording already displays more musical acculturation than those recorded in the previous generation, such as by Gillin (1936), including a broadening of pitch from more strictly pentatonic to more diatonic (1982: liner notes). The phrases above include all five lower notes in a diatonic minor scale, though the single pitch—scale degree two, B in the above transcription—that distinguishes the excerpt from the lower four notes of world pentatonic mode two (more commonly known as the "minor " configuration of anhemitonic pentatonic; see Hijleh 2012:70) is clearly more ornamental than structural. Subsets of the world pentatonic collection are featured throughout traditional folk musics of the Americas, both north and south, though whether these are actually indigenous features has been disputed, and some research points to African origins for this pentatonic flavor. At the very least, contemporary evidence shows that native musicians found these pentatonic collections ultimately conducive to their tastes, further expanded by the European tonalities introduced in the Exchange, as in the example above. This pitch orientation has achieved a prominent place in the later stages of Latin American musical development, often with modal harmonies added. The same pitchscape can be shown to underlie a number of more mature North American styles that arose from African influences, such as jazz and rock.[8]

Rhythmically, the dynamic 3 + 3 + 2 and 3 + 2 + 3 patterns—clearest in the fourth and fifth bars of the excerpt as indicated by brackets representing groups of three and slurs groups of two at various hierarchical levels—are globally ubiquitous and certainly quite common in American musics.[9] The even higher durational (formal) structure of the excerpt reflects the dynamics of twos and threes as well: 3 + 2 + 2, as the first phrase is three bars while the second phrase group reflects 2 + 2 bars due to the repeated bar.

Dale Olsen and Daniel Sheehy state that "the African presence…is probably the most obvious thread that pervades the Caribbean," noting the work of anthropologist Maya Deren on "cultural convergence" between Taino and Africans, and observing that "African-derived drums can be found in a variety of contexts, as well as Spanish-derived singing styles and construction of lyrics" (2008:104), for example.

Nowhere is this convergence stronger than in Cuba, which has been a dynamic locus for continuing Latin American musical development for more than 500 years in close connection with Haiti, the Dominican Republic, and Puerto Rico. Both Iberian and French elements have been at the center of this locus, along with some of the strongest African inputs, providing interesting parallels to certain areas of the United States, especially New Orleans, Louisiana (see Chapter 6).

The Yoruba peoples (from what is today Nigeria, Togo, and Benin) provided some of the deepest and longest-lasting African musical influence on Cuba in the form of the two-headed *bata* drum used for religious rituals, the *shekere* (bead-covered gourd), and two metallic bars for keeping the organizing rhythmic pattern or timeline, along with drums from the Congolese *ngoma* ensemble (Rodriguez 2008:108–109). The presence of *ngoma* ensemble elements reinforces the notion that the interlocking polyrhythmic texture of much West African music was present early in the process. Gerhard Kubik (2000:276) identifies a timeline in Congolese regions, linked also to parts of West Africa, of 2 + 2 + 3 + 2 + 3 (shown in the groupings above the following example), which, when superimposed on Western meter this timeline, is identical to the syncopations of the Cuban *son* clave pattern (shown in the groupings below the example):

Ex. 5.3 Congolese timeline/Cuban son clave

The rise of the Cuban *son* genre (not to be confused with the more generic Mexican *son* discussed later in this chapter) is further illustrative of the transcultural synthesis that endured well beyond its origins: Fletcher notes that it "was always a hybrid form [that] adopted African-style shifted accents...[but] also used European harmonies, guitars, and four-line verse forms," asserting further that with the addition of modern Western instruments into the twentieth century it became the basis of *salsa* (2001:518–519). Tracing its deeply rural origins to the mid-eighteenth century, Olavo Rodriguez comments that what he calls the "*son* complex, [featuring] African-derived percussion instruments" such as *bongos* combined with the *maracas* that are ubiquitous in Central and South American (and Africa), became the most important musical genre of the twentieth century in Cuba (2008:115).

Other key Cuban transcultural genres with global impact that developed from the nineteenth century onward include (1) the *habanera* and *bolero*, both with *cancion* (song) and dance origins and eventually associated with famous under-lying rhythms; (2) the celebratory *rhumba* and the introduction of tall barrel-shaped *conga* drums as part of its ensemble; and (3) arising from imported French *contredanses*, several genres of *danzon*, including what became the very popular *mambo* and *cha-cha-cha* in the 1950s as they melded with jazz elements from the United States (Rodriguez 2008:114–118, Fletcher 2001:517–519).

In Haiti (the western half of the island Columbus named Hispaniola), the strong influence of traditional religious elements from the same West African regions took the form of Vodou, while additional French influence resulted from that country's foothold on the island during the eighteenth century. The African slaves that the French imported also spread to Cuba, while others went to New Orleans in the United States. The most important tribes with distinctive musical cultures among these immigrants included the Ewe (from what is now Ghana) and Fon (from ancient Dahomey, modern Benin), which share musical similarities with the Yoruba, including use of the timeline.[10] Much like in Cuba, there are only hints of what indigenous Taino musical culture on the island may have contributed. Averill and Wilcken suggest evidence that "some traits of Haitian religion are more readily explained in Arawak than in African terms," noting that the Vodou ritual *tchatcha* rattle may have had Amerindian origins (2008:127). Meanwhile, in what became the Dominican Republic (eastern half of Hispaniola) the earliest Africans tended to come from the Senegambia, including the Wolof peoples whose instruments include the *halam* (five-string plucked chordophone) and whose "drumming is energetic, with complex polyrhythmic combinations of instruments" (DjeDje 2000:143–144). In addition, reflecting the Catholic Christianity brought by the Iberians, Dominicans created *Salves* (after the Salve Reginas sung by the Spanish, including Columbus immediately upon his arrival) and other rural/ folk religious expressions. Highlighting the transcultural nature of these genres, Davis notes that "the conservation of archaic liturgical practices in folk ritual demonstrates the importance of the oral tradition as a source of historical documentation," and that "other Spanish influences...are unaccompanied, unmetered, melismatic, [with] antiphonal vocal production,...often in the minor mode or [using] a neutral third" (2008:145–146). These features point to Arabic flavors that also correspond to some African sensibilities.

While much of the transcultural developmental story of Puerto Rico is similar to other Caribbean islands, evidence of the musical legacy of the Arawak-Taino there is perhaps clearer than on neighboring islands. Hector Drouet lists "gourd rasps with scrapers (*guiros*); conch trumpets (*guamos*); wooden trumpets; pieces of hollowed log with an H-shaped slit (similar to the [Mexican] *teponaztli*)...; shell, clay, wood, and gourd rattles (maracas); clay ocarinas; clay and bone whistles; and a bone flute" discovered on this island in archaeological digs of Arawak midden sites, and suggests that these instruments were part of the Taino *areito* ceremonies discussed above (2008:164). Although Drouet also notes that the first direct evidence of African musical influence dates from the early eighteenth century, giving rise to the *bomba* dance as a defining Puerto Rican genre (2008:169), it is interesting to consider again how a number of the *areito* instruments would have easily integrated with African sensibilities, and how many are found elsewhere in Latin America. Other genres emerging from Puerto Rico included *decima* (poetry and music) and the *seis*, the latter a "tradition

[that] includes names, rhythms, instruments, and possibly styles of singing that manifest the historical amalgamation, probably begun in the 1520s and 1530s, of African, [indigenous] Indian, and Spanish traditions" (Drouet 2008:171).

Fletcher points out that the islands of Trinidad and Tobago (just off the Venezuelan coast) were at various points "subject to Spanish, French, British, African, and East Indian influence" during the approximately 450 years prior to independence in 1962 (2001:515). The most globalized results of this history, largely driven by resistance to authorities, have been calypso and steel band music, the latter emerging when African drums and wooden sticks were banned and residents used junk metal (especially large industrial oil containers) to create new percussive instruments starting in the 1930s. The East Indians, who for most of the islands' history separated themselves musically, began to merge their traditions with calypso singing in the late twentieth century (Fletcher 2001:517), continuing the long transcultural trend.

Mexico and Mesoamerica

Figure 5.1 Folio from *Codex Azcatitlan*, c. 1550, showing the *teponaztli* and *huehuetl* (bottom center) in use during Aztec human sacrifice.

Source: Bibliothèque nationale de France. Used by permission.

Using the Caribbean as a staging ground, Hernán Cortés proceeded into the Mexican interior, penetrating the Aztec capital of Tenochtitlan by 1519, where his company encountered key Aztec instruments such as the *huehuetl*—what the Mayans called *pax*, a single-head drum carved from a sacred tree and covered with jaguar skin—and the *teponaztli*—which the Mayans labeled *tunkul*, a drum with an H-shaped slit, usually articulating two pitches, carved in sacred shapes from tree trunks, into which sacrificial blood was sometimes poured (Stevenson 1968:18). Robert Stevenson presents evidence that slit drums were also found in the Caribbean as early as 1515 (1968:72), and Jacqueline DjeDje (2000) mentions them throughout West Africa, including from Sierra Leone and Liberia, which were important coastal loci for slaving transactions. Other common Aztec instruments included the *ayotl* (tortoise shell with deer horn beaters; the Mayan *kayab*), *huilacapitzli* (clay whistle), *tepuzquiquiztli* (long wooden didgeridoo-like trumpet of the Maya), *atecocoli* (conch-shell trumpet, also found in the Caribbean) and *ayacachtli* (small gourd rattle with handles, filled with beads or other rattling material, similar to maracas which are found throughout South-Central America and which are considered to be oracles of the gods by many Amazonian tribes, including the Guarani). All these were considered sacred, or were at least used consistently for sacred purposes, and nearly all also had Mayan analogues or precursors. Stevenson (1968:8–9) notes that Aztec culture supported civic musicians and groups of professional temple musicians as well for the purpose of celebrating military glories and staging elaborate religious rituals. Thus, it was not a momentous transition for them to understand music of the same scope and in European styles meant for Christian worship, which may help explain further how these very different musical sensibilities gradually came to be combined and mutually transformed into something new.

In contrast to Castillo's horrific description of Aztec music in the context of blood rituals noted earlier in this chapter, Toribio de Motolinia (c. 1490–1565, i.e., contemporaneous with Castillo), pioneer Christian missionary to Mexico, provides a more positive appraisal of other Aztec musical contexts; his description of the instruments is similar enough to that of the Taino *areito* in the Caribbean and some elements of Amazonian music to evoke further speculation about how much contact pre-Hispanic indigenous musicians may have had with one another:

> Because [the natives in New Spain] took their festivals with extreme seriousness and set great store by them, it was the custom in each town for the nobility to maintain in their own houses choirs of singers, amongst whom some were composers of new songs and dances. Composers skilled in fashioning songs and ballads were everywhere in great demand…The singers always decided what they were going to use several days beforehand and practiced…When they were ready to begin the dance three or four sounded some shrill whistles. Then the drumming began…The crowd often united in a dance routine that would challenge the skills of the best dancers in Spain…Each verse or couplet was repeated three or four times, the singing, drums, and dancing remaining throughout perfectly coordinated…At times trumpets and also flageolets were played; but the flageolets often seemed not

too well tuned. Occasionally they also blew small bone whistles that made a bright sound.

(Quoted in Stevenson 1968:97–99)

Alejo Carpentier offers insight into the early role that Spanish musicians played as the *conquistadores* moved between the Caribbean and Mexico, centered on another interesting military-musical figure named Ortiz:

> There can be no doubt, however, concerning the early introduction of the Spanish romance (ballad) into [the Caribbean]. When Cortes went to Trinidad to seek men for the conquest of Mexico, he counted upon the support of Ortiz the musician, player of the *vihuela* and the viol, who also conducted a dancing school in the city...Ortiz ended his career in Mexico, where he re-established his school for dance and instrumental instruction.
>
> (1947:372)

Stevenson adds a few additional details about Ortiz that demonstrate the transcultural context underway in Mexico City ("New Spain") at the time:

> He was soon forced to change his studio location after three bordellos opened nearby. His clientele included numerous Indians. Had it not, his gaining such mastery of Nahuatl as to be called *Nahuatlato* ("interpreter") would be more difficult to explain.
>
> (1968:221–22)

Reflecting an interesting tension among scholars, Stevenson (1968:99, footnote 218) also mentions that "Negroes flooded New Spain with the first wave of Europeans," and suggests other African influences brought to the mainland by the Spanish from the Caribbean even at this early stage, while Fletcher (2001:503) essentially disputes any significant African influence on Mexican musics. Certainly, any such influence seems to be lesser in comparison to African influence on Caribbean and coastal Brazilian musics, though Sheehy notes that

> close analysis of [Mexican] regional music today yields strong affinities of certain musical styles, such as the *son jarocho* with its African organizational principles...[featuring] repetition of a simple, relatively short...pattern...[while in] contrast, most other *son* styles follow more European-derived songs structure.
>
> (2008:184)

The differences between the older Cuban *son* and the Mexican *son* are instructive here, as the latter is more European with its guitar or harp accompaniment, but also interesting in its inclusion of *zapateado* dancing with Gypsy/North Indian roots as well as its frequent use of rhythmic *sesquialtera*, which likely arose from Arabic influence in al-Andalus, as noted previously.

Among the Mexican musics that developed the most global influence through the twentieth century, *mariachi* is perhaps the most well-known. A celebratory genre arising as early as the end of the eighteenth century (Fletcher 2001:502), this traditionally all-male ensemble has at various times included two or three different-sized guitars, harp, and two trumpets and/or violins, while featuring singing and straightforward European tonal harmonies with motion in parallel thirds. At the same time, the *sesquilaltera* rhythms of the *son* have remained prominent in the genre. From the 1930s onward, the development of the *mariachi* image and sound was largely driven by the film and television industry (Sheehy 2008:203), augmenting its global reach and character. Some contemporaneous groups such as Mariachi Flor de Toloache now feature women and more sophisticated jazz harmonies, rhythms, and timbres.

In Mesoamerica further south, representative transcultural musical developments include the rise of the modern *marimba* (a Bantu word), dating from as early as the seventeenth century and clearly modeled on African xylophones with resonators attached below the wooden keys that are played with rubber-headed mallets (Fletcher 2001:502–503). Maya-dominated Guatemala has been the country most closely associated with the emergence of the marimba, which "could be called [its] national instrument" and which was likely present there starting in the sixteenth or seventeenth century but not before (Obrien-Rothe 2008:222, 229). The marimba became a staple of Western percussion since its expansion to a chromatic instrument by Mexican musician Corazón de Jesús Borras Moreno late in the nineteenth century and its subsequent use into the twentieth century by European composers such as Milhaud, Janacek, and Orff. Guatemala also represents an interesting mix of indigenous influences; in addition to serving as a locus for the long reign of the Maya it has since the late sixteenth century been an adopted home of the Garifuna, descendants of Arawak and Carib natives who merged with Africans post-Columbus. Not surprisingly, several *arieto* instruments as described in the Caribbean are featured in the most traditional Garifuna ensembles, though with different names and in the service of a more Afro-Cuban style (Obrien-Rothe 2008:219).

Peruvian/Andean regions

Some time ago there lived a poor man in rags named Huathiacuri, whose father Pariacaca lived in a magical giant egg on a mountain. Huathiacuri had learned many arts from his father. Hearing from two foxes that a rich man lay very ill, with two snakes and a two-headed toad lying in wait to eat his house, Huathiacuri healed the sick man in exchange for marrying his beautiful daughter, but did so by exposing adultery on the part of the rich man's wife. This, along with now having a poor man in rags as a relative, greatly embarrassed the family. One day Huathiacuri's brother-in-law, hoping to shame Huathiacuri, challenged him to a public duel of drinking and dancing. Huathiacuri accepted the challenge, asking this father Pariacaca for advice. His father told him to go to a nearby mountain, where he would be transformed into a dead huanaco llama that would attract two hungry foxes carrying with them three magical items: a jar of chicha beer, a drum, and a set of antara panpipes. Stopping to eat, the foxes dropped their items; Huathiacuri resumed his natural form, grabbed the beer and musical instruments and went to the site of the challenge, where his brother-in-law was already dancing and drinking with many friends while his drums were being beaten by two hundred women. Huathiacuri arrived with his wife, who danced with him and also filled his beer cup and played his drum. At the first sound of her drumming the whole earth began to shake and dance, as if it was keeping time to the music. Huathiacuri drank more and danced better than his brother-in-law and all his rich friends. In fact, his brother-in-law ran away so fast that he turned into a deer who at first survived by eating people, but later was eaten by people instead.

Having established himself as an explorer and *conquistador* in Panama, including accompanying Vasco de Balboa across the Isthmus of Panama to the Pacific Ocean, Francisco Pizarro first landed on the Peruvian coast in 1524, and by 1533 had successfully led the Spanish efforts to defeat the Inca who dominated the region. The indigenous peoples there had a long and venerable musical ancestry, starting as early as c. 1400 BCE with the Chavin of the central Andes (Romero 2008:439). Miriam Kolar (2013) has demonstrated fascinating aspects of Chavin use of conch shells (*pututus*), for example. The Moche (flourished c. 100 BCE–700 CE) left behind detailed depictions of musical instruments and contexts on their distinctive pottery, while the Nazca (flourished c. 200 BCE–600 CE) seem to have specialized in ancient versions of the panpipes (variously called *antara*, *siku*, or *zampoña*) and end-blown flutes (typically called *quena/qina* or *pincullu*) that continue to be a feature of Peruvian/Andean traditional music to this day. As suggested earlier, it is interesting that the more recent musics played on these aerophones tend strongly toward world pentatonicism while field research with surviving pre-Hispanic instruments that have been excavated clearly demonstrates their capability of producing highly chromatic and even microtonal pitch collections. However, since 10 of the 19 ancient *antara* for which the scales are notated by Stevenson (1968:248–9) include world pentatonic structures of at least four notes across consecutive tubes, and since pentatonic subsets seem common in indigenous American musics as the basis to which are sometimes added chromatic or microtonal ornamental variants,[11] it is worth reiterating the possibility that this was one indigenous pitch sensibility that came later to be more widespread among these regional musics, reinforced by Iberian tonal sensibilities and possibly affected also by African musics in the coastal areas.

Three examples from the fieldwork of Bishop Baltazar Martínez Compañón transcribing Peruvian music c. 1785 are instructive in this regard. The region was occupied by the Moche, Chimu, and, briefly, the Inca before conquistadores arrived and founded Trujillo, seat of Compañón's bishopric, as one of their first new cities there in about 1534. Coastal Trujillo gave rise over the 350 years between its founding and Compañón's arrival to a particular mix of Incan, Spanish, and African musical sensibilities, while more isolated communities in the highland regions further inland were slower to integrate. Among the examples Compañón notated are two different but strikingly similar indigenous dance song melodies from Cajamarca (some 150 miles inland from Trujillo) and Chachapoyas (another 200 miles inland from Cajamarca). Relevant excerpts from these are reproduced in modern notation below from Compañón's original manuscript:[12]

Ex. 5.4 Peruvian melody—Chachapoyas version.

Ex. 5.5 Peruvian melody—Cajamarca version.

In the version from Chachapoyas, furthest inland, the melody is entirely in world pentatonic mode two, the pitch structure that continues to dominate the region today, while the "harmony" (even if implying chordal improvisation *a la* figured bass) is so rudimentary—and, toward the end, so awkward—as to be nearly optional: all the pitches remain in the same scale and only the clear G major chords in the middle add anything tonal/modal.

The longer version from Cajamarca, heading toward the coast and Trujillo, demonstrates two important differences. The first of these is a clear but unexpected attempt to make it tonal using a non-scalar leading tone (D-sharp) at the end (the D-sharp is also heard in an introduction earlier, not shown here); otherwise, the harmonic structure is essentially identical to the Chachapoyas version. Closer to Trujillo, this music was also closer to Spanish influence. The second difference in the Cajamarca version, its solitary but still noticeable instance of a syncopated rhythmic figure, aligns with a third melody in Compañón's field collection, from the more cosmopolitan Trujillo, excerpted here to show African rhythmic influence:

Ex. 5.6 Pervian melody, "El Congo"—Trujillo.

The melodic and harmonic pitch materials are straightforwardly European, but the sixteenth-eighth-sixteenth rhythmic figure (bars one and five) is common in African (and Afro-Cuban) musics. Compañón clearly means to mark this association by using the label "El Congo" paired with three watercolor illustrations of transplanted Africans making music (numbers 140–142 of the collection).

These intercultural elements continued to coalesce in key Andean genres such as the *huayno* song-dance and the *zambacueca/cueca/marinera* dance (Fletcher 2001:499, 506–509). In addition to the antara/siku/zampoña panpipes and quena notched flute, various sizes of guitars (such as the *charango*) and harps prominently reinforce tonal/modal harmonies while drums and shakers/rattles provide relatively straightforward rhythmic and metric support. The European violin is also used to mirror melodies or to provide simple counterpoint (as it does, for example, in the Compañón manuscripts). Likely the most globally well-known huayno to date is Peruvian Daniel Robles's 1913 "El Condor Pasa," especially after it was recorded with English lyrics as "If I Could" by Americans Paul Simon and Art Garfunkel on their album *Bridge Over Troubled Water* in 1970.

The (urban) Brazilian coast

The intercultural dynamic that developed in Brazil after its colonization by the Portuguese in the 1530s was somewhat different from other Latin American regions in that many indigenous peoples (whom the Europeans discovered were not well suited to heavy physical work burdens) fled or were driven into the interior while the Iberians brought African labor to the coastal areas, primarily to cultivate sugar cane. As a result, significant groups of native cultures continued to flourish in the Amazonian and other interior regions rather than being as thoroughly decimated as in the Caribbean. Meanwhile, the African influence on the Brazilian coastal communities was even more pronounced. With the establishment in 1549 of Bahia (modern Salvador) as a Portuguese administrative hub very near the eastern-most coastal point of Brazil, the transcultural developmental process began in earnest.

The power of Yoruba-Fon religions in Bantu-speaking regions of Africa, combined with the power of Catholicism imposed on Brazil by Iberians, accounts for some of the most vital musical developments around religious syncretism among Africans transplanted there. In one of the most prominent and enduring of these syntheses, Candomblé, music and dance are central. Pentatonic and hexatonic pitch structures, call and response organization, and characteristically interlocking African rhythmic processes (including improvisatory passages around otherwise fixed patterns) prevail, while European and indigenous influences are less prominent. By contrast, the even more popular (and more contemporary) Umbanda, which incorporates some elements of Candomblé, has broader cultural integration and commensurately broader appeal (Behague 2008:354–356).

No musical tradition distinguishes urban (coastal) Brazil more than the *samba* and Carnaval, which arose from the syncretic religious context of Iberian Catholic Christianity and African traditional spirituality, as in Haiti with Vodou. Suzel Reily, reflecting Brazilian musicologist Jose Ramos Tinhorao, suggests one attractive theory: "that the samba was the product of a middle-class elaboration of Afro-Brazilian musical practices by professional musicians in Rio…[after which] it was then reappropriated in its more complex form by blacks and mulattos for their Carnaval parades" (2008:341). Some of the roots of the modern samba can be traced back to *batuque*, an eighteenth- and nineteenth-century group dance of Angolan/Congolese origin with drums, percussion sticks, and rattles, in which the motion is passed along the circle via bumping of bellies. Gerhard Kubik relays the story of one late twentieth-century link to the original batuque tradition in the person of Benedito Caxias, in the small town of Capivari more than 300 miles from one locus of the tradition, the coastal city of Sao Paulo (1990:119ff.). Caxias, like the music he championed, was of mixed parentage, with a Brazilian-born (Bahian) father and a mother of directly African parentage. Based on detailed transcriptions and organological analysis from films made of Caxias's playing, Kubik demonstrates that not only are there traits from a number of African traditions intermingled in the drumming style, but also that a variety of non-African characteristics are clear as well, especially (and unusually) European military marching idioms.[13] Kubik goes further in linking these marching-step rhythms to the modern urban samba that emerged into the turn of the twentieth century and continues to dominate today (1990:143–159).

Since the 1950s, samba has emerged as a truly globalized idiom, also giving rise from the early 1960s to another widely popular idiom known as *bossa nova*. Brazilian composer Antonio Carlos (Tom) Jobim is closely associated with this easygoing style which maintains the African syncopated rhythms seen elsewhere in this study in combination with sophisticated jazz harmonies. Jobim's "The Girl From Ipanema" certainly remains the most globally famous bossa nova piece, and perhaps the most well-known Brazilian musical composition to date.

Amazonian and other interior areas

Even as cultural strongholds were being established on the Brazilian coast, exploration of and influence on the inland regions—such as the famous voyages of Francisco de Orellana along the Amazon River in the 1540s—continued apace. An encounter described by one of Orellana's chroniclers, Friar Gaspar de Carvajal, is instructive. Natives appeared in numerous large boats carrying musicians with "many trumpets and drums, and pipes on which they play with their mouths, and rebecs, which among these people have three strings," along with groups of men on the bank "playing on instruments and dancing about...manifesting very great joy upon seeing that we were passing beyond their villages" (quoted in Kupperman 2012:30), suggesting that these musical displays were not meant as welcoming, but as signals of militant threat, as in Mexico. The use of the term "rebec" (Spanish descendant of the Middle Eastern *rebab* and an ancestor of both the European violin and a Brazilian folk violin called the *rabeca*, still in use) for whatever chordophone Carvajal observed is a reminder of the Arabic musical legacy these Spaniards carried with them (see Chapter 4).

The stories of Spanish Jesuit missionaries who created Christian settlements along and around the Paraná River (near what is today the intersection of Brazil, Paraguay, and Argentina) from c. 1609 until their expulsion in 1760 are interesting in that the Jesuits found the native Guarani tribes to be very musical, trained many in European classical/ecclesiastical musics (as in Mexico and other Latin American strongholds), and used such a state of affairs both as a tool for conversion and as a way of keeping Portuguese and Spanish imperial overlords from exterminating these indigenous peoples (see, e.g., Reily 2008:328–329). Though fictionally oversimplified, Roland Joffe's 1986 film *The Mission* captures the spirit of this historical moment, including the fact that European musical influence does not appear ultimately to have prevailed in the region, nor in the vast inland areas of South America generally, becoming absorbed instead into new transcultural styles. Venerable film composer Ennio Morricone tells this parallel musical story in the form of his score for *The Mission*, which carries the stylistic integration of indigenous and Spanish musics to an idealized level, demonstrating the extent of this transculturality as it continued to develop late into the twentieth century. Elements of Guarani influence continue in a transcultural context to this day in Paraguay (Watkins 2008).

Reily (2008:330) reproduces a typical *caterete* (also called *catira*, a Tupi word) dance rhythm from rural interior Brazil, featuring the same sixteenth-eighth-sixteenth African figure seen in the Peruvian interior, which also falls into the 3 + 3 + 2 grouping seen in the Carib shaman's melody earlier in this chapter. Earliest fully reliable evidence of the *caterete* dates to the nineteenth century, though legend and some scholars have traced its emergence to late in the sixteenth century in the context of the Jesuit José de Anchieta y Díaz de Clavijo (1534–1597), who was among the founders of both Sao Paulo and Rio de Janiero and who worked with Tupi tribes in South-Central Brazil (Reily 2008:329). Shrouded in the mists of time, there is no consensus on what the mixture of indigenous, African, and even European inputs to the *caterete* might have been, but it seems clear that it developed as a transcultural phenomenon. Reily produces similar rhythmic evidence against a backdrop of European harmonies in parallel thirds in a *toada de moçambique* ensemble piece used for a Christian festival in Sao Paulo (2008:340), reinforcing the regional and conceptual connections noted here.

Among contemporary Brazilian musicians, the work of Marlui Miranda (b. 1949) in albums such as *Ihu—Todos Os Son* (1996), *Ihu 2—Kwere:Rezar:Prayer* (1999), *Neuneneu Humanity* (2006), and *Fala de Bicho, Fala de Gente* (2014) stands out for its extensive field research on indigenous musics from the Xingu areas in the Brazilian interior expertly integrated into twenty-first-century transcultural contexts.

Spotlight: the rise of the guitar as a global transcultural instrument

One of the most interesting stories to take clearer contemporary shape with the coming of American transcultural musics after 1500 is that of the guitar. As noted throughout this study, plucked chordophones figured prominently from the beginning of documented global music history. Which of these influenced the others the most and when is difficult to discern. For example, as tempting as the often repeated notion is that the Greek *kithara* lyre was the ancestor of the guitar, several analytical paradigms argue against it; ancient Mesopotamian or Persian long-necked lutes seem to be better candidates (Alves 2015:7–9). The Arabs in al-Andalus contributed the *oud*, a fretless lute that closely resembles the Chinese *pipa* and its ancient Kuchean precursor described in Chapter 3, which in turn clearly influenced the design of the Western European Renaissance lute.[14] The modern guitar, with its frets and straight neck, seems to have evolved further from the Spanish *vihuela* sometime in the thirteenth or fourteenth centuries, and is mentioned in the collection of Spanish poems and songs titled *El Libro de Buen Amor* (The Book of Good Love) c. 1330. There are also at least two types of guitars featured visually in the *Cantigas de Santa Maria* manuscripts (Alves 2015:12). The *vihuela* and the guitar became key instruments in Latin America: ship's records indicate that the first vihuela arrived in Puerto Rico in 1512 and the first guitar in 1516 (Drouet 2008:164). In 1578, an English colonist in Brazil, William Whithall, lists guitar strings among the items he is ordering from a European merchant vessel (Pendle 1963:81). Africans in the New World would have been familiar with long-necked chordophones such as the *kora* (harp-lute) and the *ngoni* (most likely the ancestor of the American banjo) found in their indigenous regions, and would eventually incorporate the styles associated with some of these into the new world of the guitar in the Americas.

Over the intervening years, the character and use of the American guitar continued to develop with additional intercultural input, just as the Americas themselves did. This transcultural context is reflected strongly, for example, in the life and work of Mexican master guitarist Manual Ponce (1882–1948), who returned to his native country after further studies in Europe, lived in Cuba for a time, and determined to integrate indigenous Mexican themes into his compositions for the guitar (Alves 2015:116–119). Something similar could be said of the Brazilian Heitor Villa-Lobos (1887–1959), who wrote extensively for the instrument. Today the list of guitar virtuosos extends to all corners of the globe. Meanwhile, though it has increasingly claimed a space in the world of art music, the guitar remains at the heart of folk and popular music in both Latin America and the United States. Indeed, with the addition of electric amplification it became a foundational instrument in the story of American folk, blues, jazz, and rock,[15] which styles have spread to the rest of the world as well. The guitar thus embodies the tenets of this study in that it has become the most ubiquitous plucked chordophone globally, across styles and cultures, in some ways absorbing, consolidating, and redirecting the many other versions of itself conceptually that continue to exist: "The guitar is in every respect a global phenomenon" (Bennett and Dawe 2001:1).

Notes

1 In addition, French musical contributions were not inconsequential in the Caribbean. While Dutch and English representatives also arrived in these parts of the New World during the sixteenth to eighteenth centuries, these seem to have had a negligible distinctive effect on musical developments. Further north, they were far more important (see Chapter 6).

2 And/or possibly arrived on Pacific coastal areas of the Americas via ocean travel, potentially with Australasian origins (see, e.g., Callaway 2016, Skoglund et al. 2015). Barbeau (1934) provides an analysis of similarities between indigenous North American songs and those from Siberia and China. See also Note 3 below.

3 In all but a handful of current theories, the most relevant traits are likely to be reflective of the oldest known traditional musics of Oceania and/or northeastern Siberia. Davies (1927) and Caughie (1958) both show Australian aboriginal mono/heterophonic vocal music that includes or features world (anhemitonic) pentatonicism with micro-tuning variations, in melodic pitch-range configurations that start high and descend, as some Native North and South American musics do. This might suggest an historical global loop in which human musics of the farthest East have now met up with their descendants, so to speak. But not all aboriginal music conforms to such a profile.

4 See Chapter 4 for additional discussion.

5 Stevenson reproduces a choral work from c. 1599 by an Aztecan composer who has been fully acculturated to this same musical language, using native Nahuatl language into which has been integrated appropriate Spanish words for Christian concepts, insightfully speculating that the composer's command of the rhythmic complexities clearly exceeds that of his harmonic part-writing because of the indigenous musical context in which he was raised (1968:204–207).

6 This is not to suggest that harmony was never present, at least among the Maya and even earlier civilizations. However, harmony seems not to have survived, or at least not to have been featured, by the time of the Spanish occupations; European harmony certainly quickly came to dominate in any case (Stevenson 1968:84–85, Seeger 2008:86).

7 Especially among, for example, the Aztecs. The journals of Jean de Lery from his brief time in Brazil c. 1557 also show that Europeans were "shocked" by discoveries among other natives of musical items like "rattles and flutes made from human skulls and bones" (Reily 2008:327).

8 On the question of pentatonicism in the Americas, the findings are complex. Stevenson (1968:245–252) and Romero (2008) note that ancient Peruvian flutes, long assumed to be pentatonic in design because of current practices, allow for expanded microtonal pitch collections (but see the section in this chapter on Peruvian/Andean musics); Stevenson (1968:54) mirrors this same point with regard to preserved ocarinas. One might speculate that the generally nature-oriented pre-Hispanic indigenous soundscapes, likely imitating animals and birds, would help explain the wide range of pitch and quasi-pitch options. This does not definitively demonstrate, however, that pentatonic subsets of larger collections did not coalesce with some consistency, as they often do elsewhere in the world (see again, e.g., Kolinski 1957, Hijleh 2012 as noted earlier). Chá, for example, suggests in passing that the Andean region of Argentina originally featured pentatonicism (2008:404–405), while Romero himself notes that the indigenous Culina in the Amazonian regions of Peru also commonly use the collection (2008:454). Cohen and Wissler point out that the relatively less-acculturated Hatun Q'eros natives in the upper Andes within 100 miles of Cusco sing pentatonic

songs to their farm animals and play pentatonic melodies on six-note *pitu* flutes during the pre-Hispanic *ch'unchu* dance (2008:463–464, 467), and Seeger transcribes a Suyá song (modern but written in traditional Amazonian style) that features a four-note world pentatonic subset, though with rising and falling pitch centers and what appears to be one "chromatic" alteration (2004:88–93); Stock (1996:95) transcribes a Kaiapo corn ritual song, also Amazonian, with the same pitch collection plus the missing note that makes it fully pentatonic. Ramon y Rivera (1969) posits a more complex thesis in which fundamental pentatonic pitches are combined with overtones higher in the series as well as expressive chromatic notes in scales of three to five notes in a variety of indigenous Latin American musics. Sargeant rightly points out that the strikingly and consistently pentatonic Quechua melodies would not have received that pitch structure from the Iberian folk or church musics (1934:230–231), to which it can be added that African influence on culture in the Andean highlands has been practically nonexistent (Romero 2008:438). Returning to the Caribbean, Averill and Wilcken (2008:130) note that Haitian Vodou music also tends toward pentatonic structures, suggesting that African pentatonic influence on Caribbean musics (and, by inference, on coastal Brazilian musics) was strong and reinforcing the key point that the inter/transcultural origins of Latin American music are deep, ancient, and challenging to unravel into constituent parts—though the general evidence is overwhelming.

9   Averill and Wilcken note that 3 + 3 + 2 is, for example, one of the fundamental rhythms in Haitian Vodou (2008:129–130); it is also the *malfuf* pattern of Arabic hand drumming.

10 Played most often on a solo bell, which is likely to have been the origin of the cowbell in the modern drumset, and used in *salsa* and other Latin American genres to be reminiscent of the African timeline feature; the Yoruban-Brazilian *agogo* double bell, almost identical to the Ewe *gankoqui*, serves this same purpose.

11 Olsen (2004:283–284) demonstrates this effectively by relaying his field experience of a traditional melody played microtonally on a Q'eros *antara* (*qanchis sipas*) that is subsequently sung with a much clearer world pentatonic tuning by a native musician.

12 From the *Trujillo del Perú Codex*, public domain. The melodies appear also in Stevenson (1968:318), who includes the two different sets of lyrics and who also more or less endorses the notion that they are "authentic survivals" based "on circumstantial evidence." Stevenson (1968:319) provides one additional melody (Compañón's example 189, also from inland) that reinforces the thesis of this section in that it mixes two different aspects: the pitch structure is straightforwardly tonal but features grace note ornaments throughout that are evocative of indigenous singing, something seen also in the Cajamarca melody above. Meanwhile, other melodies in the collection from Trujillo explicated by Stevenson show African stylistic input (see, e.g., 1968:316–317).

13 Interestingly, military marches also played a key role in the development of African-American music in the United States; see Chapters 6 and 8.

14 The name "lute" traditionally derives from the Arabic "al-'ud." Alves, however, notes the important morphological distinction between short- and long-necked lutes and how these in turn created evolutionary branches important to the emergence of the guitar proper (2015:10–13).

15 See Bacon (2011) for a history of the transformation of the guitar in the United States in conjunction with these developments.

References

Alves, Júlio. 2015. *The History of the Guitar: Its Origins and Evolution*. Huntington, West Virginia: Marshall University Digital Scholar Library. Accessed 2-12-2017 at http://mds.marshall.edu/music_faculty.

Averill, Gage, and Lois Wilcken. 2008. "Haiti." In Olsen, Dale, and Daniel Sheehy (eds.), *The Garland Handbook of Latin American Music* (2nd ed.), New York: Routledge, 126–142.

Bacon, Tony. 2011. *History of the American Guitar: 1883 to the Present Day*. Milwaukee, Wisconsin: Backbeat Books.

Barbeau, Marius. 1934. "Asiatic Survivals in Indian Songs." *The Musical Quarterly* 201:107–116.

Behauge, Gerard. 2008. "Afro-Brazilian Traditions." In Olsen, Dale, and Daniel Sheehy (eds.), *The Garland Handbook of Latin American Music* (2nd ed.), New York: Routledge, 352–369.

Bennett, Andy, and Kevin Dawe (eds.). 2001. *Guitar Cultures*. Oxford: Berg.

Blades, James. 2005. *Percussion Instruments and Their History* (Revised ed.). Westport, Connecticut: The Bold Strummer (orig. published 1970 by Faber and Faber, London).

Callaway, Ewen. 2016. "Coastal Route for First Americans." *Nature* 538: 138.

Carpentier, Alejo (trans. Cohen, Ethel). 1947. "Music in Cuba (1523–1900)." *The Musical Quarterly* 333: 365–380.

Caughie, Catherine. 1958. "The Scales of Some Central Australian Songs." *Journal of the International Folk Music Council* 10: 57–61.

Chá, Ercilia. 2008. "Argentina" In Olsen, Dale, and Daniel Sheehy (eds.), *The Garland Handbook of Latin American Music* (2nd ed.), New York: Routledge, 385–407.

Cohen, John, and Holly Wissler. 2008. "Q'eros." In Olsen, Dale, and Daniel Sheehy (eds.), *The Garland Handbook of Latin American Music* (2nd ed.), New York: Routledge, 463–473.

Davies, E.H. 1927. "Palæolithic Music." *The Musical Times* 681014: 691–695.

Davis, Martha. 2008. "The Dominican Republic." In Olsen, Dale, and Daniel Sheehy (eds.), *The Garland Handbook of Latin American Music* (2nd ed.), New York: Routledge, 143–162.

DjeDje, Jacqueline. 2000. "West Africa: An Introduction." In Stone, Ruth (ed.), *The Garland Handbook of African Music*, New York: Garland, 140–168.

Drouet, Hector. 2008. "Puerto Rico." In Olsen, Dale, and Daniel Sheehy (eds.), *The Garland Handbook of Latin American Music* (2nd ed.), New York: Routledge, 163–175.

Fletcher, Peter. 2001. *World Musics in Context*. New York: Oxford University Press.

Gillin, John. 1936. *The Barama River Caribs of British Guiana*. Cambridge, Massachusetts: Papers of the Peabody Museum of American Archaeology and Ethnology, Harvard University XIV: 2.

Hijleh, Mark. 2012. *Towards a Global Music Theory*. Farnham, Surrey: Ashgate.

Kolar, Miriam. 2013. "Tuned to the Senses: An Archaeoacoustic Perspective on Ancient Chavín." *The Index* 1.3. Accessed 1-16-2017 at theappendix.net/issues/2013/7/tuned-to-he-senses-an-archaeoacoustic-perspective-on-ancient-chavin.

Kolinski, Mieczyslaw. 1957. "The Determinants of Tonal Construction in Tribal Music." *The Musical Quarterly* 431: 50–56.

Kubik, Gerhard. 1990. "Drum Patterns in the 'Batuque' of Benedito Caxias." *Latin American Music Review/Revista de Música Latinoamericana* 112: 115–181.

Kubik, Gerhard. 2000. "Central Africa: An Introduction." In Stone, Ruth (ed.), *The Garland Handbook of African Music*, New York: Garland Publishing, 260–290.

Kupperman, Karen. 2012. *The Atlantic in World History*. New York: Oxford University Press.

Markham, Clements. 1873. *Narratives of the Rites and Laws of the Yncas*. New York: Burt Franklin (reprinted from The Hakluyt Society).

Obrien-Rothe, Linda. 2008. "Guatemala." In Olsen, Dale, and Daniel Sheehy (eds.), *The Garland Handbook of Latin American Music* (2nd ed.), New York: Routledge, 216–233.

Olsen, Dale. 2004. "Aerophones of Traditional Use in South America, with References to Central America and Mexico." In Kuss, Malena (ed.), *Music in Latin America and the Caribbean: An Encyclopedic History*, Vol. 1, 261–326.

Olsen, Dale. 2008. "Studying Latin American Music." In Olsen, Dale, and Daniel Sheehy (eds.), *The Garland Handbook of Latin American Music* (2nd ed.), New York: Routledge, 13–35.

Olsen, Dale, and Daniel Sheehy (eds.). 2008. *The Garland Handbook of Latin American Music* (2nd ed.), New York: Routledge.

Oppenheimer, Stephen. 2004. *Out of Eden: The Peopling of the World*. London: Constable and Robinson.

Pendle, George. 1963. *A History of Latin America*. New York: Penguin.

Ramon y Rivera, Luis. 1969. "Formaciones Escalísticas en la Etnomúsica Latinoamericana." *Yearbook of the International Folk Music Council*, 1: 200–225.

Reily, Suzel. 2008. "Brazil: Central and Southern Areas." In Olsen, Dale, and Daniel Sheehy (eds.), *The Garland Handbook of Latin American Music* (2nd ed.), New York: Routledge, 326–351.

Rodriguez, Olavo. 2008. "Cuba." In Olsen, Dale, and Daniel Sheehy (eds.), *The Garland Handbook of Latin American Music* (2nd ed.), New York: Routledge, 105–125.

Romero, Raul. 2008. "Peru." In Olsen, Dale, and Daniel Sheehy (eds.), *The Garland Handbook of Latin American Music* (2nd ed.), New York: Routledge, 438–462.

Rouse, Irving. 1992. *The Tainos: Rise and Decline of the People Who Greeted Columbus*. New Haven: Yale University Press.

Sargeant, Winthrop. 1934. "Types of Quechua Melody." *The Musical Quarterly* 202: 230–245.

Seeger, Anthony. 2004. *Why Suyá Sing: A Musical Anthropology of an Amazonian People*. Chicago: University of Illinois Press.

Seeger, Anthony. 2008. "Musical Dynamics." In Olsen, Dale and Daniel Sheehy (eds.), *The Garland Handbook of Latin American Music* (2nd ed.), New York: Routledge, 78–89.

Seeger, Charles. 1977. *Studies in Musicology 1935–1975*. Berkeley: University of California Press.

Sheehy, Daniel. 2008. "Mexico." In Olsen, Dale, and Daniel Sheehy (eds.), *The Garland Handbook of Latin American Music* (2nd ed.), New York: Routledge, 181–208.

Skogland, Pontus, Swapan Mallick, Maria Bortolini, Niru Chennagiri, Tábita Hünemeier, Maria Petzl-Erler, Francisco Salzano, et al. 2015. "Genetic Evidence for Two Founding Populations of the Americas." *Nature* 525: 104–108.

Stevenson, Robert. 1968. *Music in Aztec and Inca Territory*. Berkeley, CA: University of California Press.

Stiffler, David. 1982. *Music of the Coastal Amerindians of Guyana: the Arawak, Carib, and Warrau* [Audio recording and liner notes]. New York: Folkways Records FE 4239.

Stock, Jonathan. 1996. *World Sound Matters: An Anthology of Music from Around the World* (Transcriptions). London: Schott.

Watkins, Timothy. 2008. "Paraguay." In Olsen, Dale, and Daniel Sheehy (eds.), *The Garland Handbook of Latin American Music* (2nd ed.), New York: Routledge, 370–384.

6 The rise of transcultural musics in the United States[1]

I am now satisfied that the future of music in [the United States] must be founded upon what are called the Negro melodies.

—Czech composer Antonín Dvořák (1893)[2]

The African race is a music-loving one, proverbially; and many there were among my fellow-bondsmen whose organs of tune were strikingly developed, and who could thumb the banjo with dexterity...Alas! had it not been for my beloved violin, I scarcely can conceive how I could have endured the long years of bondage...Often, at midnight, when sleep had fled affrighted from the cabin, and my soul was disturbed and troubled with the contemplation of my fate, it would sing me a song of peace...It heralded my name round the country—made me friends, who, otherwise would not have noticed me.

—Black American fiddler Samuel Northup (1853:216–217)

Figure 6.1 U.S. Civil War soldiers with black musicians.

Source: *Frank Leslie's Illustrated Newspaper*, January 31, 1863, p. 292. From the Lincoln Financial Foundation Collection, courtesy of the Indiana State Museum and Allen County Public Library.

Africans and Europeans in the United States together created a dynamic and ever-evolving group of transcultural musics that was rather different from that in Mexico and further south,[3] one that stemmed in part from the long interactive evolution of transplanted African cultures in a country of Protestants that united in independence against European colonial powers and in the long run provided more opportunity for black musicians to create distinctive musics and pass them along to the world (albeit sometimes in exceedingly unjust ways over which they had little control). Because it is an unfortunate but undeniable fact that the ancient indigenous cultures that settled and developed north of Mexico had little consequential influence on the most important American musics and the global hybrids that eventually resulted (as previously noted in Chapter 1), this study will not address them substantially.[4] Some of the differences between North American and Latin America musics of fusion were due in part to this lack of indigenous influence further north, and also in part to the differences between Iberian and English folk musics. Eventually, however, musicians in the United States absorbed, integrated, and transmitted the transcultural musics of Latin America as well, ultimately recognizing that all original musics throughout the Americas since 1500 CE share deep African roots.

The most globally consequential musical contributions of the United States developed almost entirely east of the Mississippi River until well into the twentieth century, when recording and broadcast technologies began to mitigate the significant distances that separated continental (and global) east and west. The western and southwestern regions, of which the territories that were to become Texas and California were the most consequential, were essentially Spanish-Mexican colonies well beyond the time that musical developments in the eastern portions of the country emphasized in this chapter were underway. European, African, and Native American intercultural musical confluence west of the Mississippi added little if anything to these eastern syntheses until much later, and even then largely built upon them.

Key moments early in the evolution of this distinctive synthesis that can be seen clearly in three important cultural centers: (1) the publication and wide use of the *Bay Psalm Book* (1640) and Isaac Watts's *Hymns and Spiritual Songs* (1739) in Boston, both of which served as models from which black musicians learned Western tonality (at first melodic and later harmonic); (2) the growth of Charles Town (Charleston), South Carolina, as a slave territory that served as "the cultural metropolis of the South, regarded by some as the musical center of the entire eastern seaboard during the early eighteenth century" (Southern 1983:26), where, for example, blacks were taught instrumental skills by professional musicians in order to provide entertainment for their households, where the Wesley brothers published their *Collection of Psalms and Hymns* (1737), and where communities of free blacks eventually exerted influence after the Civil War (Southern 1983:36, 52–53, 97); and (3), as the nineteenth century progressed into the twentieth, in New Orleans, perhaps both the "most exotic" and the "most musical city in the land," where "in 1803, the year of the Louisiana Purchase, its Spanish, French, African, English, Irish, and German traditions were fusing into something that was new and different, into a truly American culture," and in which the "Negro population, the largest of any American city, constituted more than one-third of the city's total" (Southern 1983:131–132). After the U.S. Civil War and the emancipation of slaves late in the nineteenth century, the trends begun at America's founding continued as Africans slowly became part of free society and the musical synthesis developed further into the twentieth. This chapter focuses on the precursors of the blues and jazz in the United States prior to the 1920s: African and European folk music, work songs, music for Christian worship, dance music for entertainment, minstrelsy, ragtime, and the rise of instrumental music in the military and in public education that brought key jazz instruments to the fore. In these instances especially, African and European musics interacted and evolved towards new fusions or outright transformation.

Colonies, revolution, and the seeds of civil war

The area of North America that was to constitute the original United States (that is, excluding Florida and the territory west of the Mississippi River) was colonized by British, and to a lesser extent Spanish and French, explorers from about 1570 until the thirteen British colonies conceived of, declared, fought for and won national independence in the period of roughly 1765 to 1783—though many aspects of early U.S. identity would not be resolved until about 1815. During the subsequent 50 years, until the prosecution of the U.S. Civil War from 1861–1865, elements already set in motion continued to affect the development of American music. The constancy of military contexts and the rise of public education resulted in essential contributions that took root later in the nineteenth century in conjunction with the growth of cities and a kind of urban diversity in the U.S. Cities remained racially segregated, like much of the rest of the country, yet musical integration proceeded apace.

North and South

The United States did not begin as entirely united, and its unity was fitful during the first phase of its history. In a divide that has not entirely disappeared as of this writing, North and South in the United States developed along rather different cultural lines. The famed Mason–Dixon line, first forged just prior to the American Revolutionary War in order to settle colonies' border disputes, effectively defined Pennsylvania, Delaware, New Jersey, and points north as "the North," while Maryland, Virginia, and points south became "the South," though the cultural realities were somewhat more complex and had been underway much earlier. The South remained more rural and agricultural while the North moved towards crafts and trade, emphasized education, and urbanized sooner during the eighteenth and early nineteenth centuries. In many respects these trends continued well into the twentieth century. English colonists to both the South and the North and their descendants were motivated by a complex set of religious, political, and economic factors, but real differences did emerge that affected musical developments in the respective regions.

The development of the South started a few decades earlier than the North. After multiple failed attempts, the English arrived in the Chesapeake Bay (the area that today spans essentially from Baltimore, Maryland, to Norfolk, Virginia) to stay in 1607, where indigenous tribes had driven off the Spanish several decades earlier. Meanwhile, Puritan (extremely conservative Calvinist Protestant) colonists began to arrive in what came to be called "New England" in 1620, starting with the Massachusetts Bay, at the heart of which now lies modern Boston. By 1680, the southern stronghold of Charles Town (Charleston) quite a bit further south of the Chesapeake in what came to be South Carolina was also well established. Because Boston and Charleston, both port cities, were the sites of well-documented musical activity, they may serve here as representatives of North and South. On the other hand, it is important to keep in mind that most people lived rurally rather than in towns for some time during the colonial era. Moreover, rurality and urbanity emerged rather differently in the North and South.

Differing economic opportunities in North and South created differing complexities surrounding the need for labor, though at first the colonial system revolved around those indenturing themselves voluntarily in exchange for the promise of future freedom and free land (Taylor 2001:133–134). These settlers, most of whom started out as poorer single young men (Taylor 2001:169), ended up with ever-larger plantations producing tobacco, rice, and indigo, which yielded excellent monetary returns on investment but required constant, intense labor, just as sugar did in Latin America. While African slaves arrived in Jamestown, the first stable colony, by 1619 (Southern 1983:1, 3), the drive to acquire more slaves needed for economically efficient labor in the face of declining voluntarily indentured immigrants rose dramatically in the region starting in the 1680s: "the slave numbers surged from a mere 300 in 1650 to 13,000 by 1700, when Africans constituted 13% of the Chesapeake population. During the early eighteenth century, their numbers and proportion continued to grow, reaching 150,000 people and 40% by 1750" (Taylor 2001:153–154).

Meanwhile, the economics of agriculture in the North revolved around the family farm and a stable, deeply religious life in a part of the country that was much colder and more barren than the fecund, humid South. Northern Puritans tended to be better off and more skilled prior to embarking on their journey to the New World (Taylor 2001:169). Most were less economically ambitious and more ambitious with regard to piety, which led to valuing education as a means to encourage reading of the Bible and consideration of Christianity and culture (Taylor 2001:179). "More than the colonists in any other region, the orthodox New English maintained that they had a divine mission to create a model society in America" (Taylor 2001:178). All of this added up to a far more modest approach to the problems of labor and the need for slaves. A decade into the colonization process in New England, less than 20% of immigrants were indentured servants, and, unlike in the South, Northerners declined to augment their numbers significantly with African slaves: "In 1700 less than two percent of New England's inhabitants were slaves, compared with 13 percent in Virginia" (Taylor 2001:169).

Early musical inputs and trends

North and South put aside these and other differences enough to unite against the British government, break free, and establish a stable new national government by 1783. Nevertheless, cultural differences between North and South continued to evolve into social-institutional distinctives, particularly regarding the place of Africans, but also regarding religion and economics. Each new state was fiercely independent, and each region had its character. As a result, music developed in various ways throughout the territories, though important common factors remained.

Primary source material about English art music around the beginning of the seventeenth century can be found in *A Plaine and Easie Introduction to Practicall Musicke* (1597) by the composer/theorist Thomas Morley (1557–1602) as well as the lute songs and commentaries of lutenist John Dowland (1563–1626), whose collection *The First Booke of Songes or Ayres* also appeared in 1597. Morley's treatise and his music both reflect the dominance of Italian theory and practice in sixteenth- and seventeenth-century England. String music, in the form of "viol consorts" (sometimes with keyboard added) was a multi-part alternative to choral music, and not dissimilar from it. At the same time, in Italy, the violin itself continued to develop into something more of solo virtuoso instrument. In the colonies, both the lute and the violin—with their mixed Arabic origins—also resonated with African chordophonic experiences.

Dowland carried forward some of the momentum towards a return to the solo song that was, in a different form, also driving the development of European opera. Certainly, the homophony of the lute-songs stands in contrast to the complex polyphony of the choral madrigals, though the harmonic language of each is very similar and the lute accompaniments do include modest polyphonic movement against the simpler vocal rhythms. Suites of dance movements for solo lute were also an important part of the repertoire, and these reflected more of what was being exported to the colonies, where social dancing was a prime form of entertainment. Nor was the separation of these categories rigid: folk tunes associated with the lute for all sorts of purposes—including political balladry—circulated widely. Roy Lamson (1939) found that, based on statistical analysis of records of their appearance in various period sources, the three most popular of these tunes were, in order: "Packington's Pound," "Fortune My Foe" (most well-known in an arrangement by Dowland), and the eternal "Greensleeves." Interestingly, all three of these are primarily in minor modes and are more contemplative than spritely.

Probably no other individual had as much total impact on the very earliest English musical influences in America than the London music publisher John Playford (1623–1687). Folk music and instructions for dancing were supplied by numerous editions of his *The English Dancing Master*, starting in 1651 and extending well into the eighteenth century (Crawford 2001:72–5). In addition, either the 1674 or 1679 edition of his *Introduction to the Skill of Musick* (one of eighteen editions issued between 1654 and 1730) seems almost certain to have been the musical source for the ninth edition of the *Bay Psalm Book* (1698), the first to contain tunes in notation (Lowens 1955).

As in Latin America, blacks came largely from the West African region that has been called the Senegambia (centered around Senegal and The Gambia), and would have been steeped in features that had contributed to the Andalusian-European synthesis in the previous era. Robert Palmer notes that "because of Senegambia's many centuries of contact with the Berber and Arab cultures north of the desert, the vocal music tends to reflect the Middle East's predilection for long, tortuous melodic lines" (1981:27), and, it should be added, featured the Afro-Arab singing style that came to dominate American popular music. Palmer suggests that the Wolof people "played a particularly important and perhaps a culturally dominant role in the early slave culture of the United States" (1981:31), including in its music. Interestingly, Jacqueline DjeDje (2000:143–144) notes that musical professionals in the cultural cluster of which the Wolof are a part tend to overshadow non-professionals; that chordophones (including the well-established *kora* lute-harp), flutes, and idiophones (pitched and unpitched) are prominent; that seven-note scales of various tunings as well as pentatonic scales are used; and that drumming, while socially ubiquitous and "energetic, with complex poly-rhythmic combinations," is not associated with professionals. Rather:

> Emphasis is on solo singing, with one or more instruments in accompani-ment. A high-pitched, tense quality is common in both women's and men's voices. Most songs consist of a soloist's long, rapid declamatory phrases. The melody is melismatic with much ornamentation, and when melodic instru-ments accompany singing, monophony or heterophony results. If solo sing-ing has a vocal accompaniment, the response is drone-like: a short melodic or rhythmic phrase repeats variously.
>
> (DjeDje 2000:144)

This description reinforces again the Afro-Arab singing style as well as the gen-eral West African trait of call and response. Old World monophony, heterophony, non-diatonic tuning, and droning survived into the New World through these tra-ditions. And music was understood to be socially ubiquitous: it "highlight[ed] festive occasions, work, seasonal events, religious rites…and events of the life cycle—births, weddings, and puberty rites" (DjeDje 2000:144–145). West Africans brought these sensibilities to the English colonies and embedded them into the musical fabric of American life.

Even as Africans found ways to preserve their native traditions in new forms, folk and classical styles brought from the English homeland formed the backbone of familiar musical content for the colonists. English art music had a measure of influence, but, unlike European art music in Latin America, it was significantly overshadowed by folk music and by the deliberately simplified music used for Christian worship by early settlers. The Puritans brought with them Calvinist stric-tures on music for worship—singing metrically arranged Psalms unaccompanied in unison, and nothing else. Those that settled further north were rather more staid, more educated and more socially and economically stable than their counterparts in the Chesapeake region and further south. The musical life of especially conservative Puritan strongholds such as Boston revolved around congregational singing of Psalms, from books or from memory. Meanwhile, the "worldly" entertainment of dancing was frowned upon by many for some time, but nevertheless remained generally present throughout the colonies. Less conservative Anglican (and soon, Methodist) colonists in both the South and the North accepted social dancing and more elaborate worship music—with organs and choirs—sooner and more rapidly.

> The story of the arts in seventeenth-century New England is the tale of a people trying to plant in the New World the very vines whose fruit they had enjoyed in the Old, while, at the same time, it is the chronicle of the unconscious development of a totally different civilization. The seventeenth-century history of the Bay Psalm Book is a case in point, for although the psalm-tunes sung to its texts may superficially appear to be nothing more than a provincial utilization of certain music sung in the mother country, a mysterious qualitative change took place when they were sung on different soil. Here, they proved to be the seed out of which a new, uniquely American music was later to flower.
>
> (Lowens 1955:29)

This "mysterious qualitative change" included (though was not entirely defined by) the influence of Africans who sang Psalms alongside their masters' families, both in the meeting hall and at home (Southern 1983:32–33), no doubt adding their own inflections with decreasing subtlety.

Many devout whites in the North saw the education and spiritual development of black slaves more clearly as a Christian duty, which included musical instruction for the purpose of cultivating Christian worship. In the South, musical education of blacks too often tended more towards opportunities (sometimes illicit) to develop skills so as to serve as entertainers—though this did offer many of African origin in the South a chance for a better life of sorts (see Southern 1983:25–53; Palmer 1981:39–40). Black musicians seem to have been more valued for their abilities with European music, as might be expected, and whites had some suspicion about African musical styles since they represented identification with freedom and pride outside of the accepted paradigms, but it is likely that even at this early stage these musicians were beginning to integrate idioms from both musical worlds.

Something of the odd mix of condescension and veneration with which the white ruling culture regarded black slave musicians can be seen in the newspapers, court and other government records, and the personal accounts of interaction in which whites expressed their perspectives (Southern 1983:27–30). The following example from the *Virginia Gazette* in 1767 makes this especially and poignantly plain:

> TO BE SOLD a valuable young handsome Negro Fellow about 18 or 20 years of age; has every qualification of a genteel and sensible servant and has been

in many different parts of the world...He ...plays on the French horn...He lately came from London, and has with him two suits of new clothes, and his French horn, which the purchaser may have with him.

(Southern 1983:27)

Many were fiddlers, and some, no doubt of necessity, made their own instruments, as another notice in the *Gazette* the following year demonstrates: "RUN AWAY...a black Virginia born Negro fellow named Sambo, about 6 ft. high, about 32 years old. He makes fiddles, and can play upon the fiddle, and work at the carpenter's trade" (Southern 1983:29). Fiddling became a common feature of dance accompaniment in the colonies, as it did in English folk music, and thus once again skilled black musicians found significant demand for their abilities.

In Boston, the diary of Samuel Sewall (1674–1729), a Puritan court judge, reveals much about the carefully orchestrated musical encounters further North. A fervent devotee of Psalm singing and other musical pursuits, Sewall's close association with the famed preacher Cotton Mather connected him closely to efforts to treat slaves humanely as Christian brothers and sisters. Though both owned slaves and stopped short of advocating true emancipation, Sewall's 1700 tract *The Selling of Joseph* argued for cessation of the active slave trade. Thus, both Sewall and Mather were in favor of full black participation in Christian musical activity and the education necessary to advance it. Sewall's descriptions of singing clearly imply that African sensibilities were involved, including at least one slave wedding in which he participated as well as other public community events in which slaves would have been participants (Southern 1983:33).

The life of early American-born composer William Billings (1746–1800) has been much celebrated, with good reason, but David McKay (1971) has demonstrated that accomplished English musicians such as William Selby (c. 1738–1798) were highly influential in New England. Selby's career in Boston as everything from prominent church organist to music and dancing instructor to concert performer epitomizes the context in which European immigrants continued to influence the colonies musically. McKay is also quick to point out in how much tension the "essentially secular" (1971:609) realm of instrumental music—even high art music, let alone music for dancing—was held with the Puritan/Congregationalist views on how musical resources should be deployed: the latter were clearly convinced that music should be devoted to Psalm (and to some extent hymn) singing. Since African transplants and their descendants found much opportunity in playing for social dancing, while at the same time they were being instructed in music for the purpose of Christian devotion and worship, this dynamic was especially interesting. Moreover, the African traditional music that slaves, servants, and free blacks continued to preserve in evolving forms during sanctioned and unsanctioned musical activities (Southern 1983:53–59) would have reflected some of the rhythmic, physical, textural, and tuning boisterousness that many white conservative colonists found most alienating. Not the least of this energy came in the form of drumming—which, because it had been used as a form of signaling during slave insurrections, was prohibited for Africans in most colonies by the mid-eighteenth century (Palmer 1981:33).[5]

Yet there were confluences between English folk and religious music and West African music that facilitated integration. Assuming it has not changed much over 400 years, van der Merwe asserts that European folk music differed from art music in that the former lacked harmony (polyphony) outside of droning (and, one would assume, at least accidental heterophony); retained diatonic modality and a wider range of variety within those modes (i.e., resisted "tonalization"); embraced flexible intonation, including the flatter thirds, sixths, and sevenths of the scale that are found in some African musics; and embraced repetition and variation rather than the more sophisticated developmental techniques of art music. Moreover, steady rhythm was for dancing rather than for singing (1989:21–22). To these, the early twentieth-century analyst Cecil Sharp added "irregular rhythms," by which he meant metrical freedom with changing combinations of two- and three-beat groupings; "non-harmonic passing notes," or a penchant for first stepping out of a chord and then leaping, akin to what has been called an "escape tone;" and syllabic rather than melismatic word settings (Sharp and Broadwood 1908). These features would be quite conducive to integration with some African features, and in fact may already display them from earlier encounters. Since both folk tunes and psalm tunes were learned by rote, a tendency to embellish over time was evident in both traditions—and created significant controversy as singing in some churches "devolved" into improvisatory chaos (in the English countryside no less than in the colonies; see Temperly 1972:430), leading to a concerted effort at regularizing congregational singing through the use of notation and careful instruction (Crawford 2001:24–34).

Africans embraced the development of non-psalm hymns such as those put forward in collections by Isaac Watts in England in 1707, 1717, and 1739, about the same time as the Wesleys' *Collection of Psalms and Hymns* appeared in Charleston (1737) during the "Great Awakening" Christian revival in the colonies, because they offered livelier music and more vibrant texts (Southern 1983:35). Hymns came to replace psalmody. In combination with the development of singing schools intended to promote a better, more "regular" musical offering, this led to more harmonized choral music in worship, including full anthems. These dynamic tensions between worship music and folk/dance music from both England and Africa created the crucible from which a particular Euro-African synthesis emerged in the United States.

The Revolution itself created a whole new military musical context for whites and blacks alike, since political songs were promoted to the general public as propaganda while official military fifers and drummers led marching and raised the patriotic spirits of the troops. The most famous of these tunes, *Yankee Doodle*, appeared in many versions that pre-dated the Revolution on both sides of the conflict. Instrumental military music for marching was an important precursor to the marches of the later nineteenth and early twentieth centuries, including those of the famed John Philip Sousa (1854–1932)—for these marches served as an important input to the birth of jazz, as will be discussed later in this chapter.

Full military bands were commissioned by the United States Congress starting in 1792, and played an expanded role in the War of 1812 and the Civil War of 1861–1865. These ensembles included a variety of European brass, woodwind, and percussion instruments that African-Americans learned to play, as evidenced by the formation of highly accomplished black bands throughout the nineteenth century (Southern 1983:67, 132–133, 254–255). There was early precedent for black musicians in the American military: public records indicate that one Nero Benson of Framingham, Massachusetts, apparently one of only a handful of "servants for life" in the town at the time, served as a trumpeter in a colonial militia commanded by Captain Isaac Clark in 1725, one of the first black American musicians named in any official context.

Antebellum America

During the approximately 50 years from the end of the Revolution and securing of the domestic peace to the outbreak of the Civil War, the Afro-European musical synthesis in the newly formed United States was accelerated by urbanization and the fading of slavery in the North—creating more opportunities for racial intermingling and the expansion of free black musical enterprise—coupled with economic growth and the expansion of slavery in the South—which meant more African-Americans in bondage but also a rise in expendable income that could be directed to culture-building. The flourishing of New Orleans in the former French territory of Louisiana (part of the United States starting in 1803) was especially important to American and global music history, and would continue to be so well into the twentieth century. From 1810 to 1860, the population of New Orleans grew nearly tenfold, while the nation's population as a whole grew by considerably less than half that rate. Boston grew 20% faster than the country as a whole during the same period. From 1790 to 1840 (after which it fell out of the top 10 cities), however, Charleston's influence diminished as its population slightly less than doubled while the nation's quadrupled. Nevertheless, overall, the percentage of Americans living in cities nearly tripled. Meanwhile, the percentage of Southerners living in cities only doubled—because slave populations on plantations were soaring. By 1860, overall population in the South consisted of 66% whites, 32% black slaves, and only 2% free non-whites. The surge in Southern slavery arose largely from the Industrial Revolution and the invention of the cotton gin just before 1800, because cotton became very lucrative but its harvesting required the same intense manual labor that tobacco and rice had previously. Thus, the lot of Southern blacks changed very little, and music-making remained largely a rural activity for them while Northern blacks reaped the benefit of increased opportunity—with New Orleans remaining the Southern urban exception. Around 1800, about 10 % of American blacks lived in urban communities where, even when slavery continued, sensibilities were more relaxed and levels of freedom typically greater. By 1827, most Northern blacks, rural or urban, were legally free.

Southern black slaves in particular "developed a hybridized musical language that distilled the very essence of innumerable African vocal traditions"

(Palmer 1981:33). Field hollers and other work songs reflected this phenomenon, as did other communicative, sometimes coded, cries of expression (Southern 1983:156). The American architect Frederick Law Olmsted (a Northerner), traveling in South Carolina in the 1850s, described an impromptu experience:

> At midnight I was awakened by loud laughter, and, looking out, saw that the loading gang of negroes had made a fire, and were enjoying a right merry repast. Suddenly, one raised such a sound as I never heard before; a long, loud, musical shout, rising, and falling, and breaking into falsetto, his voice ringing through the woods in the clear, frosty night air, like a bugle-call. As he finished, the melody was caught up by another, and then, another, and then, by several in chorus...After a few minutes [of silence] I could hear one urging the rest to come to work again, and soon he stepped towards the cotton bales, saying, "Come, brederen, come; let's go at it; come now, eoho! roll away! eeoho-eeoho-weeioho-i!"—and the rest taking it up as before, in a few moments they all had their shoulders to a bale of cotton, and were rolling it up the embankment.
>
> (Olmsted 1856:394–395)

Blacks also began to form their own churches during this period, allowing them to develop their own musical sensibilities based on the previous synthesis. By this point, those of African origin in America had fully absorbed Western European harmony and had many generations of experience with its power. Black Christians took English-American hymnody and its associated keyboards—the organ and piano—and made them their own; or rather, made them something new in the nation and eventually around the world. The Rev. Richard Allen (1760–1831), who later helped to found the all-black African Methodist Episcopal Church in Philadelphia in 1816, published *A Collection of Hymns and Spiritual Songs from Various Authors* in 1801. Some of the formats, such as verses interposed by refrains, are conducive to African call-and-response singing, allowing the congregation more freedom to embellish (Crawford 2001:110; Southern 1983:168). Once untethered from conservative white sensibilities in worship, black churchgoers adapted Euro-American hymnody further towards the transformed styles that had been developing in American communities since colonial times. A visitor to Allen's Philadelphia church in 1820 documents the use of popular tunes and improvisatory elements in the worship; the later development of Black Gospel music clearly stems from these directions (Southern 1983:78, 444ff.). About the same time as black congregations were forming, the Spiritual (from "spiritual song") also began to emerge as a new, freer Christian song combining European tonality with black rhythms and singing styles. After the Civil War, these grew into a major genre that spread the integrated style broadly (Crawford 2001:412ff.).

Meanwhile, in Philadelphia and New York, already centers of intellectual and artistic refinement for blacks and whites alike, black performers such as singer Elizabeth Greenfield (1824–1876) and trumpeter/concert band leader Francis Johnson (1792–1844) offered European-style music to enthusiastic audiences.

These contexts facilitated continuing musical integration in other forms, with black performers adding subtle stylistic touches to otherwise "straight" literature (Southern 1983:103–109).

Two black fiddlers, one from the South and the other from the North, represent some of the typical regional distinctions but also some exceptions to these general milieus during the Antebellum period. Both frequently played for social occasions in which middle and upper-class whites enjoyed the "Virginia Reel" and other popular lively dances, such as the perhaps aptly named "Negro Jig." A passage from the journal of one Nicholas Cresswell conveys something of this phenomenon. Cresswell, an Englishmen traveling in Maryland in the late eighteenth century, seemed astonished to have observed couples jigging "to some Negro tune"—which reinforces the notion that whites perceived this music as "Negro music" in some way (Southern 1983:45–46). It is possible that these tunes were Africanized to various degrees from English sources such as Playford's *Dancing Master* and *Introduction to the Skill of Musick*.

Simeon Gilliat, who died in 1820 but was performing during the reign of his owner Norborne Berkeley, Fourth Baron Botetourt, who was royal governor of Virginia from 1768–1770, would have had ample high-profile opportunity in this regard as the slave of a prominent politician. After the Revolution, Gilliat continued as "the leading figure at [Richmond's] balls," likely even maintaining his eighteenth-century courtly dress that included silk coat, vest, breeches, and stockings as well as a brown wig: "His manners were as courtly as his dress and he elbowed himself and his fiddle-stick through the world with great propriety and harmony" (Mordecai 1856:311). Thus, despite being a Southern slave, Gilliat's musical abilities kept him associated with the trappings of aristocracy: a sexton (groundskeeper) in his local Anglican church, he remained celebrated and in the company of local gentility nearly all his life.

From a different perspective, the astounding story of Solomon Northup (c. 1808–1863) reveals even more. Northup, a free-born musician and farmer living in Hebron, New York (about 200 miles north of New York City, near the resort town of Saratoga Springs), garnered a considerable reputation as a paid performer in the towns around him—"Wherever the young people assembled to dance, I was almost invariably there"—though he only made a portion of his living by means of the violin (Northup 1853:24–25). The details of how he came to learn to play have not surfaced, but he was provided the opportunity for what was considered an excellent overall education by his father, and had the leisure both to read literature and to pursue music, "the ruling passion of my youth." (19–20). Having been lured first to New York City and then on to Washington, DC, by two men promising lucrative playing engagements, Northup was kidnapped and forced into subjugation. Taken to the slave market in New Orleans, he demonstrated his skills as a violinist early on, playing a "Virginia Reel" tune for the slave pen holder there (79). His name was changed (more than once during his captivity), and he was first sold to William Ford, whose plantation was near the Red River in northern Louisiana, not far from the Mississippi River along the border between the states. Northup's experience in this region included firsthand encounters with Southern black and white musical contexts that were being fused. Hired or sold to more than one master, and for the most part subjected to the intense agricultural labor and mistreatment of all slaves, he was nevertheless provided a violin—"frequently...called into the house to play before the family" for dancing and other entertainments—and was actually paid in some circumstances (179–182, 196).[6] In general, fiddling was a welcome and sometimes modestly lucrative consolation for Northup, especially during the phase of his captivity along the Louisiana Bayou:

> My business on these gala days [such as Christmas] always was to play on the violin...My master often received letters, sometimes from a distance of ten miles, requesting him to send me to play at a ball or festival of the whites. He received his compensation, and usually I also returned with many picayunes [NB: small Spanish coins] jingling in my pockets—the extra contributions of those to whose delight I had administered. In this manner I became more acquainted than I otherwise would, up and down the bayou. The young men and maidens...always knew there was to be a jollification somewhere, whenever [I] was seen passing through the town with [my] fiddle in [my] hand...[My violin] introduced me to great houses —relieved me of many days' labor in the field—supplied me with conveniences for my cabin—with pipes and tobacco, and extra pairs of shoes, and oftentimes led me away from the presence of a hard master, to witness scenes of jollity and mirth. It was my companion—the friend of my bosom triumphing loudly when I was joyful, and uttering its soft, melodious consolations when I was sad...On holy Sabbath days, when an hour or two of leisure was allowed, it would accompany me to some quiet place on the bayou bank, and, lifting up its voice, discourse kindly and pleasantly indeed.
>
> (1853:216–217)

While in the Red River region, Northup collected a tune titled *Roaring River, A Refrain of the Red River Plantation* that he published in his account (1853:322). The tune is instructive in that it is pentatonic but with the tonal inflection of the raised seventh scale degree added to reinforce the tonality. The tune sounds much like the country fiddling that has survived to this day in the United States, and Northup also mentions the technique of "patting juba" in this context, a substitute for other percussion that was not allowed, "performed by striking the hands on the knees, then striking the hands together, then striking the right shoulder with one hand, the left with the other—all the while keeping time with the feet, and singing" (219). The rhythm of the tune itself is in straight duple divisions, no doubt to aid in dancing. Thus, it does not directly exhibit African rhythmic influence, but we do not know what the accompanying instruments, such as the banjo that Northup mentions, may have added; judging from the banjo styles that have survived, it is likely that the complexity of African rhythm would have played a role in addition to the patting.[7]

New Orleans prior to the Civil War deserves special note due to the astonishing combination of French, Spanish, English, and African musics interacting there in both concert/classical and vernacular contexts. Ted Gioia has even proposed a fascinating way of seeing in this city the culmination of elements that contributed to the musical character of al-Andalus, continued forward into the creation of jazz over the course of the millennium between the coming of the Arabs to Europe in c. 718 and the founding of New Orleans in 1718 (2011:5–6). "The complex culture of New Orleans offers us an opportunity to rethink the concept of diaspora, to discern the ways in which New Orleans is always African—but never only African" (Lipsitz 2011:261). With a population more than 30% black and a strict caste system that distinguished whites, blacks, and creoles (at various percentages of mixed race and nationality), African musical elements tended to exert an especially profound influence, as did already transcultural musical fusions arriving from Latin America. French control of Louisiana prior to 1803 brought Africans from Haiti and Cuba before, during, and after the Haitian revolution of 1804, bringing Vodou religious practices to the area in a particularly significant way (Southern 1983:138–140). In addition, while black instrumental music was more prominent than vocal music in New Orleans, longstanding French Catholic contexts created milieus that shared elements with Latin America. In the same city, Mardi Gras and opera flourished alongside these genres. New Orleans thus integrated some elements of northern American cities with those of southern living and more original African elements, including gatherings of blacks on Sundays and other festival days in a location called Place Congo for public African-oriented group dancing with drums and chordophones (Southern 1983:136–138). As a key waterfront port town at the origin of the Mississippi River, New Orleans was the scene of constant arrivals, departures, and concomitant entertainments—many of which traveled further up the River into the heartlands of America, from which blues would emerge and in which jazz would flourish.

In the years leading up to the Civil War, however, it was the Louisiana native Louis Moreau Gottschalk (1829–1869) who perhaps most creatively fused the European, African, and Latin American musics swirling around him in New Orleans into a distinctively transcultural voice (Crawford 2001:331–350). Gottschalk, a white pianist and composer whose heritage included French-Haitian aristocracy as well as English-Jewish blood, and who grew up in a household where blacks and whites intermingled freely, studied in Paris as a teenager and then toured Spain before returning to the U.S. in the early 1850s. Compositions of his such as *Bamboula* (1846) reflect Louisiana creole culture, while his virtuosic and highly innovative piano piece *The Banjo* (1855) imitates its title namesake in distinctively African-American ways while referencing Stephen Foster's "Camptown Races" (see next section). Gottschalk subsequently spent considerable time in Cuba and other parts of Latin America which influenced his music profoundly. Works from the later 1850s such as *Souvenir de la Havane* and *Souvenir de Porto-Rico* reflect his absorption of these musics and likely some of the Arabo-Spanish influences he encountered previously (*Souvenirs d'Andalousie* dates from 1851, for example). His performances of these original compositions caused a sensation across the United States during his lifetime and well after: scores of his piano pieces remained in print as late as 1915, the American pianist

Eugene List (1918–1985) championed them throughout much of the second half of the twentieth century, and in the 1970s the New York City Ballet staged a work titled *Cakewalk* based on his music. Nevertheless, Gottschalk's music has not survived the judgment of cultural history, likely due to a pronounced rejection of its transcultural sensibilities by German influence in United States art music history as well as its genre-crossing qualities (Crawford 2001:347–350). By the time the transculturality of global music history began to come into focus, Gottschalk's pieces may have seemed outdated. Or perhaps the fact that he was a white male in a time of great injustice in the Americas led to a rejection of his prescient innovations in favor of the later work of musicians of color. Whatever the reasons for its current obscurity, his music represents an extraordinary moment in music history: it is certainly an important and culturally respectful precursor to the explosion of energetic transculturality in America that dominated musical development through the twentieth century and beyond.

Minstrelsy and its influence

Ironically, black New Orleans street peddlers such as the popular "Signor Cornmeali" (d. 1842, real name unknown) also participated in early forms of something that came to be called "Ethiopian minstrelsy" starting in the 1820s—whites, with blackened faces, parodying African-American slave music and mannerisms. Christopher Smith (2013) rightly argues that minstrelsy represented a significant culmination of early "creolization" of culture in the U.S., and that a good deal of evidence is available in the visual art of white painter and fiddler William Sydney Mount (1807–1868).[8]

Both Northern and Southern blacks were often parodied by whites in the form of two characters, "Jim Crow" (a naive plantation bumpkin) and "Zip Coon" (an urban quasi-sophisticate). Both spoke and sang in exaggerated African-American accents (Crawford 201ff., Southern 228ff.). Yet, musically, this unflattering genre gave blacks another entre into the majority white culture. Indeed, through black participation in minstrelsy, with or without blackening their faces to match the white performers, even more authentically African-influenced musical styles made further inroads into minstrel shows and the culture at large. Among the most successful black minstrels were William Henry Lane, known as Master Juba (c. 1825–1852), and James Bland (1854–1911), who garnered a reputation as "The World's Greatest Minstrel Man" (Southern 1983:234). The white songwriter Stephen Foster (1826–1864) also composed a number of songs that came to define the genre, including "Camptown Races," "Oh! Susanna," and "Old Folks at Home." Many of these were introduced to the public by the white Christy's Minstrels, the founder of which, Edwin Christy, was born in Philadelphia but spent time experiencing music in New Orleans before striking out in the direction that would catapult him to considerable fame (Crawford 2001:210–217). One reasonable interpretation even traces the roots of American musical theater to works such as John Gay's *The Beggar's Opera* (London 1728, New York 1750), influenced later by the music and forms of minstrel shows. Musical theater then settled more deeply into popular hybrid styles, rather than retaining its quasi-classical English roots, as it came of age into the 1920s.

The road to expanded freedom and transcultural musical growth

The Civil War created a defining moment in American history, though cultural changes were slower in coming than many hoped. In addition to the participation of black and white musicians in military bands, political songs were in abundance on both sides and many Christian hymns about freedom were appropriated to advocate for and then celebrate emancipation. The economic lives of many freed blacks, especially in the South, did not immediately improve; in some ways all were worse off as the country recovered from the privations of a bitter war and the South slowly attempted to adjust to an entirely different economic paradigm. Black musicians had essentially the same musical opportunities as before the War, one of which was growing opportunity in minstrelsy, which slowly expanded its idioms beyond black parody and became a major source of entertainment in the newly reintegrated nation. Nevertheless, "minstrels" such as James Bland—born in New York City and educated at Howard University in Washington, DC, who sang and played the banjo—used the platform to reach huge audiences, some of whom did not know they were hearing music of a black composer. Bland's "Oh, Dem Golden Slippers" and "Carry Me Back to Old Virginny" became national-level hits that carried the transcultural synthesis in sound to millions in the decades following the war (Southern 1983:234–237). Freedom ultimately created the opportunity for many more black musicians to garner the fruits of their labor while the impact of their creativity expanded. As noted, white musicians such as Stephen Foster also benefitted from the rising popularity of the American musical styles. In a phenomenon that would unfortunately continue, whites often either stole from or paid geniuses such as Bland for work that they then passed off as their own—still, an ultimate compliment.

Black colleges, particularly Fisk University in Nashville, Tennessee (est. 1866), also began to sponsor ensembles that capitalized on the public's growing taste for legitimized African-influenced music. Fisk choral groups toured with concerts of classical anthems and arrangements of spirituals, the latter of which grew into a choral genre that remains a vibrant part of the repertoire as of this writing.

Meanwhile, the foundational work of Lowell Mason (1792–1872) was crucial to the rise of music in public education, which in turn made possible opportunities for a new generation of young musicians who might not otherwise have had the means to pursue them. After spending time in the antebellum South, Mason successfully expanded the realm of American Christian hymnody, and the training of singers for that purpose, into the world of the secular as a developmental enterprise through co-founding the Boston Academy of Music in 1832, eventually becoming a musical leader in the Boston public school system, where he taught until 1855: "Having made himself the first American expert on how children learn music, [Mason] enlisted and trained the teachers of those children, supplying them not only with ideas and techniques, but with publications to meet their practical needs" (Crawford 2001:151). These methods and systems eventually spread across the country: the New Orleans public school system, modeled on that of Boston, was established by 1842, and before the end of the century at least some schools included music in their curricula (Kennedy 2005:1–27). As a result, musical instruments and various forms of instruction on them were available in the city during the critical years leading up to 1920. Without the vision of Mason, these contexts might not have arisen as early or as strongly. Instrumental music education added to the already robust collection of instruments from popular brass bands and military bands.

Ragtime and Scott Joplin

Sometime in the 1890s, ragtime emerged as a stylistically coherent genre that creatively brought together already well-established elements—certainly one of the first Afro-European musical products to be so fully defined. The African-inspired Southern dance called the Cakewalk, with its characteristic short-long-short rhythmic pattern—and sometimes the reverse (both seen in many earlier musics)—against a steady duple beat was a clear precursor, while the steady beat was emphasized in nineteenth-century military music and its concert versions such as popularized in the works of John Philip Sousa (1854–1932), suggesting an instrumental rather than a vocal context and perhaps even reflecting black influence on marches from more than a century of involvement in American military bands. Van der Merwe dates the ragtime phenomenon to 1896 and two vocal/piano pieces by Southerner Ben Harney—sometimes purported to be a mulatto passing as white, but most likely entirely white—that touched off a craze with New York audiences (1989:279–280), while Southern credits the song "All Coons Look Alike to Me" from the same year, by black minstrel composer Ernest Hogan (Southern 1983:311).[9] Compositions continued to evolve, with piano rags being the most common, combining upper hand rhythmic groupings of $3 + 3 + 2$, $3 + 2 + 3$ and other "syncopations" against the oom-pah back and forth of the left hand. The ragtime form itself also came from marches, with a short introduction typically followed by three or four themes ("strains") presented with repetitions and a return to at least the first theme somewhere before the end. One of these sections is usually more relaxed (without changing tempo) and legato, deriving from the "trio" section of the European instrumental tradition. In addition, a shorter, louder, and more dramatic section that in a march is sometimes called the "dogfight" often breaks up the more tuneful thematic strains. Harmonic relationships, also derived from European instrumental traditions, typically revolve around a tonic key and its subdominant (the key of the fourth scale degree from the tonic); in minor keys the modulation is to the relative major. In short, ragtime fuses foundational African and European characteristics into sometime new.

Pianist and eventual concert composer Scott Joplin (1868–1917) came to be called the "King" of ragtime. Around 1885, Joplin began to garner this reputation in St. Louis, Missouri, and in 1895 resettled to the small Missouri town of Sedalia (closer to the state's western border), where he studied music at a local college for blacks. His first characteristic piano rags were published in 1899 by Carl Hoffman in nearby Kansas City. With the publication of the *Maple Leaf Rag* that year, Joplin's reputation soared. The work features sophisticated, ornamentally chromatic harmonies that seem to try to capture the microtonality inherent in African singing on an instrument of fixed pitch, a trend that would continue with the development of jazz into the twentieth century. In 1907 Joplin moved to New York, two years after completing an opera, *Treemonisha*, that reflects both the challenges and aspirations of Southern blacks in the late nineteenth century. The work remained unperformed until 1972, but has since been recognized as significantly and importantly predating another "first American black opera" of note, *Porgy and Bess* (1935), by white Jewish New Yorker George Gershwin, which also features a nearly all-black cast and similar narrative themes. By the time of *Porgy and Bess*, the American Afro-European synthesis had developed to a greater level of sophistication, but Joplin's weaving of European grand opera traditions with the ragtime elements evident in his other compositions is extraordinary. Nevertheless, as with the music of Gottschalk—though likely for very different reasons—the vagaries of history have thus far relegated *Treemonisha* to a status far below its importance in global music history.

The Blues

The Blues represented something of the Southern black American experience that no other genre captured as well, and eventually propelled black musicians into a level of commercial success that outstripped their previous economic achievements in the musical realm. Origins in and around the Mississippi Delta region— where Solomon Northup was confined—have been most celebrated, though Blues evolved regional variations across the South from East Texas to Virginia and quickly migrated much further afield (Palmer 2001:43–47). Typically a slow, mournful song accompanied by guitar (or sometimes played by guitar alone), Southern Blues combines complex African vocal style—further shaped by centuries in the New World, such as in the field hollers and spirituals—with a quintessentially European harmonic structure built around the primary chords of a given key: four measures of the tonic (I) chord, two measures of the subdominant (IV) chord, two measures of the tonic, then one measure each of the dominant (V), subdominant and two final measures of tonic to round out the 12-bar sequence. The qualities of the chords can vary, but most often each consists of a major triad with a minor seventh on top, requiring chromatic notes for the I and IV. The term "blue notes" derives from the genre, referring primarily to neutrally tuned third and seventh scale degrees—somewhere between unflatted and fully flatted from a chromatic perspective—that is not uncharacteristic of West African music.[10] The pitch and rhythmic complexities of the melody are superimposed over the relative regularity in this harmonic sequence, creating a dynamic and highly expressive process that can be endlessly and subtly varied, giving the genre both its power and its longevity.

Blues texts tend to revolve around heartbreak, poverty, injustice, and other troubles, though they can be humorous, and sexual innuendo is common. Quadruple repetition eventually settled into an AAB poetic form arranged evenly across the 12 bar cycle (4 + 4 + 4 bars). "Father of the Blues" W.C. Handy (1873–1958) is usually credited with bringing the genre to the level of attention and organization that allowed it to break out into an economic and cultural powerhouse within the first few decades of the twentieth century. Handy's 1914 "St. Louis Blues" became a huge commercial hit and a standard part of the repertoire. Interestingly, the song also features a "Spanish tinge,"[11] the term commonly used for explicit interpolations of Latin American rhythms into American jazz and blues: in this case, it is the Cuban habanera/tango rhythm (dotted quarter, eighth, quarter, quarter) that appears from time to time throughout. Discussion of the Blues and its impact continues in Chapter 8.

On the verge of jazz

Thus, minstrel songs, ragtime, and the Blues were the most definitive genres emerging from intercultural convergence, fusion, and transformation in the United States during its first century and a half. These were also the most important inputs to two mature genres that overtook the globe: jazz and rock. Jazz was already beginning to take shape prior to the turn of the twentieth century, and is typically seen as originating in New Orleans. In addition to the elements cited above, black brass bands and dance orchestras permeated both the city and more rural areas beyond its outskirts (Southern 1983:338–343). The brass band was also (and remains to this day) popular in England, and had migrated to the proto-United States during colonial times. The dance orchestras typically included six or seven instrumentalists: cornet, trombone, string bass, guitar, drums, and one to two clarinets or violins—an instrumentation from whence the earliest jazz ensembles emerged. Of the New Orleans band leaders just prior to 1900, cornetist Charles "Buddy" Bolden (1877–1931) had the mostly lasting impact, as his "hot" style became the one to emulate: "it incorporated blues and ragtime and his men improvised as they played" (Southern 1983:341). "Bolden…combined the rhythms of ragtime, the bent notes and chord patterns of the blues, and an instrumentation drawn from New Orleans brass bands and [dance] ensembles" into what would soon be called jazz (Gioia 2011:34). Southern goes on to note that one Bill Johnson and his Original Creole Band were responsible for taking these rapidly coalescing elements out of New Orleans to the rest of the country during the years between 1911 and 1917 (1983:343), though it would be "King" Oliver (1885–1938) and his most famous protégé Louis Armstrong (1900–1971) who would catapult jazz to national prominence and beyond in the coming decades. The creole (racially and culturally mixed) complexity of New Orleans gave rise to these phenomena.

A turning point

In his biography of Edward "Duke" Ellington, Terry Teachout identifies 1920 and the Volstead Act (prohibition against the sale of alcoholic beverages) as a turning point in American history, musical and otherwise (2013:55–56); Southern marks this same year as a musical turning point (1983:357ff.). The development of recording and broadcast technologies were also critical to the moment. Before diving into the heart of what was to be dubbed by some as "the American century," however, a look at how multi/inter/transcultural Western European musical tastes were developing across the globe in the form of exoticism and the colonial/imperial era that facilitated it are in order.

Notes

1   Since the musics featured in this chapter and those following are well-documented in pictures and notation, they will not be reproduced further here; the reader is referred to Southern (1983), van der Merwe (1989), Crawford (2001), Hijleh (2012:37, 92–94, 127, 160, 200) and DeVeaux (2015) in addition to examples referenced directly and many others readily available.
2   For context and analysis on this moment in American musical history, see Levy 2012:2–6.
3   In the very first issue of the *Journal of the American Musicological Society*, Richard Waterman (1948) suggested a number of reasons for these differences that are consonant with the analysis given herein.
4   Interestingly, Stevenson (1968:90) suggests this may have happened because North American indigenous musics did not resonate emotionally with European listeners in the stronger, more positive ways that some indigenous South-Central American musics did. The 2017 documentary film *Rumble: The Indians Who Rocked the World* puts forth a rather different thesis in which Native American music did in fact deeply affect the nature of music in the United States (Fon and Bainbridge 2017).
5   Interestingly, percussion in the United States evolved around striking instruments with sticks rather than with hands, which had been the medieval European military tradition starting in Switzerland and extending to England; Wolof drumming typically uses one stick and one hand. Use of stick percussion continued into American band (military and concert) and orchestra music, and made feasible the development of the American drum set starting in the mid-nineteenth century; the drum set, which mixes various drums and cymbals and sometimes small idiophones—all played with an increasing variety of stick types and making further use of the feet through a system of pedals—became ubiquitous in musics of the Euro-African synthesis into the twentieth century. As Latin American influence on popular music in the United States increased, the cow bell was often added to drum sets along with a greater variety of drum sizes to reflect the sounds of the different traditions involved. Even some Asian influence can be seen in the variety of cymbal sizes and additional drums/idiophones used. (For an excellent illustrated global history, see Berger 2014.) Late in the twentieth century, electronics were introduced to increase the sonic capabilities of the drum set even further, though the triggering of sounds typically continues to be accomplished by striking some sort of surface.
6   Southern provides several other accounts of black fiddlers on Southern plantations (1983:185–186)
7   As mentioned in Chapter 5, the banjo was almost certainly a descendant of the West African *ngoni* (Duran 1999:545). Hans Nathan (1956) demonstrates possible African rhythmic features that were integrated into published banjo tunes ("jigs") during the mid-nineteenth century; his analysis would apply equally to fiddle tunes and other

similar dance music in which blacks participated consistently. Nathan also suggests that these features may have been suppressed in print (1956:466, note 26); given the nature of African musicianship, we can be certain that far more Africanization took place in real time—and that this vitality is one very likely reason why these musicians were in such demand. Van der Merwe also provides considerable analytical evidence for such a view, in all its transcultural complexity (1989:52–90, 156–170).

8 Whereas "creole" in Latin America tended to mean "one of pure Spanish blood" born in the New World, the same term in New Orleans suggested anyone born in the region, regardless of the racial mix of Spanish, French, and African heritages; indeed, it really meant one who represented the complex mixture of cultural elements that came to define the area. Thus there were Louisiana Creoles who were more "colored" than European, and everything in between.

9 Interestingly, Hogan (born Ernest Reuben Crowdus, 1865–1909) also produced and starred in two early Broadway musicals, *Rufus Rastus* (1905) and *The Oyster Man* (1909), "and was reputed to be the highest-paid black vaudevillian of his time" (Southern 1983:297). See also "Minstrelsy and its influence" in this chapter.

10 See, for example, Hijleh 2012:89–94; van der Merwe (1989:119–120, 131–145) examines further details and suggests confluences with Arabic and British folk styles, including improvisatory elements.

11 The label "Spanish tinge" is attributed to Ferdinand "Jelly Roll" Morton (1890–1941), whose musical leadership figured prominently in the first half of the twentieth century.

References

Berger, Matthew. 2014. *A Cultural History of the Drum Set: Proliferation from New Orleans to Cuba* (unpublished master's thesis). Prescott, Arizona: Prescott College.

Crawford, Richard. 2001. *America's Musical Life: A History*. New York: W.W. Norton.

DeVeaux, Scott. 2015. "North American Jazz." In Michael Church (ed.), *The Other Classical Musics*, Woodbridge, Suffolk: Boydell and Brewer, 199–215.

DjeDje, Jacqueline. 2000. "West Africa: An Introduction." In Stone, Ruth (ed.), *The Garland Handbook of African Music*, New York: Garland, 140–168.

Duran, Lucy. 1999. "Mali/Guinea: Mande Sounds." In Broughton, Simon, Mark Ellingham, and Richard Trillo (eds.), *World Music: The Rough Guide, Vol. 1: Africa, Europe and the Middle East*, London: Rough Guides Ltd., 539–562.

Fon, Christina (Producer), and Catherine Bainbridge (Director). 2017. *Rumble: The Indians Who Rocked the World [Motion Picture]*. Canada: Rezolution Pictures International.

Gioia, Ted. 2011. *The History of Jazz* (2nd ed.). New York: Oxford University Press.

Hijleh, Mark .2012. *Towards a Global Music Theory*. Farnham, Surrey: Ashgate.

Kennedy, Al. 2005. *Chord Changes on the Chalkboard: How Public School Teachers Shaped Jazz and the Music of New Orleans*. Lanham, Maryland: Scarecrow Press.

Lamson, Roy. 1939. "English Broadside Ballad Tunes of the 16th and 17th Centuries." *Papers Read by Members of the American Musicological Society at the Annual Meeting*, 112–121.

Levy, Beth 2012. *Frontier Figures: American Music and the Mythology of the American West*. Berkeley: University of California Press.

Lipsitz, George. 2011. "New Orleans in the World and the World in New Orleans." *Black Music Research Journal* 31.2:261–290.

Lowens, Irving. 1955. "The Bay Psalm Book in 17th-Century New England." *Journal of the American Musicological Society* 8.1: 22–29.

McKay, David. 1971. "William Selby, Musical Émigré in Colonial Boston." *The Musical Quarterly* 57.4: 609–627.

Mordecai, Samuel. 1856. *Richmond in By-Gone Days*. Richmond, Virginia: George M. West.

Nathan, Hans. 1956. "Early Banjo Tunes and American Syncopation." *The Musical Quarterly* 42.4: 455–472.

Northup, Solomon. 1853. *Twelve Years a Slave: Narrative of Solomon Northup, a Citizen of New-York, Kidnapped in Washington City in 1841, and Rescued in 1853*. Buffalo, New York: Derby, Orton and Mulligan.

Olmsted, Frederick Law. 1856. *A Journey in the Seaboard Slave States; With Remarks on Their Economy*. New York: Dix and Edwards.

Palmer, Robert. 1981. *Deep Blues*. New York: Penguin.

Sharp, Cecil, and Lucy Broadwood. 1908. "Some Characteristics of English Folk-Music." *Folklore* 19.2: 132–152.

Smith, Christopher. 2013. *The Creolization of American Culture: William Sydney Mount and the Roots of Blackface Minstrelsy*. Chicago: University of Illinois Press.

Southern, Eileen. 1983. *The Music of Black Americans* (2nd ed.). New York: W.W. Norton.

Stevenson, Robert. 1968. *Music in Aztec and Inca Territory*. Berkeley: University of California Press.

Taylor, Alan. 2001. *American Colonies: The Settling of North America*. New York: Penguin Books.

Teachout, Terry. 2013. *Duke: A Life of Duke Ellington*. New York: Gotham/Penguin.

Temperley, Nicholas. 1972. "John Playford and the Metrical Psalms." *Journal of the American Musicological Society* 25.3: 331–378.

van der Merwe, Peter. 1989. *Origins of the Popular Style: The Antecedents of Twentieth-Century Popular Music*. New York: Oxford University Press.

Waterman, Richard. 1948. "'Hot'" Rhythm in Negro Music." *Journal of the American Musicological Society* 1.1: 24–37.

7 Expanded acceleration

Empires and exoticism

During the eighteenth-century "Enlightenment," educated Europeans assumed that the universe of both mind and matter obeyed predictable natural laws, rather than the arbitrary dictates of an inscrutable God. Rejecting ancient texts as a sufficient proof, enlightened Europeans sought more systematically to collect and organize new information about everything on earth (and beyond). European leaders increasingly concluded that wealth and power accrued to nations that discovered and analyzed new information. In publications circulating through the learned circles of the European elite, new discoveries became a medium for the competitive pursuit of national prestige.
—Alan Taylor (2001:446)

Partly because of empire, all cultures are involved in one another; none is single and pure, all are hybrid, heterogeneous, extraordinarily differentiated, and unmonolithic.
—Edward Said (1994:xxv)

Figure 7.1 Johann Zoffany (1733–1810)—Indian musicians with the Impey family, Calcutta c. 1783.

Source: © Museo Nacional Thyssen-Bornemisza/SCALA, Florence. Used by permission.

"New information about everything on earth" certainly included music, not least music of non-European cultures. While the pivotal American musical convergence was in progress and the work of several German/Austrian composers—J.S. Bach (1685–1750), F.J. Haydn (1732–1809), W.A. Mozart (1756–1791), Ludwig van Beethoven (1770–1827), Richard Wagner (1813–1883), and Johannes Brahms (1833–1897)—was being created and epitomized within the European "classical" art music tradition, the growing colonies and empires of European nations outside of the Americas between c. 1600 and 1920 were milieus both for attempts to globalize developing European music and for (re)encounters with musical elements and other cultural features from China, Japan, India, Africa, and West and Central Asia (and later, America itself). These features were exported after a fashion to broader audiences and thus (re)globalized in new ways, though not without significant cultural mitigation and sometimes outright transformation. Europeans who had the opportunity to incorporate "exotic" musics into their sensibilities considered them fascinating and primitive oddities at first, sometimes even as unpleasant cacophonies. Later, legitimate tastes for these new stylistic flavors developed further nonetheless. Though not giving rise to any pivotal convergences, this phenomenon—facilitated by technological advances and European scientific approaches to analysis and synthesis—laid the groundwork for the next level of musical globalization that exploded into the twentieth century and beyond, ultimately exemplified by and flowing from the Americas.

Musical instruments were one relatively convenient (though certainly imperfect) way through which these encounters could be accomplished. David Irving, surveying "comparative organography in early modern empires" (2009), has demonstrated that intercultural encounters around musical instruments rose to levels of transculturality in some instances due to the organological principles underlying nearly all of them. The objectification of instruments apart from deeper knowledge of their cultural contexts may have allowed Europeans to consider those transculturalities in more detail, undisturbed by undesired associations. Yet in other ways, Irving notes, these confluences drew Europeans to hearken back to pre-historic universal musical underpinnings, and sometimes even transcended cultural tensions. Musical instruments were often understood as rare, exotic, and valuable representations of the cultures from which they came. Moreover, both the characteristics of the instruments themselves and the techniques used for playing them seem to have flowed back and forth between cultures (Irving 2009:389–390, 392ff.).

Folk musics of both the colonized and the colonial homeland were another source of what was emerging as "comparative musicology,"[1] especially in Britain and India (Clayton 2007). Even though Indian music historians seem to have been less interested in their own vernacular heritage, their British overlords intuited a possible convergence around nationalist themes. Moreover,

> [though] the folk traditions of Indian rural life…were often the subject of Raj administrators' investigations…primarily for administrative purposes…, the suggestion that the collectors were consequently uninterested in the artistic

dimension of rural songs, dance, poetry, and proverbs is not entirely borne out by an examination of a wider range of sources…On the contrary, some colonial officials appeared to approach the music and culture of India with sensitivity, and their works are sometimes gems of social and musical anthropology long before such concepts entered scholarly discourse. Their papers and publications show that they themselves were changed by their encounter with Indian culture, sometimes encouraging within them universal sentiments about the deep human connections between all peoples, regardless of race or creed.

(Farrell and Sorrell 2007:110)

Interestingly, though perhaps not surprisingly, theatrical music emerged during this period as one of the genres in which both cultural distinctions and inter/transcultural possibilities were most clearly manifested. Later this phenomenon would also be transferred to film and television. Certainly Indian music has deep and ancient roots in the concerns of the theatrical, as the *Natyasastra* demonstrated, and this integration continued in myriad forms throughout the modern period, of which the twentieth- and twenty-first-century "Indywood" film genre is only the latest manifestation. The work of composer-playwright Rabindranath Tagore (1861–1941) provides a notable example. As with all Indian music, Persian and later Western influences were considerable as Indian theatrical-musical styles developed (see, e.g., Schramm 1969), and this may be attributed to some of the same cultural-historical forces surveyed in this chapter. Highly popular Indonesian *wayang kulit* (shadow puppetry), like Indian theater, integrates music at the deepest levels. In a completely different way the short-lived but powerful Indonesian popular musical theater genre Komedie Stambul synthesized musical elements and cultural themes from across Eurasia (see van der Veur 1968; Cohen 2006). Until the mid-eighteenth century, highly developed Jesuit drama, often including music, served Christian missionary purposes in India, Japan, and the New World; Japanese theatrical influence flowed back to the West as a result (Wetmore 2016:13–14). Japanese musical-theatrical *noh*, *bunraku* (puppet plays), and *kabuki* which, like Chinese opera, seem to have solidified during the fourteenth century (Hughes 2015; Miller and Church 2015), developed apace during the European colonial period, though far more isolated in Japan. Gilbert and Sullivan's *The Mikado* (1885) can be seen as a parody of these forms—but also, it should be noted, as a parody of the foibles of British society along with its invented Orientalism—though with decidedly English nineteenth-century music.[2] In the West, musically and theatrically, Giacomo Puccini's operas *Madame Butterfly* (1904–1907)[3] and *Turandot* (unfinished in 1924; completed by composer Franco Alfano) are interesting examples of the proto-globalized synthesis emerging from this age of empires and exoticism. Apart from musical style itself, Giacomo Meyerbeer's *L'Africaine* (1865) and Giuseppe Verdi's *Aida* (1871) are earlier manifestations: *Aida* has garnered some interesting analysis with regard to whether it is imperialist/orientalist in the way it handles Egyptian and Ethiopian concerns (see Robinson 1993), while *L'Africaine* revolves around the explorer

Vasco De Gama and makes reference to Hinduism rather than anything specifically African. Puccini attempted to evoke Asian musical sounds in *Butterfly* and
Turadot, while Meyerbeer and Verdi ignored non-Western music in their respective works.

Yet these forays would not have been made unless Europeans had been fascinated by what they had heard (and increasingly seen) of Asian and African
cultures. Musicologist of India Gerry Farrell has observed that by the nineteenth century "the naive musical heart of the West became entranced by the
Orient" (1997:79). Even if this comment is taken as cynical or at least rueful, too
much emphasis has been placed on the (primarily economic) power differentials
involved in Europe's exoticism, and too little on whether any genuine mutual
interest—not to mention mutual influence—was present. In fact, both colonizers
and the colonized developed something of a musical fascination with one another.

In *Beyond Exoticism* (2007), Timothy Taylor, going all the way back to the
beginning of the seventeenth century, argues that the very rise of opera and even
of tonality itself was Europe's vehicle for expression of power and domination
over the Other—that is, the rest of the globe. Opera and tonality, Taylor asserts,
separated Europe and gave it the opportunity to portray other cultures in the ways
it preferred, primarily as oddities needing "civilization." In Taylor's view, use
of exotic characters and locales cannot be a legitimate expression of interest and
respect, whether multicultural, intercultural, or transcultural. Indeed, for Taylor
"globalization" itself "is the term most commonly used to refer to the recent
regime under which nonwestern peoples are dominated and represented by the
West" (2007:113).

This is a bleak and altogether too-convenient picture, cleverly precluding any
positive view of intercultural convergence, fusion, and transformation. Jonathan
Bellman puts it well:

> What postcolonial criticism is not equipped to do is address transcultural
> music where there is no perceived power differential, or at least none of
> interest…Spain offers an [especially] problematic example; Spanish exoti-
> cism via musical markers is an old, old tradition, but the power differen-
> tial kept changing. "Spain" might evoke the glories of Moorish Al-Andalus,
> the Spanish imperial cruelty in the new world, the rigidity of Most Catholic
> Spain in the Counter-Reformation, Enlightenment condescension about the
> decrepitude of a long-vanquished and formerly feared power, a colorful but
> harmless tourist spot of later decades, or (going full circle) the remnant of
> an ancient and glorious golden age of power, civilization, and even con-
> vivencia…Unless the relationship between the cultures being musically jux-
> taposed is of an exploitative kind, postcolonial criticism has little to offer,
> and is thus of marginal relevance—shrill denials to the contrary—for the
> vast majority of transcultural music… "Who is colonizing who?"…seems
> almost quaintly out of date if one considers the omnidirectional globalism of
> musical dissemination.

(2011:433)

This also applies to music as commodity: "In reality, the question of who is exploiting whom is often a complicated one as non-Western musicians find access to markets hitherto only dreamt of" (Lancashire 2003:21; this is one of the key points in Cowen 2002 as well).

Further, even if Taylor is partly correct, the idea that musical cultures have always been in congress—and that very interesting new musics emerge as a result, however one sees the justness of their origins—can no longer be denied. Taylor's view precludes any notion of musical universals being manifested in ever-changing cultural milieus, perhaps because acceptance of such an idea would threaten cultural autonomy and open the possibility that cultures could profoundly and even fundamentally affect one another musically. In fact, it has been the power of these myriad expressions of qualified musical universals that has held sway to an ever-increasing degree, even over the course of the rise and fall of Europe's presumed cultural hegemony. Hence, one way to see things is that, musically, the Other has won and Europe's "classical" attempts to dominate have lost.[4] Despite being firmly poised to reinforce Otherness, musicians in the United States rather rapidly (in global historical terms) bowed to Afro-European fusion in real terms—musically, "who colonized who?" indeed. "Pure" European music (if such a thing ever existed) was subsumed under the inexorable power of transcultural transformation and the human creative spark. Jann Pasler put it eloquently in observing a now normative "postmodern and postcolonial preoccupation with hybridization…as well as the notion of Western culture as *a product of the colonized and the colonizers*" (2006:459, emphasis added).

In his incisive and revealing article "Creole Europe: The Reflection of a Reflection," Christopher Pinney notes that

> with the passing of the Rococo, which [art historian and critic Bernard] Smith described as its last 'original art style', European art modelled itself on others, in the form of the past, or the exotic. 'In European colonies settled during the nineteenth century', Smith concludes, 'art was *the reflection of a reflection*' (emphasis added). One way of comprehending this *reflection of a reflection* is in terms of the refracted nature of colonial enunciation. We have come to accept this enunciation as split by a process of hybridization, partialization, or creolization but have not yet fully come to accept, I think, that this colonial enunciation is a double splitting of an originary Europe *that is itself already creolized or hybridized.*
>
> (2002:125–126)

This leads Pinney to assert plainly that Europe "was always a reflection of other times and places, never a self-present unity awaiting its replicatory colonial enunciation" (2002:126–128). It is an analysis in keeping with the thesis of this book, namely that global music history is rooted in inter/transculturation, which in turn sheds a different light on the importance of modern-period European musical exoticism: however inconvenient or awkward, it was simply another continuation of an old story.

Debussy: a culmination?

The music of Claude Debussy (1862–1918, French) after his encounter with Javanese gamelan at the 1889 Exposition Universelle in Paris is especially instructive. Importantly, it was the Dutch who, having had long intercultural experience in Indonesia, brought the gamelan to Paris in 1887 and put it on public display in 1889. Debussy's exoticism was perhaps more important than Puccini's: the French composer's entire corpus was fundamentally transformed by the Asian elements he apprehended. As Richard Mueller has demonstrated, the effect on Debussy of his "many fruitful hours…spent in the Javanese *kampong* of the Dutch section listening to the percussive rhythmic complexities of the gamelan with its inexhaustible combination of ethereal, flashing timbres" (1986:158) was immediate: over the subsequent 20 years it caused him to rethink, for example, his *Fantasie* for piano and orchestra that had initially been in composition during 1889–1890. In 1895 Debussy wrote to the poet Pierre Louÿs, "Do you not remember the Javanese music, able to express every shade of meaning, even unmentionable shades, and which make our tonic and dominant seem like ghosts?" (quoted in Mueller 1986:158). Mueller notes that Debussy translated what he heard into Western musical terms, materials, and processes; for example, transmogrifying the Javanese *slendro* and *pelog* pitch collections into world pentatonic and whole tone scales within 12-EDO, and featuring them more prominently in the *Fantasie* and thereafter (1986:159–161). Mueller goes on to demonstrate how some of the particularities of Javanese melodic periodicity ended up in the DNA of Debussy's ostinati, and how the composer heard resultant extended tertian harmonies emanating from the gamelan as well (Mueller 1986:171). By the time of Debussy's vocal setting of Verlaine's "Claire de Lune" (1891), the absorption and transformation was complete, not only in the way pentatonicism occurs, but also in the textural arrangements of the piano accompaniment (Mueller 1986:1973ff.), textures that would characterize Debussy's music henceforth.

By 1903, Debussy had expanded these sensibilities further. Sylvia Parker, for example, shows how "Pagodes" represents "a remarkably successful rendition of the Eastern gamelan on the Western piano" (2012:1). Debussy continued to comment on his appreciation for Javanese music as late as 1913, noting that it "obeys laws of counterpoint that make Palestrina seem like child's play. And if one listens to it without being prejudiced by one's European ears, one will find a percussive charm that forces one to admit that our own music is not much more than a barbarous kind of noise more fit for a traveling circus" (quoted in Parker 2012:4). Parker goes on to demonstrate how "within Pagodes aspects of both Eastern and Western musical thinking merge" (2012:7), notably in Debussy's use of harmony that retains creative elements of tonality while emphasizing sonority over function—one of the composer's trademarks—and in his addition of triplets of various kinds to the otherwise even rhythmic doublings (e.g., quarter-note, eighth-note, sixteenth-note relationships) that characterize gamelan *irama*. That Debussy had expanded his thinking to Asian sensibility more generally is shown in a 1926 comment from the composer's friend Robert Godet that "one had the occasion to submit to the composer numerous documents collected in diverse places of Asia" that subsequently resided in Debussy's "memory or fantasy" (quoted in Parker 2012:8)—pagodas are, after all, something of a representative, mystical pan-Asian phenomenon, especially in the Western mind.[5] Farrell suggests that Debussy was also influenced by the Indian musician Hazrat Inayat Khan (1882–1927), a Sufi immigrant to Europe who "had wanted to unite the East and West through music" (1997:145). And it is important to remember that Debussy, always looking for fresh ideas, also knowingly embraced the black American ragtime rhythms of the cakewalk dance in his "Golliwog's Cakewalk" of 1908.

In other words, Debussy's experience represented intercultural encounter that evolved into transcultural phenomena. In that sense, his music, though still Western, challenged the European conceptions from whence it first sprang. Debussy was only one of the first Westerners to do so as the twentieth century unfolded. Yet he emerged late in the period under discussion. A survey of how Europe and its colonies arrived at such a moment by processes underway in the era leading towards the turn of the twentieth century is therefore in order.

Missionaries

The European Christian missionary impetus was strong, and, outside of lucrative trading voyages, the chance to spread the Gospel was considered a good cause for the investment involved. One of the earliest of these missionaries, Portuguese Dominican Gaspar da Cruz (c. 1520–1570) recorded his observations of Chinese music, based on direct experience hearing it, for publication in 1569. Da Cruz notes that "they began not all together, but the one tarried for to enter with the other, making many divisions in the process of the music, some staying, other playing; and the most times they played all together in four parts"—perhaps a reference to heterophonic texture—and mentions plucked, bowed, and possibly even hammered chordophones that the musicians gave attention to tuning in advance (Clarke 2010:545). This is not an insignificant comment given a tendency for Europeans to think most non-Western music to be out of tune.

Jesuits fostered as much intercultural congress in East and Southeast Asia as they did in the Americas. Francisco de Xavier (1506–1552, Navarrese-Basque), one of the original founders of the Jesuit order, became a missionary for the Society after extensive education at the University of Paris, where he would almost certainly have been instructed in music as one of the seven liberal arts. Though early Jesuit attitudes towards music were complex (see Bertoglio 2017:482–490), the approach to evangelism abroad that all Jesuits eventually adopted reflects Francis's understanding and appreciation of music as a means of human nonverbal communication as well as a way to teach Scripture and doctrine. A missionary pioneer from 1542, Francis worked in Goa, India and in various Southeast Asian islands before journeying to Japan in 1549, where he presented a European clavichord to the local nobility in 1551. By 1562, there is evidence that Japanese boys were playing violas da gamba at a high level (Takahashi 2001:116–117). Meanwhile, one wonders whether Francis and his successors (some of whom were Franciscans and Dominicans) heard beggar Zen Buddhist priests playing their proto-*shakuhachis* (possibly *hitoyogiris*) in the streets (see Lee 1992, section 3.2.2) during the relatively brief time Japan initially remained open to Christian missionaries (until about 1613). Not until the opening of the Meiji period in 1868 did the West again have significant access to the traditional Japanese music that had continued its development.[6]

No doubt the combination of complex harmonic partials being emitted from the "gong-chime" ensembles (Fletcher 2001:273), alternate tuning systems, and heterophonic textures made Southeast Asian music especially challenging to Western ears. Yet according to the Jesuit Guy Tachard, writing in 1688 about Siamese (Thai) music, "There was nothing extraordinary, neither in the Musick nor Voices; yet the novelty and diversity of them, made them pleasant enough not to prove tedious the first time" (quoted in Miller 1984:32). Indeed, predisposed to seek or create intercultural syntheses in order to propagate the Christian message, some Jesuits learned to appreciate the music of their host countries as well as possible confluences with European musics and instruments, and to communicate their findings back to Europe.

Writing on Chinese music by two French Jesuits, Jean-Baptiste Du Halde (1674–1743) and Jean Joseph Marie Amiot (1718–1793), attracted attention from musically and culturally influential compatriots. Du Halde, who never visited China but based his information on the reports of Jesuit brothers who had, included five transcriptions of Chinese music along with some commentary in his *Description geographique, historique, chronologique, politique, et physique de l'empire de la Chine et de la Tartarie chinoise* (1735). Du Halde's comments on these tunes and on Chinese music overall in the publication are fairly typical of Europeans in the period, reflecting a general sense that music had degenerated from its heights in the ancient glory days of the civilization under Confucius, and was now heard as primitive. Du Halde specifically mentions that he heard monks sing without half-steps, but only in thirds, fifths, and octaves—no doubt a strong focus on the anhemitonic world pentatonic collection in what he heard reinforced this perception: "They all sing the same tune as it is practiced in all Asia." Moreover, because of the continued focus on monophony from ancient times, the complexity of Western harmony and contrapuntal textures "seems to [the Chinese] a disagreeable confusion" (Du Halde 1735:266). Apparently, however, the complexity of Asian heterophony was not noticed (or perhaps not appreciated) by the Westerners. The use of notation as an aid to preservation was highly impressive to the Chinese as well: in the context of the commentary, it appears that Du Halde consulted with Father Tomas Pereira (1645–1708, in China from 1673), who had captured the five "Airs Chinois" as a result of these demonstrations. Numbers one, four, and five are firmly in world pentatonic mode one, while numbers two and three are essentially in world pentatonic mode two with a few additional passing tones. In addition, interesting syncopated rhythms (short-long-short patterns) are included in numbers two, four, and five; the commentary suggests these were accurate depictions of the rhythms played by the Chinese musicians, and not editorial additions.[7] Du Halde's work provided important reference material on Chinese music and culture to Voltaire (François-Marie Arouet, 1694–1778) and Jean-Jacques Rousseau (1712–1778), among others (Clarke 2010:545).

Following the general example set by Jesuit Matteo Ricci (1552–1610; in China from 1583) with regard to a respectful, personal, and strategic approach to cultural synthesis, Amiot studied Chinese music extensively in-country and wrote about it in positive detail in works that theorist and composer Jean-Philippe Rameau (1683–1764) made reference to in his *Code de Musique practique* (1760).[8]

> When he had first reached Beijing Amiot had tried to win over new listeners for Rameau…But…in his letters [of 1776–1789], he assumes the role of an apologist for traditional Chinese musical practice. He now identifies himself with the Chinese, and, by implication, condemns the French spirit of levity that had proved so alien to his first audience in China.
>
> (Wah 2005:131)

Amiot was actually the last in a line of Jesuit musician-priests in residence at the Chinese court that essentially started with Father Pereira (noted above), whose knowledge of both Western and Chinese music inclined emperor Kangxi to appoint him to the position of palace musician. Amiot's "*Memoires de la musique des Chinois tant anciens que modernes* (Beijing, 1776) proved to be an important contribution to the understanding of Chinese music in Europe, and was widely read in France" (Lindorff 2004:408, 410).

Interestingly, the strong and ancient culture of Christian Ethiopia and its connections to the Alexandrian patriarchate ultimately prevented the efforts at Catholic Romanization by Jesuit missionaries that began in the late sixteenth century (see Caraman 1985), preserving a distinctive musical culture in the process. Indeed, as Anne Damon-Guillot (2017) has detailed, music was far from inconsequential to the story, for the Jesuits seem to have heard the indigenous music as extremely disturbing—perhaps "a sonic hell" (2017:41)—and in need of an "Edenification" that a European Christian style would presumably bring. One of the European sonic elements (aside from tonal harmony) was apparently the complexity of ringing bells,[9] whereas the sistrums and drums of the Ethiopians (still in practice as of this writing) were like the dreaded "bacchanals" of pagan Greece (2017:46–48). By the 1630s, Catholics were effectively expelled from the area, not to return until the early nineteenth century. Yet even these rough beginnings raised intercultural contact to a new and serious level. By the 1960s recordings of Ethiopian music were on the rise for new generations of Westerners to discover (Betreyohannes 2010).

In a section of his 1650 *Musurgia Universalis*, the Jesuit Athanasius Kircher had perhaps a laudable idea for the time—he attempted to wed texts based on the Ethiopian traditional Christian liturgy that he had written in the indigenous language (Ge'ez) with European music. His methods, however, were not inter/transcultural; rather, seen charitably, they stemmed from the best universal vision of music he could muster (see Damon-Guillot 2017:51–52). Twenty-first-century

Ethiopian popular music—including most of its contemporary Christian music—is highly intercultural, reflecting centuries of West Asian and traditional indigenous influences integrated with American jazz-rock elements. It is a reconciliation of sorts, perhaps at least in the true spirit of Kircher, many centuries in the making. Moreover, in a fascinating twist, Ethiopia's most celebrated twentieth-century art music composer, Ashenafi Kebede (1938–1998)—trained in the United States and a prominent ethnomusicologist as well—made it "one of his major objectives…to compose works using musical concepts distilled from many cultures and expressing the humanity of humankind…inspired by the musics of countries spanning several continents including his native Ethiopia, Japan, the Middle East, India, Eastern Europe notably Hungary, and the USA" (Kimberlin 1999:323–325). Kebede merely exemplified the long inter/transcultural milieu of his homeland.

Trade and colonization

"China, India and Japan were at something of a cultural peak in the sixteenth and seventeenth centuries. The land blockade of Eastern Europe by the Turk made them even more attractive to Europeans than they had been before" (Roberts 2004:631). It was therefore inevitable that attempts at lucrative trade, and eventually control, would be made.

Indonesia

The arrival of the Portuguese in Indonesia during the sixteenth century opened the door to a greater influx of musical influences from Indian, Arabic, and African slaves, though prehistoric animism along with Hinduism and Buddhism from India and China remain at the heart of the culture of the region. Sufi Islam provided a later but still powerful additional color from the fifteenth century onward: among the instruments likely entering the traditional gamelan from this direction is a version of the Arab rebab (Sorrell 2015:52–56). The Dutch followed the Portuguese to the area beginning in the seventeenth century, and though European and other influences continued (including integration of the violin and the Portuguese-Hawaiian ukulele along with Western harmony), just as important was the fact that the Dutch allowed traditional gamelan music to flourish in the Javanese courts—and then became enamored with it themselves, eventually exporting it to rest of the globe as in the story of Debussy and the Exposition Universelle, above.[10] In Bali, *gamelan gong kebyar* slowly diverged stylistically from ancient Javanese gamelan and emerged as another example of Indonesian music going global over the course of the twentieth century (see Tenzer 2000).

China

Just as Rome saw the Silk Road as access to Chinese goods, so was much of the age of European empires directed towards facilitating and continuing this goal once Central Asia was no longer a viable route. Europe thus remained in full engagement with China, with cultural as well as material commerce proceeding apace in both directions. Chinese visitors to Europe and Europeans to China were therefore not especially uncommon as the nineteenth century progressed—though as late as 1757, the idea of "an encounter with Chinese music…in London," for example, would still have been exceedingly rare, and likely not very musically enlightening (Clarke 2010).

Perhaps a watershed moment for broader European understanding of and appreciation for Chinese music is to be found in the 1884 publication, in Shanghai under the auspices of the British government, of the book *Chinese Music* by the Belgian J.A. van Aalst (1858–1914), which went on to be reprinted five times through 1965 (Han 1988:127). Van Aalst was one of multiple Europeans employed by the Imperial Maritime Customs service, situated in a diplomatic-trade enclave that China still officially governed, where he served as both a cultural expert and Postal Secretary. A graduate of the Conservatory in Ghent, he was stationed at several different locations in China beginning with Guandong Province from 1881 (Han 1988:128). Thus, his musical qualifications and Chinese experience were considerable, and his analysis of Chinese music is enlightening. A master of tact, van Aalst opens his book by noting that

> amongst the subjects which have been treated with the least success by foreign writers, Chinese Music ranks prominently. If mentioned at all in their books, it is simply to remark that "it is detestable, noisy, monotonous; that it hopelessly outrages our Western notions of music," etc. I do not wish to create any discussions by contradicting these and many other erroneous statements found in descriptions of Chinese Music: it would take too long a time…In the description I give here I will endeavour to point out the contrasts or similarity between Western and Chinese Music, to present abstruse theories in the least tiresome way, to add details never before published, and to give a short yet concise account of Chinese Music.
>
> (1884:iii)

Here van Aalst is acting the consummate bureaucrat who must navigate both Chinese and European contexts (his supervisor in Shanghai was the British diplomat Sir Robert Hart), but the message is clear: Europe's views on Chinese music need at least some correction. Early on he notes that "it cannot be denied that the national music of every country, however simple it may be, has a mystic influence on the passions of its inhabitants," and wisely portrays Chinese music as being commensurate with other ancient musics such as those of Greece and Egypt (1884:1–3).

With scientific precision, van Aalst proceeds to explain why Chinese tuning does not correspond exactly to 12-EDO Western tuning, causing aural dissonance to Western listeners. But he carefully avoids any clear statement on the inherent superiority or inferiority of either system in this context, observing instead that Chinese notes "could not possibly be rendered on our Western tempered instruments" (1884:12). He neutrally comments that the Chinese "remain faithful to their pentatonic scale, and find therein all the variations necessary to satisfy their ear" (1884:19), going to imply that the types of tuning and the limitation of the pitch collection used is appropriate to the continued monophony of Chinese music (1884:22). Van Aalst is perhaps less neutral about Chinese rhythmic notation, noting that "incontestably the weakest point in Chinese musical notation…[is] the total absence of signs showing the value, the rests, the time, etc., [making] it quite impossible to learn a tune by merely reading the written notes"—yet even here he seems to understand that this is due to a different system, one requiring aural traditions rather than notation alone: "The best Chinese musician could only conjecture the general form of a written piece shown to him for the first time; to be able to decipher it he must first hear it played" (1884:18).

Van Aalst also correctly transcribes an Imperial March (1884:26) in world pentatonic mode three (M2, m3, M2, m3, M2), now known to be quite common in Chinese musics over many centuries. His book covers ritual/religious music, popular music, instruments, singing, and lyrics; it is lavishly and attractively illustrated and populated with many musical transcriptions as well. Van Aalst cannot entirely escape the age in which he lives, concluding that "it is incontestable that Chinese music compares unfavourably with European music" (1884:84). Yet he tempers this in the same breath:

> Why does not Chinese music leave a better impression on the ears and minds of foreigners? Most naturally because it has not been made for foreigners… From our point of view it certainly appears monotonous, even noisy-disagreeable, if you please; but what matters this if the Chinese themselves are satisfied with it?
>
> (84)

And the very last sentence is revealing: "According to the Chinese themselves, music proceeds from the heart of man; it is the expression of the feelings of the heart" (84) This is remarkably balanced and open language for a colonial conservatory-trained European to be using in 1884. For one man at least—one whose book influenced at least two subsequent generations—Chinese music had made an intriguing impact.[11]

Britain and India

Perhaps no part of this era in global music history has been as well documented and analyzed as the relationship between colonial Britain and India. That story begins with the founding of the (British) East India Company (EIC) by the English under Queen Elizabeth I one day before 1601, more than a century before the forging of Great Britain and its "empire on which the sun never sets" (23% of the world's population at its height in 1913). About the same time that the first British colonists were headed towards the Chesapeake Bay in America, the EIC was moving ahead with its plans to wrest a portion of the spice trade with the "East Indies" (South/Southeast Asia) from the Spanish and Portuguese who had dominated it throughout most of the sixteenth century. The Dutch too seized the opportunity left by a Spanish/Portuguese decline in the region, though the Dutch ended up focused more on Indonesia while the British gravitated towards India, and to a somewhat lesser degree China, as the eighteenth century unfolded, assuming colonial rule of India by the middle of the nineteenth century. Within 50 years of the collapse of the Mughal empire in 1707, the same year that England and Scotland united into Great Britain, the British took the region of Bengal and assumed dominance of the Indian subcontinent.

Katherine Brown (Schofield) provides a complex and nuanced snapshot of European-Indian (and, secondarily, Persian) musical interactions during the seventeenth century through the eyes of European travel writers, some of the main historical sources readily available, noting that

> it would seem that the patronage of Indian musicians by Europeans and vice versa was widespread, and that Indian musicians at least began to play European instruments, possibly even developing hybrid styles. On the other hand, Indian instruments were adopted into the military bands of the Europeans, which were used in Mughal style. The travel literature also provides documentary evidence of the continuing contact between Indian and Persian musicians, especially in Esfahan.
>
> (2000:26)

Clearly this mutual congress continued throughout the eighteenth century, despite considerable ineptitude (perhaps colonially willful at times) on the part of the British with regard to the apprehension of Indian music (Head 1985).

The notion that what is today regarded as "Indian classical music" was invented during British colonial rule (see, e.g., Schofield 2010:487ff.; J. Katz 2015:166) warrants close scrutiny, but from a different perspective than might be assumed: that is, the extent to which such a notion is true is actually a testimony to the power of inter/transculturality rather than a path to declaring the music "inauthentic." That Indian music might have been reinvented through its encounter with European "intrusion" is a sign of its strength, not its weakness. The same could be said, as noted in detail in Chapters 5 and 6, of African music in the Americas. In fact, as Schofield shows, the "classical" (art, courtly) music of the Mughals in the North—Muslims from Central Asia who were successfully integrated into ancient Hindu cultural structures ("subsumed in a vision of a universal God of Love; Persian Sufism blended with Hindu *bhakti*" (Fletcher 2001:233))—that the British encountered upon their arrival in India was already well developed, and convenient commonalities with European music were found on which to focus.

Meanwhile, in the South, Carnatic music centered more on pure Hindu devotion emerged, though it too was stylistically mutually influential with the North. The British attitude towards Indian culture was similar to that of the Romans: refrain from interference except as needed to ensure structures for profitable trade (Roberts 2004:639). As a result, Carnatic music in South India seems to have continued to develop its own distinctives (Fletcher 2001:239).

The story of Muttusvami Dikshitar (1775–1835) is highly instructive, as he was one of the "holy Trinity" of Carnatic composers who also had meaningful dealings with European music and studied Hindustani music seriously. Dikshitar is closely associated with the introduction of the European violin into Carnatic music, for example (Balachandran and Bhardwaj 2001:692). His "Shakti Sahita Ganapathim" is a catchy popular tune arranged around Western tonality and British style (almost like a sea shanty in 6/8 meter), while his numerous devotional songs, which use both Carnatic and Hindustani ragas, are entirely Indian and of the utmost complexity. In the generations following his death, the book of music and composers' biographies *Sangita Sampradaya Pradarshini* (1904) by Dikshita's nephew Subbarama (1839–1906) helped to solidify the legacy. Thus, a rather transcultural Indian composer remained at the heart of the "classical" Carnatic tradition that continued to be promoted to the West.

Sir William Jones's (1746–1794) *On the Musical Modes of the Hindoos*, written in India in 1784, a year after his arrival there, "based on his reading of Sanskrit and Persian music treatises...was to prove influential not merely on later scholars of Indian music, but also on intellectuals and composers in Europe" (Schofield 2010:504). As in Du Halde's inferences about the Confucian glory days of Chinese music, many Europeans, led by Jones, were most interested in recapturing "purely Hindu" Indian music from what they imagined to be a lost noble civilization.[12] Meanwhile, Hindoostannie (Hindostanee, Hindustani) Airs, which Ian Woodfield has defined as "a short piece derived from an Indian original but arranged in a European idiom" beginning in the 1780s (1994:189), "represented the first serious attempts to transcribe Indian music, and the first tangible evidence of how Europeans viewed and understood, or misunderstood, the living sound of Indian music" (Farrell 1997:28). In other words, however much corrupted the original Indian music was in these attempts, they were at least based on observable practice and not on ancient Sanskrit texts. Hindustani Airs were in fact loosely based on North Indian music that was heavily influenced by centuries of Persian/Arab/Islamic input—that is, reflective of the inter/ transculturality that characterized earlier global music history eras, not least across Central and West Asia, and continued therewith. With its additional European input, the Hindustani Air can be seen as propagating this same inter/ transcultural transformation.

Perhaps most important to global music history was William Hamilton Bird's collection of his own Hindustani Airs, *The Oriental Miscellany* (1789), which reached a broad and influential public that included Belgian musicologist and critic François-Joseph Fétis (1784–1871)—Bird's collection was still referenced in works a century later (Farrell 1997:32). It is likely that Bird researched the material for his work in Lucknow, in the broader Awadh region, which featured both Hindu and Muslim musical influences. Indeed, Lucknow "had become a cultural meeting ground between the British and Indians, unlike anywhere else in India at that time...[and] came to exemplify the amalgamation of two cultures in a number of areas, including architecture, painting and music" (Farrell 1997:35–36). This material was interpreted through thoroughly Western sensibilities. Yet faint "hints of the original Indian melodic and rhythmic structures can also be discerned in *The Oriental Miscellany*" and other collections, including the use of pedal tones as something of a substitute for Indian drones, ornaments inspired by Indian *gamakas*, rhythmic arrangements that mirrored the *talas* associated with the "lighter" Indian dance music that served as inspiration, and occasional scalar alterations that suggest expressive elements within certain *ragas* (Farrell 1997:37–44). That the Hindustani Air genre traveled back to England not long after its inception is evidenced by the publication of a collection by former Captain Thomas Williamson (1759–1817) of the British army in London c. 1800 (Edwards 1980:680). The practice also extended to the dissemination of "airs" from other countries (see Farrell 1997:84–86).

It is with this genre that Farrell begins insightfully to draw a distinction between scholarly and popular approaches to Indian musicology as a global entity (1997:78ff.), a distinction that can be drawn for other musics as well: though globalization came to both art music and vernacular music, to scholarly study and to popular entertainment, it came differently to each. Perhaps the most important point in this regard is that popular musics have seemed to incorporate transcultural elements sooner and more readily. Certainly, this was the case with African elements in the Americas as well as with Indian music in Britain and beyond.

Yet it is also worth noting that the British art music composer Gustav Holst (1874–1934) was entirely and sincerely fascinated with Indian philosophy and the hymns of the Rig Veda, which aspects found their way substantially into the subject matter of his compositions from about 1907 onward. What is less clear is whether Holst's (likely rather limited) experience with Indian music itself had any effect on his deliberate efforts to break away from the Wagnerian traditions that tended to hold sway at the turn of the twentieth century. Through brief but fascinating evidence, Raymond Head subtly suggests the possibility that some of Holst's innovations in the areas of rhythm, pitch contour, and process (including improvisatory textures) may have been the result of both Indian philosophical and aural elements (1988:38–40). If so, Holst would only have been following the path taken more directly by Debussy in response to gamelan music.

Africa (and France)

The exportation of African musics to the Americas through the slave trade was the main way in which their global influence would be felt. Yet colonization of Africa itself formed another part of the story, one that brought other nations into the milieu, especially France in North and West Africa (in addition to a large part of North America prior to 1800). This trend accelerated precipitously during the last nineteenth-century "scramble for Africa" in which the occupation of the African continent by outside powers went from approximately 10% in 1870 to nearly 90% in 1914. Eurasia had a long history of African coastal contact, but exploration of the interior of sub-Saharan Africa by Europeans did not commence until very late in the eighteenth century—and musics such as that of the Aka and Mbuti (formerly called "pygmies") did not reach a wide audience until the 1960s, after which they gained significant popularity. With England ruling over some 30% of the African population and France some 15%—and both countries long involved with Africans in their New World territories as well—African congress with Anglo-French cultures was especially strong. The French presence in North Africa from about 1830 was notably consequential in bringing attention back to the Afro-Arab musical syntheses that had continued to develop there under the Ottomans since the seventeenth century—eventually giving rise to the globally popular, politically charged genre called Rai beginning in the 1920s (Noor Al-Deen 2005). Egypt too was to become a key influence in the forging of nineteenth-century French worldviews, despite France's failure to secure the territory from the Ottomans.

Perhaps no single European figure was more influential in documenting and propagating the continuation of Arab-Andalusian music in North Africa than the Baron Rodolphe d'Erlanger (1872–1932). D'Erlanger, based in Tunisia (a French protectorate from 1881), started his work in 1914 and was instrumental in producing the First International Congress of Arab Music in Cairo in 1932, in which, among others, Henry George Farmer also featured prominently (Davis 2004:41–50; I. Katz 2015).

Jann Pasler paints an unflattering picture of how the French viewed the music of Africa and Asia, but admits that

> exotic [musical] instruments…allowed the French to come closer to something more authentic in a foreign culture than what was offered to their imaginations by stories…French desire to experience the unknown, the incomprehensible, the impenetrable, possibly the unknowable, undoubtedly created a tension when coupled with their inclination to reduce instruments to stereotypes.

> (2004:30)

And, after detailed analysis of late nineteenth-century illustrations of Asian and African instruments and musicians in the popular elite magazine *L'illustration*, revealing a complex range of depictions, Pasler also notes that

> instrumental similarities, to French readers, may have seemed to transcend racial differences and to suggest that human differences are bridgeable, at least when it comes to music. From this perspective, the images support the hypothesis of a unified human race, and one showing remarkable flexibility over time.

> (2004:63)

That is, the biases of those who practice(d) comparative musicology cannot in the end overshadow what the exercise reveals: the transcultural brilliance of human musicality. The increasingly (re)globalized world of empires and exoticism made this ever more plain, despite itself.

The Ottoman Turks, Russia, and Europe

The Ottoman Empire—forged at the turn of the fourteenth century, annexing Byzantium a century and a half later, and (at its height in the late seventeenth century) encompassing cultures from Arab to North African to Eastern European—exemplified and facilitated an East-meets-West milieu for centuries into the modern age. What was considered a Turkish musical style, based on military march rhythm and noisy, ringing percussion, was all the rage in Europe during the time of Mozart and Beethoven.[13] Beethoven also attempted to recreate a Sufi (Mevlevi) Whirling Dervish dance in his incidental music to *The Ruins of Athens* (1811): the chromatically angular melodic material in a minor key is clearly meant to evoke an imagined exotic Arab sound, and no doubt contributed to additional music stereotypes that endured well into the twentieth century. For their part, Ottoman elites embraced a variety of European musical elements (Kosal 1999). Influential in the process, for example, was Giuseppe Donizetti, brother of the famed nineteenth-century Italian opera composer Gaetano Donizetti (Aracı 2002). During the eighteenth and nineteenth centuries, the borders of the Ottoman empire continued to shrink until only the current nation of Turkey remained as of 1923, with ancient Istanbul (Byzantium) still at its heart. Nevertheless, West and Central Asian musical legacies, now informed by centuries of intercourse with Europe, continue to constitute a globalized living tradition there.

Ottoman culture was in dialogue with and exerted influence on both Eastern and Western Europe. This included the Russia empire, with which the Turks were in significant political tension from the latter's emergence early in the eighteenth century. The Rus, Christianized by Byzantium and effectively brought into the developing European world nearly a millennium earlier, wedded Central Asian folk influences with the conservatism of Orthodox Christian worship and greater aspirations towards European art music beginning in the sixteenth century. By the nineteenth century, composers such as Peter Ilyich Tchaikovsky (1840–1893) and Nicolai Rimsky-Korsakov (1844–1908) were advancing this synthesis to a high level. A similar synthesis was growing across Eastern Europe, especially in Hungary and Bulgaria, where an even stronger Central Asian legacy was present.[14]

The rise of the Soviet Union from the Russian revolution (beginning c. 1917), with its heavily state-controlled approach to music rigidly designed to promote a unified nationalism, unfortunately put a damper on this intercultural creative spark in Eastern Europe and eventually in much of Central Asia as well for many decades. Communist China from the 1920s also promoted nationalistic music bureaucratized around something of a homogenized Chinese-European style (see Gong 2008:53–69) rather than encouraging a freer interculturality. Yet folk musics survived across Eurasia, and eventually global popular music broke through this attempted wall of creative control from about the 1980s on, aided significantly by the American convergences.

Musical transmission accelerated

Music notation—in use to varying degrees across times, places, and cultures in global music history but eventually taken to new levels of detail by the West—was in many ways a blunt tool in the age of empires and exoticism, standing in tension with the emerging technologies of sound recording and broadcast. While the latter two will be explored in further detail in Chapter 9, a word on this tension is in order here, since it shaped the transmission of non-Western musics back to the West so profoundly.

European efforts to capture the broader musics of its empires certainly changed them. In the case of Hindustani Airs, for example, Farrell suggests that it all but eliminated any of the original Indian basis (1997:42), and no doubt this applied to many parallel situations. This phenomenon still can and should be seen as another instance of intercultural convergence, fusion, and transformation. Moreover, the issue of the nature of transmission outside of direct performance should not be ignored—after all, transformed musics are transmitted as well. The advent of sound recording suitable for music, in the form of Thomas Edison's phonograph cylinder from 1878 and Emil Berliner's gramophone from c. 1890, changed this circumstance dramatically. Very soon thereafter, musics from around the globe were being recorded—for example, Benjamin Ives Gilman's wax cylinders of Javanese gamelan made at the 1893 World's Exposition in Chicago (Mendonça 2011:56, 75). The challenges resulting from "freezing" a single performance of music in time and declaring that moment to be representative are multitudinous, not least the implications inherent in its subsequent interpretation,[15] but there was still much to be gained from hearing at least one manifestation of a music in a form less subject to (though certainly not entirely without) interpretive mitigation. The attending issues are still being debated, but general agreement has emerged that preserving the world's variety of musics in this way is better than not doing so. Perhaps most importantly for this study, sound recording of music has enabled us to experience the effect of its continuous global transformation far more readily. It has, as will be explored, also accelerated that transformation. Both of these aspects were born in the imperial period.

The Great War

The "war to end all wars" (World War I, 1914–1918) was in some ways a rude surprise in an age of considerable optimism about the future of prosperity and social harmony, at least for Europe. Yet in the European world of art and art music some voices were sounding alarm bells: a certain sort of decadence had set in and there was an uneasiness that expressed itself in a trend away from the moorings of Western tonality and forms/processes. In music this had essentially started with Debussy and his challenge to the European paradigms. What is most interesting is that that challenge came through a realization of something that was crystal clear in the Americas and might have been just as clear in the story of global music history, had a broad enough view been taken: the answer to European musical decadence lay in a return to a global inter/transcultural perspective on the nature of music, its universals, and their manifestation across cultures, the endless possibilities of human recombination and reinvention. Igor Stravinsky (1882–1971, Russian), who was to be one of the leading lights of the twentieth century, realized this just as Debussy had. Stravinsky's appropriation of an imagined ancient Central Asian "primitive" music combined with the power of European orchestral forces in his pivotal work, the ballet *Le Scare du Printemps* (*The Rite of Spring*, 1913), first offered to a Parisian audience on the eve of the Great War, brilliantly captured all of these elements in tension and more: It was modernist, pre-modern, and post-modern all at the same time, stepping outside the Western tradition significantly enough to be a "third way" between tonal-chromaticism-on-the-verge-of-atonality and unregulated chaos. In many ways, Eastern Europe had been waiting in the wings with these answers, long accustomed to Eurasian interculturality: Stravinsky and Bela Bartok (1881–1945, Hungarian)—and many composers inspired by them—would dominate the twentieth-century art music world, reflecting syntheses that began centuries earlier in Byzantium and eventually inspiring others along even broader global lines. That Bartok became something of an ethnomusicologist, traveling around the Hungarian countryside and nearby environs making audio recordings, transcriptions, and arrangements of Hungarian, Slovak, Romanian, and Bulgarian folk music, and later as far afield as Algeria, is telling in this regard, as these materials later found their way meaningfully into his compositions (Suchoff 1987; Parker 2008). Meanwhile a different form of musical globalization was, as noted, about to burst forth from the Americas. Both streams were a continuation of global music history and a breaking free from what Europe had attempted to impose on the world, yet both also relied on Europe's distinctive contributions. The Great War gave the world pause, but musical development continued unabated.

Notes

1 For comment on the concept of comparative musicology and its history, see Savage and Brown 2013:148–150.
2 The work also makes two pointed references to blackface minstrelsy (see Chapter 6).
3 It is illuminating that Puccini also crafted something of a musical mash-up for his operatic tribute to U.S. history, *The Girl of the Golden West* (1910); the work features Impressionist, African American, and even Native North American musical references (see Ross 2007:31).
4 This is generally true despite the fact that a sizable part of East Asia seems to have embraced the older standard repertoire of Western European classical music with a vengeance as of this writing. This suggests that that music may not disappear or be subsumed entirely; but what is more interesting is that more recent Asian art music composers have largely embraced the inter/transcultural approach for inspiration—putting them in the same camp as Euro-American art music composers fighting against the last resistors of change in art music, now their own compatriots.
5 See, for example, Ling 1974.
6 The Edo (Tokugawa)-period shakuhachi especially came to represent Japanese music to the West, as both a classical instrument and a Buddhist instrument for meditation (Keister 2004), and today is one of the most commonly used "exotic" wind instrument

sounds in popular and theatrical-cinematic music (along with the Armenian *duduk* and South American panpipes). Terence Lancashire (2003) also explores recent attempts to recontextualize traditional Japanese gagaku for a new global age.

7 Interestingly, another transcription of an Asian melody, one from Siam [Thailand] made by Simon de La Louber late in the seventeenth century, features very similar characteristics, and there is additional evidence from various French encounters that Chinese and Siamese musics were in dialogue during the period (Miller 1984:34–37).

8 Lam Ching Wah (2005:129) reports that the work in question was understood to be Amiot's translation of Li Guangdi's treatise *Guyue jingzhuan* (Canonical Book and Commentaries on Ancient Music), but François Picard (2001) identifies it as original writing.

9 Perhaps this is why the French Jesuit Joachim Bouvet (1656–1730) also registered his attraction to the Siamese *kawng wong*, a set of suspended bells he heard at a performance in-country, noting that it "gave a quite harmonious sound" (Miller 1984:35).

10 Maria Mendonça (2011) has also commented on this phenomenon in the context of an inspiring World War II story about the Dutch gamelan ensemble Babar Layar.

11 Among the many so influenced was Puccini, who used *Chinese Music* as a reference for the Chinese portions of *Turandot*.

12 Interestingly, this "Hindu purity" approach was also used by Indian nationalist musicians such as Vishnu Narayan Bhatkhande (1860–1936) in an attempt to "rescue" Indian music from centuries of Persian-Muslim influence (see Clayton 2007:90).

13 William Lichtenwanger (1948:55) traces Turkish military band music back to Central Asia and the records from the Han Chinese around the beginning of the first millennium CE; see also Knechtges and Chang (2010:370), and the section titled "China looking west" in Chapter 3 of this study.

14 The Romani people, who migrated from Northwest India and became the Gypsies in both Hungary and Spain, also contributed elements to Iberian musical culture that were exported to Latin America (see Chapter 5).

15 See, for example, James Badal (1996) on how the interpretation of Western classical orchestral music was transformed (flattened, he contends) by recording technology. Anthony Seeger (1986) discusses the issues in the context of ethnomusicology.

References

Araci, Emre. 2002. "Giuseppe Donizetti at the Ottoman Court: A Levantine Life." *The Musical Times* 143.1880: 49–56.

Badal, James. 1996. *Recording the Classics*. Kent, Ohio: Kent State University Press.

Balachandran, Chandra, and Surinder Bhardwaj. 2001. "Geography as Melody in Muttusvami Dikshita's Indian Musical Works." *Geographical Review* 91.4: 690–701.

Bellman, Jonathan. 2011. "Musical Voyages and Their Baggage: Orientalism in Music and Critical Musicology." *The Musical Quarterly* 94.3: 417–438.

Bertoglio, Chiara 2017. *Reforming Music: Music and the Religious Reformations of the Sixteenth Century*. Berlin: De Gruyter.

Betreyohannes, Simeneh. 2010. "Scholarship on Ethiopian Music: Past, Present and Future Prospects." *African Study Monographs* Suppl.41: 19–34.

Brown (Schofield), Katherine. 2000. "Reading Indian Music: The Interpretation of Seventeenth-Century European Travel Writing in the (Re)construction of Indian Music History." *British Journal of Ethnomusicology* 9.2: 1–34.

Caraman, Philip, S.J. 1985. *The Lost Empire: The Story of the Jesuits in Ethiopia*. London: Sidgwick & Jackson.

Clarke, David. 2010. "An Encounter with Chinese Music in Mid-18th-century London." *Early Music* 38.4: 543–557.

Clayton, Martin. 2007. "Musical Renaissance and Its Margins in England and India, 1874–1914." In Clayton, Martin and Bennett Zon (eds.), *Music and Orientalism in the British Empire, 1780s to 1940s: Portrayal of the East*, Aldershot: Ashgate, 71–93.

Cohen, Matthew 2006. *The Komedie Stamboel: Popular Theater in Colonial Indonesia, 1891–1903*. Athens, Ohio: Ohio University Press.

Cowen, Tyler. 2002. *Creative Destruction: How Globalization is Changing the World's Cultures*. Princeton, New Jersey: Princeton University Press.

Damon-Guillot, Anne. 2017. "Sounds of Hell and Sounds of Eden: Sonic Worlds in Ethiopia in the Catholic Missionary Context, Seventeenth and Eighteenth Centuries." In Guillebaud, Christine (ed.), *Toward an Anthropology of Ambient Sound*, New York: Routledge, 39–55.

Davis, Ruth F. 2004. *Ma'luf: Reflections on the Arab Andalusian Music of Tunisia*. Lanham, Maryland: Scarecrow Press.

Du Halde, Jean-Baptiste. 1735. *Description geographique, historique, chronologique, politique, et physique de l'empire de la Chine et de la Tartarie chinoise* (vol. 3). Paris: P.G. Le Mercier.

Edwards, Owain. 1980. "Captain Thomas Williamson of India." *Modern Asian Studies* 14.4:673–682.

Farrell, Gerry. 1997. *Indian Music and the West*. New York: Oxford University Press.

Farrell, Gerry, and Neil Sorrell. 2007. "Colonialism, Philology, and Musical Ethnography in Nineteenth-Century India: The Case of S. W. Fallon." *Music & Letters* 88.1: 107–120.

Fletcher, Peter. 2001. *World Musics in Context*. New York: Oxford University Press.

Gong, Hong-Yu. 2008. "Music, Nationalism and the Search for Modernity in China, 1911–1949." *New Zealand Journal of Asian Studies* 10.2: 38–69.

Han, Kuo-huang. 1988. "J. A. Van Aalst and His Chinese Music." *Asian Music* 19.2: 127–130.

Head, Raymond. 1985. "Corelli in Calcutta: Colonial Music-Making in India during the 17th and 18th Centuries." *Early Music* 13.4: 548–553.

Head, Raymond. 1988. "Holst and India (III)." *Tempo* 166: 35–40.

Hughes, David. 2015. "Japan." In Church, Michael (ed.), *The Other Classical Musics*, Woodbridge, Suffolk: Boydell and Brewer, 75–103.

Irving, David. 2009. "Comparative Organography in Early Modern Empires." *Music & Letters* 90.3: 372–398.

Katz, Israel. 2015. *Henry George Farmer and the First International Congress of Arab Music (Cairo 1932)*. Leiden: Brill.

Katz, Jonathan. 2015. "South India." In Church, Michael (ed.), *The Other Classical Musics*, Woodbridge, Suffolk: Boydell and Brewer, 161–177.

Keister, Jay. 2004. "The Shakuhachi as Spiritual Tool: A Japanese Buddhist Instrument in the West." *Asian Music* 35.2: 99–131.

Kimberlin, Cynthia. 1999. "The Scholarship and Art of Ashenafi Kebede (1938–1998)." *Ethnomusicology* 43.2: 322–334.

Knechtges, David R., and Taiping Chang (eds.). 2010. *Ancient and Early Medieval Chinese Literature: A Reference Guide, Part One*. Boston: Brill.

Kosal, Vedat (trans. E. Gürol). 1999. *Western Classical Music in the Ottoman Empire*. Istanbul: Istanbul Stock Exchange.

Lancashire, Terence. 2003. "World Music or Japanese—The Gagaku of Tôgi Hideki. *Popular Music* 22.1: 21–39.

Lee, Riley. 1992. *Yearning for the Bell: A Study of Transmission in the Shakuhachi Honkyoku Tradition* (unpublished doctoral dissertation). Sydney, Australia: University of Sydney.

Lichtenwanger, William. 1948. "The Military Music of the Ottoman Turks." *Bulletin of the American Musicological Society* 11/12/13: 55–57.

Lindorff, Joyce. 2004. "Missionaries, Keyboards and Musical Exchange in the Ming and Qing Courts." *Early Music* 32.3: 403, 405–414.

Ling, Amy. 1974. "The Pagoda Image in Henry James's The Golden Bowl." *American Literature* 46.3: 383–388.

Mendonça, Maria. 2011. "Gamelan Performance Outside Indonesia 'Setting Sail': Babar Layar and Notions of 'Bimusicality'." *Asian Music* 42.2: 56–87.

Miller, Terry. 1984. "Reconstructing Siamese Musical History from Historical Sources: 1548–1932." *Asian Music* 15.2: 32–42.

Miller, Terry, and Michael Church. 2015. "Chinese Opera." In Church, Michael (ed.), *The Other Classical Musics*, Woodbridge, Suffolk: Boydell and Brewer, 127–137.

Mueller, Richard. 1986. "Javanese Influence on Debussy's "Fantaisie" and Beyond." *19-Century Music* 10.2: 157–186.

Noor Al-Deen, Hana. 2005. "The Evolution of Rai Music." *Journal of Black Studies* 35.5: 597–611.

Parker, Sylvia 2008. "Béla Bartók's Arab Music Research and Composition." *Studia Musicologica* 49.3/4: 407–458.

Parker, Sylvia. 2012. "Claude Debussy's Gamelan." *College Music Symposium* 52. Accessed 9-2-2017 at https://symposium.music.org/index.php?option=com_k2&view=item&id=22: claude-debussys-gamelan&Itemid=124.

Pasler, Jann. 2004. "The Utility of Musical Instruments in the Racial and Colonial Agendas of Late Nineteenth-Century France." *Journal of the Royal Musical Association* 129.1: 24–76.

Pasler, Jann. 2006. "Theorizing Race in Nineteenth-Century France: Music as Emblem of Identity." *The Musical Quarterly* 89.4: 459–504.

Picard, François. 2001. "Music (17th and 18th centuries)." In Standaert, Nicolas (ed.), *The Handbook of Oriental Studies, Christianity in China* (vol. 1), Leiden: Brill, 851–860.

Pinney, Christopher. 2002. "Creole Europe: The Reflection of a Reflection." *Journal of New Zealand Literature* 20:1 25–161.

Roberts, J. M. 2004. *The New Penguin History of the World* (4th ed.). New York: Penguin.

Robinson, Paul. 1993. "Is 'Aida' an Orientalist Opera?" *Cambridge Opera Journal* 5.2: 133–140.

Ross, Alex. 2007. *The Rest Is Noise: Listening to the Twentieth Century*. New York: Picador.

Said, Edward. 1994. *Culture and Imperialism*. New York: Vintage (Random House).

Savage, Patrick and Steven Brown. 2013. "Toward a New Comparative Musicology." *Analytical Approaches to World Music* 2.2: 148–197.

Schofield (Brown), Katherine. 2010. "Reviving the Golden Age Again: "Classicization," Hindustani Music, and the Mughals." *Ethnomusicology* 54.3: 484–517.

Schramm, Harold. 1969. "Musical Theatre in India." *Asian Music* 1.1: 31–40.

Seeger, Anthony 1986. "The Role of Sound Archives in Ethnomusicology Today." *Ethnomusicology* 30.2: 261–276.

Sorrell, Neil. 2015. "Java." In Church, Michael (ed.), *The Other Classical Musics*, Woodbridge, Suffolk: Boydell and Brewer, 51–73.

Suchoff, Benjamin. 1987. "Ethnomusicological Roots of Béla Bartók's Musical Language." *The World of Music* 29.1:43–65.

Takahashi, Minoru. 2001. "A Portuguese Clavichord in Sixteenth-Century Japan?" *The Galpin Society Journal* 54: 116–123.

Taylor, Alan. 2001. *American Colonies: The Settling of North America*. New York: Penguin Books.

Taylor, Timothy. 2007. *Beyond Exoticism: Western Music and the World*. Durham, North Carolina: Duke University Press.

Tenzer, Michael. 2000. *Gamelan Gong Kebyar: The Art of Twentieth-Century Balinese Music*. Chicago: University of Chicago Press.

van Aalst, J.A. 1884. *Chinese Music*. Shanghai: The Statistical Department of the Inspectorate General of Customs.

van der Veur, Paul. 1968. "Cultural Aspects of the Eurasian Community in Indonesian Colonial Society." *Indonesia* 6: 38–53.

Wah, Lam Ching. 2005. "A Highlight of French Jesuit Scholarship in China: Jean-Joseph-Marie Amiot's Writings on Chinese Music." *CHIME (Journal of the European Foundation for Chinese Music Research)* 16/17: 127–147.

Wetmore, Kevin., Jr. 2016. "Jesuit Theater and Drama." *Oxford Handbooks Online*. Accessed 9-14-2017 at http://www.oxfordhandbooks.com/view/10.1093/oxfordhb/9780199935420.001.0001/oxfordhb-9780199935420-e-55.

Woodfield, Ian. 1994. "The 'Hindostannie Air': English Attempts to Understand Indian Music in the Late Eighteenth Century." *Journal of the Royal Musical Association* 119.2: 189–211.

Part III

The Global Web and continuous transformation, since c. 1920 CE

8 The full flowering and influence of the American musical convergence

Jazz is a good barometer of freedom.
—Duke Ellington, c. 1957 (quoted in Ward and Burns 2000:vii)

Mis canciones son de la re-revolución. (My songs are from the re-revolution.)
—from the song "Americano" (2011), as sung by Lady Gaga (Stefani Germanotta, b. 1986)

Indie Rock Embraces an African Invasion.
—*New York Times* newspaper headline (January 30, 2011:AR16)

America, you great unfinished symphony, you sent for me; You let me make a difference; A place where even orphan immigrants can leave their fingerprints and rise up.
—Lin-Manuel Miranda ("The World Was Wide Enough," from the hit Broadway musical *Hamilton*, 2015)

The increasing globalization of the human musical story, both artistically and commercially, began to be seen more clearly due to the nature of the acceleration in tandem with technological advances as the twentieth century unfolded, and, in so being seen, was embraced or resisted more intentionally. Musical developments in the Americas and especially in the United States led—or at the very least fully energized—that process, not only through the direct exportation of American musics but also in the way these musics inspired other musicians across Afro-Eurasia. This chapter examines how key musical elements, genres, and certain sociological factors unfolded through the twentieth century in that context. The technological advancements that facilitated the spread and sustenance of these factors will be taken up in Chapter 9.

The birth of the most globally influential popular musics in the United States—those that had the strongest effects both across the Americas and back across both oceans—can be conveniently traced geographically, though in overlapping paths, from New Orleans, up the Mississippi River, through Mississippi and Memphis, Tennessee, to St. Louis and eventually Chicago. By the 1920s New York city had emerged as the cultural capital of the United States,[1] and so it too served as a major developmental center. Latin American musics became a fundamental part of the expanded continuing convergence and synthesis as well. Since the details of these individual musics and their development have been thoroughly documented elsewhere, this study need not replicate that work;[2] rather, general reference will be made to aspects and figures that illuminate how they became situated in the broader global music history outlined herein.

It would be convenient to say that America's main musical contribution to the story was in the form of black music that subsequently took the rest of the world by storm. That is certainly true at one level, but it is too narrow a vision for the global music history outlined in this study. In fact, American music must be seen as predisposed—perhaps like no other music prior to it, for reasons that will be explored—to consist of, to generate, and to inspire ever-new syntheses of syntheses. In his masterful *History of Jazz*, Ted Gioia points out that "much is lost" by a refusal to acknowledge that

> the modern age is marked by the tendency for distinct styles to coalesce and cross-fertilize. In music, purity is a myth…The historian who hopes to come to grips with *the powerful currents of creativity in modern times* must learn to deal with these composite art forms on their own terms or not at all.
>
> (2011:84–85, emphasis added)

The evidence suggests that much—perhaps even most—of the power of American music has come from its transcultural synergies. Those that "draw an implicit delineation between popular music, jazz and classical composition" are missing something critical, says Gioia (2011:84). This makes figures who dared to cross genres and cultures—rather than embracing and propagating the Western Romantic myth that achievement within narrow stylistic boundaries is better than achievement by synthesis—far more historically important than has sometimes been acknowledged. And it was this spirit that the Americas, especially the United States, sent forth into the rest of the world throughout the heart of the twentieth century and beyond.

Three American musical streams

American Afro-European genres finally transcended their roots to become a powerful set of ever-newly-blossoming fusions. Their trajectories can be helpfully considered in the context of three overlapping sets of streams, just as North and South were overlapping streams in the earlier era of United States musical history. What follows next is an outline of these streams with brief reference to a few key figures; the section thereafter will consider further the lives and work of five pairs of American musicians embedded in these currents.

Blues, jazz, and rock

The first set of streams consists of the relationships between American blues, jazz, and rock musics, all of which had common roots but developed individually and in different mutually influential combinations. The Blues, the earliest and in many ways the bedrock of the synthesis in the United States, predating jazz but then developing in tandem with it, was largely considered the domain of blacks, whose personal experiences in the American South better matched the sentiments of the music. In addition to W.C. Handy, blues singers such as Gertrude "Ma" Rainey (1886–1939), Bessie Smith (1894–1937), and Lemon Henry "Blind Lemon" Jefferson (1897–1929),[3] along with later Chicago-style blues guitarists such as Muddy Waters (McKinley Morganfield, 1913–1983) expanded the genre into a commercial powerhouse in tandem with the developing music recording industry, with members of the black community clamoring to buy new "race records" marketed directly to them (Southern 1983:365ff.) and whites eventually embracing the genre as well. Henrietta Yurchenco sums it up well:

> The blues has been the signature American music, the basis of almost all of America's popular music, and the core ingredient of jazz, its more elaborate art form. It left its imprint on Tin Pan Alley, on 1960s white rock, and on the theater. Even Appalachian fiddling and vocal style became bluesy through constant contact between blacks and whites.
>
> (1995:450)

The breakthrough music that came to be called jazz first coalesced in New Orleans, spurred by innovations from Buddy Bolden and others. It was later exemplified by the work of musicians such as King Oliver and Louis Armstrong, both of whom had moved up the Mississippi River to Chicago by 1922. Armstrong would eventually branch out further to New York, becoming a widely celebrated American musical figure who transcended racial and national barriers (Southern 1983:373–6). The expansion of jazz into a broader American cultural context, from which it could be exported to the world, can be traced to gifted artists such as Ferdinand "Jelly Roll" Morton (1885–1941) and Fletcher Henderson (1897–1952), who composed and notated essential elements of the music so as to provide a growing repertoire of standard pieces upon which others could build or which they could imitate. The use of notation also allowed jazz ensembles to grow from the small New Orleans–style combos into complex "big bands"(Southern 1983:366, 376–80) that provided worked-out arrangements featuring a steady "swing" beat to which patrons could dance.

The next phase of jazz veered away from popular music that could be readily danced and sung, towards a far more complex instrumental style called bebop that continued in the direction of art music. Saxophonist Charlie "Bird" Parker (1920–1955) and trumpeter John Birks "Dizzy" Gillespie (1917–1993) are the best-known representatives of the genre, which features faster tempos; smaller ensembles; syncopated rhythms across the ensemble that travel very far from the beat and drive straight ahead rather than swinging along; longer and more extensively improvised solos accompanied only by the rhythm section (bass, drums, and piano or guitar); and more complex harmonies with melodies entwined among less stable chord and non-chord tones. "Cool" jazz (as opposed to the "hotness" that had come to define the energy of the music over several decades) essentially slowed down the speed of bop but kept the other ambiguities (tonal, harmonic, textural, rhythmic) more or less intact. The 1949 recording by Miles Davis and his ensemble of the cut *Boplicity* (bop simplicity?), which later appeared on his album *The Birth of the Cool*, likely says a lot about this development. On the other hand, "free" jazz moved even further away from tonal, rhythmic, and textural stability towards a kind of controlled chaos. None of these genres was music for mass appeal. Instead, they were understood as a reaction against the commercial focus of big band swing. Whether they were also an attempt by black musicians to assert independence from whites is less clear, as many bop and cool ensembles were racially mixed.

The addition of electric amplification to a combination of the blues, Gospel, the Southern United States folk music (largely white) called "country," and elements of jazz in the late 1940s and into the 1950s by musicians such as guitarists Chuck Berry (b. 1926) and Bo Diddley (Ellas McDaniel, born Ellas Otha Bates, 1928–2008), and pianist "Little" Richard (Richard Wayne Penniman, b. 1932), resulted in new genres with names like "rhythm & blues" and "electric blues." These coalesced around the name "rock 'n' roll" and eventually simply "rock" in many later forms. Early white musicians in this same arena included guitarist Bill Haley (1925–1981) and the man who became a cultural icon of rock in America and internationally, Elvis Presley (1935–1977).

Inspired by 1950s American jazz, blues, folk, and rock, a "British invasion" of bands flowed from the United Kingdom, beginning in earnest in 1960 with the formation of The Beatles, who first caused a sensation in the United States in 1963 and appeared on American prime-time television in 1964. A steady stream of influential groups followed over the subsequent decades, including The Rolling Stones, The Who, and The Police. British rock musicians also tended to be on the cutting edge of such stylistic trends as heavy metal (Led Zeppelin), jazz-rock fusion (Cream), art rock (Emerson, Lake, and Palmer; Pink Floyd), punk rock (The Sex Pistols), and new wave (Duran Duran). Perhaps because the United Kingdom had closer colonial ties to many global regions, it served both as an inter/transcultural musical incubator within its borders and as an accelerator of global pop trends.

From the 1960s on the pop music world was fully international, though American global musical influence through black musicians and their integrated styles remained significant. The global success of superstars such as Stevie Wonder (Stevland Hardaway Judkins, b. 1950) and Michael Jackson (1958–2009), who are as of this writing consistently cited among the top 10 commercial recording artists of all time, is notable.[4]

Latin American influences came to have a more prominent place in these hybrids as Hispanics became an increasingly larger minority in the United States (at about 18% as of this writing, eclipsing African-Americans at 13%). This movement starting gaining ground with Cuban music in the United States from the 1940s onward, culminating in Salsa styles, along with other popular genres such as Argentine Tango since the 1930s and Caribbean Reggae from the 1960s. Latin American music certainly developed further in its own right well into the twentieth century, yet it began to be integrated across the Americas much earlier, such as in New Orleans from the eighteenth century. With the emergence of jazz and rock, this integration accelerated rapidly and boundaries began to dissolve even more readily. Reflecting the special inter/transculturality of his native New Orleans, Jelly Roll Morton had for some time encouraged what he called the "Spanish tinge" in jazz, and the interest of Dizzy Gillespie in Afro-Cuban jazz beginning in the late 1930s was also noteworthy. While in the Cabell "Cab" Calloway orchestra, Gillespie was mentored by Cuban native Mario Bauzá, a key figure in bringing Latin elements to New York jazz. Bauzá also introduced Gillespie to Cuban conga drum player Chano Pozo, who appeared with Gillespie at Carnegie Hall in 1947 and deeply influenced his thinking (Gioia 2011:205). Bauzá's brother-in-law, Cuban-American singer "Machito" (Francisco Grillo), provided additional leadership to a number of black and white musicians in this direction. Other Latino/Latina musicians exemplifying the success of these pan-American trends in the United States include drummer Ernesto Antonio "Tito" Puente (1923–2000, Puerto Rican-American), a member of Bauzá's and Machito's band the Afro-Cubans before striking out as a major independent figure; rock musician Ritchie Valens (Richard Steven Valenzuela, 1941–1959, of Mexican-American descent), whose eight-month recording career produced the ever-popular "La Bamba"; rock guitarist Carlos Santana (b. 1947, Mexican-American); and singers Julio Iglesias (b. 1943, Spanish), Gloria Estefan (Gloria María Milagrosa Fajardo García, b. 1957, Cuban-American), and Selena Gomez (b. 1992, whose Texas-Mexican father named her after a Tejano singer).

Black and white

The second set of streams has to do with different ways that black and white American musicians were able to make their way culturally and commercially, as seen in the condensed stories of selected pairs of figures to follow. The distinctions of race have not disappeared in America, even in music, yet music has absorbed and transformed them in a way no other medium has yet, just as it has across cultures for millennia. For obvious reasons, this topic has been a most sensitive one, spawning a vast array of research and commentary. Indeed, it often forms the primary lens through which American musical history is viewed. Ever-present concerns with human social justice remain at the heart of the controversy. In this study, the notion has been advanced that music ultimately transcends these concerns and, on the whole, enhances the lives of all despite the less-than-ideal conditions in which it too often flourishes. But the deep commercial commodification of music since the twentieth century has tended to exacerbate inherent tensions. The real lives of the musicians to be highlighted in this chapter illuminate some of these issues.

The conventions, tensions, and confluences
of art music and commercial music

The third set of streams concerns the tensions and confluences of art music and commercial popular music, both of which were transformed by the American convergence and its implications. The concept of "transculturality" thus also took on more clearly than previously an additional meaning in the twentieth century: as straddling, bridging, or integrating not only musical nationality or ethnicity, but also musical subcultures within a broader culture. And especially, in this instance, successfully navigating both the continuing legacies of the European art music tradition and the new global possibilities of popular music. Alex Ross deftly demonstrates, for example, how few of the leading twentieth-century white European and American art music composers were left untouched by jazz and other African-American influences, and how many of the leading black popular musicians of the 1920s and 30s had aspirations to and abilities in art music (2007:130–170).

Because harmony around a tonal center remained a significant global legacy of the West into the twentieth century, it is important to note its continued development in these contexts. Western harmony had evolved around two general intervallic relationships: (1) movement of chord roots (function) by fifths and fourths (though this continued to evolve to include third-related roots and sometimes stepwise root movement as well); and (2) chord structures (quality) based on thirds. As Debussy and others intuited, the addition of pitches an interval of a 2nd, 6th, 7th, 11th, and 13th above the chord roots, as well as chromatic alterations of these and other chord tones, made twentieth-century harmony more reflective of the complexities of non-Western timbres and tuning. To this was eventually added the construction of chords in fourths, or quartal harmony. These developments constituted the sophisticated language of jazz harmony, which seems ultimately to have contributed to situating jazz in the realm of art music. Broze and Shanahan (2013) have demonstrated the evolution of jazz away from clear tonality, for example, making it parallel to what happened in at least one stream of Western art music. On the other hand, harmony in musics such as the blues and rock was often simplified functionally to the three chords that defined a tonal center: the I, IV, and V, sometimes with the addition of the respective "blue" notes from African tuning[5] to each to add expressive color. The functions of these chords were the same in minor modes, though the qualities were dramatically different, raising the level of perceived dissonance and potential emotional impact.

The power of the three "primary" chords was nothing new in of itself—they were the bedrock of European music from at the least the 1650s on—but in these new musics, the primary chords were often left unimpeded by other harmonies in the tonality, giving their use a kind of stark effect. Moreover, in the typical blues-rock progression, the expected cycle of chords (I-IV-V-I) was expressively thwarted to produce a more immediate emotional response. The V-IV-I sequence often found at the end of each cycle (as opposed to IV-V-I), for example, separated the series from a key element of its long-established tonal moorings:

I (1 bar) – IV (1 bar) – I (2 bars) | IV (2 bars) – I (2 bars) | V (1 bar) – IV (1 bar) – I (2 bars)

Later, the use of the vi chord—and, in minor modes, the VI and VII chords—was added regularly, in ways that raised or altered the harmonic (and emotional) tension even further. This phenomenon can be seen encapsulated in the main theme of the 1976 hit song "Turn the Beat Around," by Gerald and Peter Jackson for which the harmonic "hook" consists of i-VI-VII, VII-VI-i arranged in heavily syncopated rhythms and parallel root position streams that add to the stark, energetic quality.

As in jazz, the progression towards complexity continued (see, e.g., Capuzzo 2004), yet a vast array of pieces continued to draw on the power of "raw tonality" as expressed by the primary triads. Meanwhile, the other Western legacy, counterpoint around a tonal center, was absorbed into a more flexible continuum of textures that included ancient Afro-Asian-inspired heterophony.

Many composers in the esoteric/academic European art music stream during this period resisted inter/transcultural possibilities in favor of what they perhaps thought was Eurocentric high-mindedness. The tonally ambiguous chromaticism of the nineteenth century deliberately followed what was then seen as a logical path into chromaticism without any tonal center. A number of composers avoided what ultimately proved to be a dead end—in a way, atonality was eventually overcome by the global human awareness of organization around one or more central pitches as a musical universal—or managed to successfully integrate some of its elements into more broadly conceived styles. For example, Olivier Messiaen (1908–1992, French), following in the footsteps of Debussy and Stravinsky in his fascination with musics from many cultures, brilliantly fused Indian elements, especially in the area of rhythm, with a range of pitch approaches from other non-Western musics to complex post-tonal techniques, keenly aware of the jazz in which Paris was awash from the 1930s on, where he spent most of his life. As Ross insightfully puts it, Messiaen "presided over the transfiguration of tonality" (2007:496) while bringing a brilliant interpretation of birdsong to bear on the problems of sterility facing many streams of art music in his time.

But this inter/transcultural approach was more rare in Europe than in the Americas. In the United States, Leonard Bernstein (1918–1990) intentionally carried jazz-classical integration forward into the next generation, exemplified in his musical theater-opera piece *West Side Story* (1961), which demonstrated significant integration between Latin American, African-American, and contemporary classical styles, setting the stage for later American musical theater to continue those trends. A relatively short-lived but influential genre dubbed "minimalism"—with techniques discovered and developed primarily by the American composers La Mont Young (b. 1935), Terry Riley (b. 1935), Steve Reich (b. 1936), and Philip Glass (b. 1937), all nearly absolute contemporaries who were highly conversant in and energized by popular and art musics of many kinds and cultures—sought from the 1960s through the 1990s to capture the phenomenon of repetition that features prominently in many non-Western musics,[6] especially those of India and Africa. Reich expanded the minimalist concept into something more stylistically flexible in his music, and Glass even more so. Other composers such as Aaron Copland (American, 1900–1990, whose earlier works also draw on jazz), Darius Milhaud (1892–1974, French), Carlos Chavez

(1899–1978, Mexican), Heitor Villa-Lobos (1887–1959, Brazilian), and Alberto Ginastera (1916–1983, Argentine) integrated Latin American and European classical elements in their concert works, while John Cage (1912–1992, American) and Toru Takemitsu (1930–1996, Japanese) found ways to effectively blend complex East Asian and Western European elements. The latter two especially, it should be noted, abandoned tonality in doing so. Cage also explored extensively the elements of chance rather than control in music, creating a resultant level of perceptual complexity that can seem both "hyper-improvisatory" and difficult to distinguish from pieces meticulously organized at a granular level. Meanwhile, Lou Harrison's (1917–2003, American) *Song of Quetzalcoatl* (1941), *Threnody for Carlos Chávez* for Gamelan and Viola (1978), and *Concerto for Pipa with String Orchestra* (1997) demonstrate the extent to which all these globally integrative trends could be followed.

More recently, the stylistic globalization of art music has been exemplified by two of the world's most successful living art music composers. John Adams (b. 1947, American) represents a further evolution of minimalism into a bright, general energy of rhythm, timbre, and process that is nevertheless still inspired by repetition in various world musics, as well as a stark condensation of broad tonality. Tan Dun (b. 1957, Chinese-American) integrates traditional Asian musical elements with nearly every variety of Western music. The works of both transcend easy identification as "multicultural." Rather, they each bring global musical sensibilities to fresh, seamless twenty-first-century styles. Adams's opera *Nixon in China* (1987) and Tan's score to the international hit film *Crouching Tiger, Hidden Dragon* (2000, set in eighteenth-century China)—along with concert pieces like Tan's *Water Passion After St. Matthew* (2002) and Adams's *Gnarly Buttons* (1996)—exemplify their globally integrative gifts.

In some of the stories that follow, examples of the art-pop music convergence from the other direction can be gleaned. Either way, seeing all the critical developments of the twentieth and early twenty-first centuries as various dynamic responses to global musical interchange, transcending what are sometimes too-rigid categories, provides an extraordinarily coherent way of making sense of their wide disparities.

Five American musical pairs

The three streams outlined above can be seen operating to varying degrees among five pairs of prominent American musicians living and working through overlapping periods during the heart of the twentieth century. That one member of each pair is black and the other white (Asian-American in the final pairing) is a deliberate choice to demonstrate the level of musical transcendence that emerged across these decades. Though several of them embodied connections to art music traditions, the first four pairs of these figures have been understood to have operated largely in the realm of popular music. It has been in the realm of popular music that America has had the most direct global influence, and these figures are therefore appropriately representative of that influence. By the end of the twentieth century, however, it was becoming clear that the pop-art dividing lines were beginning to fade. The final pair of musicians below demonstrate even more the profoundly transcultural direction towards which America pointed the way in transcending these categories.

Armstrong and Beiderbecke

Louis Armstrong (1901–1971) and Leon Bismark "Bix" Beiderbecke (1903–1931) shared the trait of being among the group of jazz cornetists who broadened the scope of that instrument beyond its military (and even more limited classical) profile. But, whereas Armstrong grew up New Orleans, Beiderbecke hailed from America's rural white heartland: Iowa. It was through hearing gramophone recordings of the "Original Dixieland Band" out of Chicago—brought to the Beiderbecke household by his brother directly from World War I service, incidentally—that Bix was initiated into the art (Gioia 2011:68). In a fateful decision designed to redirect the younger Beiderbecke from his passionate interest in jazz, his parents enrolled him in 1921 in a private boarding school just outside of Chicago. Meanwhile, by 1914 Armstrong had dropped out school to begin making music on the streets and with a number of very fine ensembles in New Orleans. By 1923 he was in Chicago playing and recording with King Oliver's Creole Jazz Band. The following year—1924, the same year that the Paul Whiteman orchestra premiered George Gershwin's *Rhapsody in Blue*—Beiderbecke was making recordings with another Chicago group, the Wolverines. Beiderbecke was recruited to Whiteman's traveling orchestra in Indiana, which took him to New York. The stock market crash of 1929 brought an end to the hey-day of Beiderbecke's career (and that of many others). He died of pneumonia in 1931, likely exacerbated by alcoholism.

During this same period, the latter half of the 1920s, Armstrong's new bands the Hot Five and the Hot Seven made a series of immortal recordings in which his concept of jazz solo playing began to emerge, eclipsing the previous focus on ensemble interaction in New Orleans Dixieland style. In the midst of touring around the country and in Europe, Armstrong also made a transition to New York, where the majority of the rest of his long career was to be based. Armstrong and Beiderbecke certainly knew each other and moved in the same early jazz circles. Both were well-regarded, rising exemplars of the jazz soloist, though very different in their approaches, and well aware of these facts (see, e.g., Gioia 2011:70). Their stories demonstrate the close community of American jazz musicians, a world that early on allowed for racial transcendence despite the tensions that plagued the country in that regard (and still do), a world driven by both art and commerce. Armstrong became an American icon, an epitome of international success and influence. His appearance to over 10,000 fans in Ghana in 1956 on the eve of that country's independence from Britain is an example of this. Beiderbecke's full potential was cut short, yet he lives on in an extensive collection of period recordings, by which his contributions continue to be deeply appreciated.

Ellington and Goodman

Pianist, composer, and bandleader Duke Ellington (1899–1974) may represent the quintessential American musician to date by virtue of the combination of his original transcultural creativity across genres, commercial success, and popular and critical regard—and this in the wake of a Louis Armstrong. Yet it is also instructive to consider one of Ellington's contemporary white peers, the clarinetist and band leader Benny Goodman (1909–1986) in these same contexts. Both men straddled the pop-art music divide expertly throughout the heart of the twentieth century, well past the days in which their original realms of achievement were challenged by new forms and sounds. Ellington was born in Washington, DC, but established himself early in New York, becoming part of the Harlem Renaissance of the 1920s and 30s. Goodman hailed from another major jazz city, Chicago, but also moved to New York by the late 1920s (and played and recorded with, among others, Beiderbecke). Both were essential figures to the establishment and success of big band swing music, the most commercially successful manifestation of jazz in American history to date (Gioia 2011:135–136).

Ellington wrote what many consider to be masterpieces that transcend the jazz-art music distinction, from hit singles like "In a Sentimental Mood" (1935) and "Ko Ko" (1940) to works of symphonic proportions such as *Black, Brown and Beige* (1943) and the Sacred Concerts of the 1960s. Meanwhile, using the means gained from his commercial success, Goodman commissioned original works by the likes of Bartok, Copland, and Paul Hindemith (1895–1963, German; emigrated to the United States in 1940). But for most recording musicians, the 1930s and 40s were tough: during the Great Depression record sales in the United States declined more than 90% from over 100 million in 1927 to just six million in 1932 (Gioia 2011:127). A steady engagement at Harlem's Cotton Club from 1927–1931 both shielded Ellington from some of the effects of this Depression and provided a prestigious venue; Gioia notes that the Cotton Club was "Carnegie Hall for those who could not perform at Carnegie Hall" (2011:118), meaning especially for talented blacks not welcome in elite white society. Goodman, meanwhile, actually did perform at Carnegie in 1938. The Cotton Club also served alcohol during prohibition, attracting all sorts of characters including those in organized crime and politics—and thereby imparting to jazz an aura of enticing, forbidden danger. When the Volstead Act was repealed in 1933, this aura disappeared and business suffered: one could now drink in the comfort of one's own home, and by this time the radio waves were awash with jazz (Gioia 2011:127).

Both Goodman and Ellington joined in working regularly with the best of both black and white musicians to produce the finest musical product possible (Southern 1983:393). Among the key artists who connected these two figures was Fletcher Henderson (who had also employed Armstrong)—Ellington's main competitor in New York and Goodman's head arranger after his band was selected for NBC's radio show *Let's Dance* in 1935. Ellington also employed Puerto Rican trombonist and composer Juan Tizol from 1929 to 1944, from which collaboration came Latin American-inspired jazz hits just as *Caravan* (1936) and *Perdido* (1941), both substantially co-written by Tizol, and other pieces in the same genre such as *Conga Brava, Moonlight Fiesta*, and *Jubilesta*.

One interesting difference was the performance focus and level of achievement of each: Goodman rose to be a first-rate clarinetist, recording not only many jazz solos with multiple groups, but also works by Mozart and the original pieces he commissioned, while Ellington is considered to have been more talented as a composer and band leader than as a pianist (Crawford 2001:644). Musicians in the bands of each emerged as key figures in the bebop movement during the late 1930s and early 40s, including Ellington's bassist Jimmy Blanton and Goodman's guitarist Charlie Christian, but it was Goodman who tried briefly (and unsuccessfully) to make a transition to the new style. Among the notable experiments underwritten by Goodman during this stint was the original Latin jazz-influenced composition *Undercurrent Blues* by Arturo "Chico" O'Farrill (1921–2001, Cuban-American).

Davis and Getz

The next pair of musicians each accomplished significant stylistic transitions over their almost exactly contemporaneous lives and careers. Trumpeter Miles Davis (1926–1991) and tenor saxophonist Stan Getz (Stanley Gayetski, 1927–1991) both started at the end of the swing era but quickly turned to bebop and eventually to cool jazz before striking out in varying directions.

A fateful meeting occurred in 1944 in Davis's hometown of St. Louis when the 18-year-old Davis won an audition to play with the Billy Eckstine ensemble at the famous jazz club The Riviera—in which boppers Dizzy Gillespie and Charlie Parker were also playing. Later that year, Davis, who had a background as a classical trumpeter, enrolled at the Julliard School in New York (then known as the Institute of Musical Arts), but promptly set out after Parker, giving up his studies to be fully immersed in the New York jazz scene (Owsley 2006:86). Eventually, Davis took Gillespie's place in the Parker Quintet and later worked directly with Gillespie again. St. Louis, one of the early Mississippi River jazz towns, had also been the home of Scott Joplin from 1901 to 1903, before the composer moved to Chicago, and over the decades, The Riviera hosted an A-list of jazz greats including Louis Armstrong, Ella Fitzgerald, Cab Calloway, Stan Kenton, Art Tatum, Buddy Rich, Red Norvo, Dizzy Gillepsie, Lionel Hampton, Count Basie—and Stan Getz.

Getz, born in Philadelphia but relocated to New York as a child (where he also studied and played orchestral bassoon), performed with Goodman during the latter's foray into bop as well as proto-bopper Woodrow "Woody" Herman and a host of other name bands, leading to a noteworthy recording career as a soloist and ensemble leader. Getz and Davis played together in a landmark 1950 radio broadcast from New York. In 1953 Getz was part of a dually-eponymous sextet with Gillespie. Meanwhile, in the years just prior, Davis had finished out his time with Charlie Parker's ensemble and associated himself with talented arranger Gil Evans—during which "cool" was born in a series of recordings in

1949–50 (including *Boplicity*) that were not widely released until 1957 in the compilation *Birth of the Cool*. Getz never played in Davis's Nonet, but remained a prominent cool jazz figure nonetheless, joining a number of jazzers who brought the sound to California (Gioia 2011:260–262), where the musical ethos matched the more relaxed lifestyle. Davis's 1959 album *Kind of Blue*, exploring various tonal modalities, was certified in 2008 by the Recording Industry of America as quadruple platinum, indicating at least four million copies sold and making it the best-selling jazz album of all time as of this writing.

Davis and Getz headed in somewhat different directions beginning in the 1960s. For Getz the shift was to representing a growing Latin jazz genre called *bossa nova*, in collaboration with the Brazilian singer/songwriter/guitarist closely associated with the style, João Gilberto (b. 1931). Their 1964 album *Getz/Gilberto*, featuring Carlos (Tom) Jobin and his hit single "The Girl from Ipanema," won a Grammy and nearly ousted The Beatles from the top of the charts. Another piece on the album, "Desafinado," had been recorded by Gillespie in 1961 and vaulted Getz to fame in the genre with his 1962 recording just prior to *Getz/Gilberto*. Davis meanwhile pursued what came to be called the "fusion" of jazz and rock, exemplified by his album *Bitches Brew* in 1969–1970 that went on to sell four times the number a typical Davis album would at that time (Gioia 2011:326), winning a Grammy award in 1971. Along with Davis, musicians from the recording group including Joe Zawinul and Armando "Chick" Corea carried the genre forward independently for several decades, joined by earlier Davis group alumnus Herbie Hancock. Other popular rock bands, including Chicago and Blood Sweat and Tears, adapted the approach to great success. Getz briefly flirted with fusion, recording with Corea and others in the 1970s and 80s before returning to classic jazz, ending his career with a Grammy for best solo jazz performance in 1991.

The commercial and popular success of Davis and Getz is perhaps more analogous to that of Armstrong and Beiderbecke respectively, though the career of Getz was not cut short. Davis became an international superstar for many decades, while Getz had briefer flashes of recognition. Yet Getz deserves credit for helping to bring bossa nova to a wider audience, solidifying a key pan-American phenomenon that came to have significant and lasting global appeal.

Rock emerges: Berry and Presley

Richard Crawford insightfully notes that scholars were essentially compelled by the advent of advanced recording and broadcast technology and the concurrent rise of American popular musics to "[treat] performances as the equivalent of compositions" (2001:715); that is, the sound elements that distinguished one performance and performer from another were just as important as the melodies, harmonies, rhythms, and processes of the pieces themselves. This also clearly grew out of a strong emphasis on improvisation, which was further definitive in distinguishing one musician from another. Such an analysis is essential to understanding the shift of emphasis away from the nature of the music itself (though not entirely, of course) to its performance, for it meant that one recording of the same song could be significantly different from another, and thus in many ways a different piece of music. It also lessened the pressure for musical styles to be highly original from an objective compositional perspective. All of this was no more true for any of the new convergent American musics than for rock 'n' roll.

Crawford also rightly asserts that "no social fact about [post–World War II] American music is more noteworthy than the growing influence of teenagers in the musical marketplace" (2001:716). Rock music was for the most part, and certainly early on, consumed by American teens, though it quickly spread to other parts of the globe. The rise of light jazz crooners such as Harry Lillis "Bing" Crosby (1903–1977) and Frank Sinatra (1915–1998) presaged the rock icons of the 1950s and beyond—and the fact that they were white made them more acceptable to the parents of white teens. Yet Crosby and Sinatra still belonged to the parents' generation. "A key moment in American music history took place when teen-agers' hunger for a music they could call their own combined with the popular music business's hunger for profits" (Crawford 2001:722), at a time when jazz had veered towards complexity and lost its broad commercial appeal. Thus, for better or worse, although rock music first emerged from urban black contexts in the form of "rhythm and blues" and "electric blues," the rise of at least some white performers accelerated its shift into mainstream music in majority-white America. At the same time, for these teens, the sense of forbiddance inherent in black rock and its performers was an essential part of its appeal—in many ways like the con-fluence of jazz, alcohol, politics, and crime at the Cotton Club had been for New Yorkers two decades earlier. Thus, in fact, original black rockers had the opportu-nity to thrive as well. Moreover, like the blues, this was a music that at first flowed from the South and its blues roots to the North and its urban contexts.

One of the earliest black rock superstars, electric guitarist Chuck Berry (1926–2017), hailed from St. Louis and Chicago but had the imprimatur of noted Mississippi blues musician Muddy Waters, who had moved to Chicago in 1943 and bought his first electric guitar by 1944 (Palmer 1981:15). Berry did not meet Waters until 1955, but the conversation was to prove fateful—by later that year, Berry had his first breakout hit recording, "Maybellene." The single proved to have crossover appeal, climbing the Rhythm and Blues, Country, and Pop charts—which meant it was being bought and listened to by both blacks and whites. A year earlier, a white rock group called Bill Haley and His Comets, com-ing out of Country-Western Swing music, released the classic "Rock Around the Clock," which also topped the R&B and Pop charts and served as the theme song for the film version of *The Blackboard Jungle*. That same year, the black group the Chords recorded yet another early hit, "Sh-Boom," further proving that the new genre had wide appeal across racial lines. Yet there is evidence that it was white performers producing cover recordings (that is, unauthorized versions of hit songs in a time when copyright of varying recorded arrangements was not in force) that drove the economic growth in this arena (Southern 1983:504–506). Berry contin-ued with a string of hits in his style—including "Roll Over Beethoven" (1956), "Rock and Roll Music" (1957), and "Johnny B. Goode" (1958)—that defined the budding rock genre by its electrified guitar riffs and other grungy sound elements, un-swung driving beat, and lyrics that referred to forbidden teen topics such as sex, car racing, fashion, and other consumer style-oriented concerns.

In a humorous bit in his film *Back to the Future* (1985), director Robert Zemeckis captures the essence of a cultural moment by having a fictional Marvin Berry, cousin to Chuck, call Chuck up while guitarist-from-the-future Marty McFly is performing "Johnny B. Goode" at a high school dance in 1955, three years before the song was composed in the real world. The comedic implication is that Chuck Berry hears the "new sound" of his own future song and is thereafter inspired to write it. McFly goes well beyond Berry's style, into what sounds like the heavy metal rock of the 1960s and later. The white teen audience is not (yet) impressed, but "your kids are gonna love it," quips McFly (Canton and Zemeckis 1985).

Meanwhile, the white performer who would surpass all other early rock musicians in terms of success, Elvis Presley (1935–1977), burst onto the scene with even wider appeal, likely drawn in part from his use of black and white styles ranging from Pop to Country, Gospel, Blues, and R&B (Southern 1983:506). Born in Mississippi—important to his earliest musical experiences—but relocated to Memphis, Tennessee (on the Mississippi River), Presley listened to both black music on the radio and white Gospel quartet music in town. In light of the commercialization of music in America (and the globe) over the twentieth century, some have lamented the loss of the musically "numinous" or "spiritual" (see, e.g., Fletcher 2001:680–695). Yet strong Christian musical traditions emerged from America's transculturalities from the beginning (see Chapter 6) and continued through the twentieth century into the present.[7] Black Gospel music, for example, was exemplified by contributions of artists such as Thomas A. Dorsey (1899–1993) and Mahalia Jackson (1911–1972), but an earlier version of the style based on the same African-American roots was also used among white Christians to great effect by hymn writers such as Ira Sankey (1840–1908). This was the Southern Gospel-style milieu in which Elvis Presley was immersed in Memphis, while, via radio broadcasts, he also absorbed the classic Blues and R&B sounds of blacks such as guitarist B.B. King and heard a wide array of other musics, including the Metropolitan Opera from New York (Crawford 2001:728). In his own way, Presley thus benefited from and later retransmitted America's transcultural musical DNA. Sam Phillips, whose Sun Records studio produced Presley's first commercial recordings, intuited that Presley was able to capture the same energy and many stylistic traits of black performers, but tailored to a wider audience (Crawford 2001:731). Just or not at the onset, Eileen Southern notes that black pop musicians ultimately gained from markets and styles opened up by white trailblazers to majority demand (1983:504).

Berry's 1972 cover of the 1952 song "My Ding-a-Ling," by black New Orleans music leader Dave Bartholomew (b. 1918), proved to be one of his last hits, but he appeared on television and toured extensively, including a set of appearances in Europe in 2008. His last album was recorded in 2017. Southern suggests that while the Beatles produced their own highly influential rock style, The Rolling Stones "retained a kind of fidelity to black-music traditions" (1983:506). Indeed, the cover of Jack Hamilton's *Just around Midnight: Rock and Roll and the Racial Imagination* (2016) features The Stones's lead singer Mick Jagger in friendly conversation with none other than Chuck Berry in 1969, and Jagger paid public homage to Berry upon the latter's death in 2017. Berry's status as a rock icon was recognized by *Rolling Stone* magazine and the Rock and Roll Hall of Fame, and his "Johnny B. Goode" is the only rock song included on the Golden Record that was sent into space with the Voyager spacecrafts in 1977 (along with a single piece of jazz, "Melancholy Blues," by Louis Armstrong and his Hot Seven).

The rest of Presley's story is perhaps more well-known. Usually accorded status among the three to five top recording artists of all time (with the Beatles invariably at number one), Presley was also a hit on television and in the movies. As of this writing, *Rollingstone.com* reports that "he is believed to have sold more than one billion records worldwide, about 40 percent of those outside the U.S." (2017). Andy Bennett sums up the further implications of these facts:

> If mediated [television] images of Elvis and the Beatles [as rock 'n' roll icons] were instrumental in securing loyal and enthusiastic audiences for these artists, they also ensured the popularity of Elvis and the Beatles on a global scale…Similarly, the demand for rock 'n' roll music resulted in the appearance of 'home grown' rock 'n' roll artists in many different countries throughout the world.
>
> (2001:15)

Before delving further into this kind of global impact, however, a look at one final pair of relatively recent musical figures who have carried the transcendence of America's musical profile further in different ways is in order.

Ma and Marsalis

Wynton Marsalis (b. 1961, African-American) has in many respects come to exemplify the consolidation of America's transcultural musical identity, serving as a first-rate classical and jazz trumpeter, Pulitzer-prize winning composer, educator, author, critic, commentator, and global ambassador. In this, Marsalis's profile is entirely commensurate with that of the global musician with whose words this study began: cellist Yo-Yo Ma (b. 1955, Chinese-American). Both Ma and Marsalis were awarded the United States National Medal of Arts early in the twenty-first century at relatively young ages, signaling the extent to which America's elite understood their influence. Neither of these men is a pop superstar, yet they project the broader musical spirit of the New World across the globe in other ways. Ma especially has been an active and articulate proponent of understanding music and music history globally, both through his Silk Road project— reviving and resynthesizing transcultural traditional Old World Afro-Eurasian musics and new musics that they have inspired—and through his work as a musical ambassador in World Economic Forum meetings in Davos, Switzerland (for which he serves as a Trustee) and with the United States State Department, in countries such as Lithuania, Korea, Lebanon, Azerbaijan, and China. Born in Paris to Chinese parents but raised in New York, Ma regularly performs and records everything from Western European standard repertoire (a genre in which he has achieved the highest honors) and newly-composed works, to Brazilian and U.S. Appalachian music, in addition to the Silk Road project (the subject of the 2015 documentary *The Music of Strangers*).

Marsalis, born and raised in greater New Orleans and a fierce proponent of traditional jazz styles as opposed to fusion and beyond,[8] has, like Ma, been a classical superstar from at least the age of 14 (when he played Haydn's *Trumpet Concerto* with the New Orleans Philharmonic). But he also emerged as a prominent jazz figure from nearly the same age: while studying at the Julliard School, he began playing with top jazz figures in New York, and, at the age of 20, signed an unprecedented recording contract in both the classical and jazz areas with the CBS label (Gioia 2011:349). Marsalis subsequently won several Grammy Awards in both categories during the 1980s. In 1997 Marsalis broke another barrier by winning the Pulitzer Prize for his composition *Blood on the Fields*, which integrates a range of traditional African-American styles. As director of the jazz programs at Lincoln Center and the Julliard School, he is New York's leading jazz educator and advocate.

Like all celebrities since the 1950s, both Ma and Marsalis are media personalities. Yet they are representatives of a relatively small share of the musical world in the twenty-first century, advocates for a level of sophistication that is laudable and exceptionally important to music history but not currently determinative of global culture. Even the power of the media does not put them on a level playing field with the pop music personalities that garner the attention of millions upon millions across the world—but it does allow them a voice in the conversation. That conversation continues to focus on the various ways that music has impacted global culture: socially, politically, and economically, certainly, but also creatively.

Convergent impact

Musical forms, styles, practices, and instruments associated with the African Diaspora dominate the global landscape at the beginning of the twenty-first century. The global circulation of African Diasporic styles has a long history and complex dynamics. The circulation of rumba, tango, rock, blues, jazz, and various other forms of Western-hemisphere popular music has, among other things, returned techniques developed in the African diaspora to Africa—Martin Stokes (2004:66).

Most important to the subject of this study, therefore, are the ways in which the American convergences have been (re-)exported to and inspired the rest of the globe. One perspective has been that this phenomenon is yet another manifestation of cultural imperialism, largely driven by economic power. Certainly economics continues to play a central role in the globalization of music in the twentieth century and beyond, just as it has in every previous era (albeit when "the globe" was smaller in scope). To call this cultural imperialism, though, is a misnomer, for the globalization wrought by the American musical enterprise has actually opened the world to a wider variety of musical opportunities for many more of its citizens, both creatives and consumers—far more than the Silk Road, al-Andalus, or the European imperialism of the previous eras did—due primarily to the particular democratizations that technology has brought. In addition to the stunning evidence presented by economist Tyler Cowen (2002), demonstrating the advantages that musicians and other artists in developing countries are enjoying due to the "creative destruction" of art styles and the subsequent birth of new hybrids in a globalized milieu, Penny von Eschen deftly argues that "the production, circulation, and reception of American culture abroad cannot be reduced to a notion of "Americanization"" (2006:57), noting that Afro-Eurasian tours of popular musicians from the United States during the 1970s—ranging from Louis Armstrong to the rock band Blood, Sweat and Tears to the soul group The Jackson Five (featuring rising young pop superstar Michael Jackson)—resulted not in wholesale local imitation but rather in "processes through which genres, products, and corporations once viewed as quintessentially American [became] "global" and "transnational"" (60), and that this effect was in concert with the tendency of the American cultural message to promote a re-examination of both personal and political freedoms. Indeed,

> Not only did [visiting American] musicians bring their own agendas from promoting civil rights and challenging State Department priorities, but their desire to connect with musicians in other countries and learn new musical styles also promoted a globalization of popular music that destabilized the purported distinctiveness of national cultures promoted by governments.
>
> (2006:60)

This effect can be seen in tandem with what Nick Bromell and others have called the "cultural work" of the Blues and its offspring, early Rock: the creative tension between the European and African elements operating in the music—tonally, timbrally, intonationally, rhythmically, with regard to expectation and fulfillment (or lack thereof) in the combinations of repetition and improvisation—convey

> a condition of being free yet unfree, of being released into new possibilities of individuality yet more deeply tied to community identity than ever before, of feeling happy and feeling unspeakably low, of transcendence and immobility, of connection and isolation, of being both inside and outside, of possessing a dynamic and powerful sense of self while at the same time experiencing a construction of others.
>
> (2000:200–201)

This was the condition, Bromell argues, that American blacks felt just after legal emancipation through the mid-to-late nineteenth century. It is this powerful cultural expression that is captured in blues and rock and translated to various new contexts, from white American youths' feelings of rebellion to the forces that led to the fall of apartheid in South Africa and the fall of the Berlin wall in the 1980s, and beyond. The fact that blues and rock—and, it should be added, their various derivatives and cousins such as Southern country music and, later, rap, hip hop, and beyond—were embraced by American whites and the rest of the globe should be seen as a testament to their power rather than as yet another reason to lodge protests about the negativities of "appropriation" and "exploitation."

Whether the "cultural work" of the Blues and rock are more often ennobling or destructive is beyond the scope of this study. Admittedly, jazz is generally a more complex, sophisticated, and subtle music than these, and therefore does its work in somewhat different ways. Gioia (2011:380–388) provides a substantial summary of how jazz has gone global, almost from its inception, most prominently in Europe, but also in India, Japan, and even (in more limited ways) in Africa. If jazz is indeed the representative original art music of the United States, then "America's classical music is now the common property of the whole world" (381). The complexities of jazz (and rock) in Latin America are also highly relevant, hearkening back to the general American synthesis. Rodriguez notes, for example, that over the first half of the twentieth century, "early contacts of Cuban musical genres—particularly the *son*—with American jazz left marked effects on Cuban genres and jazz, and on the popular music of the United States" (2008:111–112). Averill and Wilcken comment that "after the popularity of North American jazz in urban Haiti in the 1930s, jazz bands began to arrange *merigues*, leading in the 1940s to "the genre *mereng-vo-dou* or *vodou-jazz*...[in which] the instrumentation resembles that of Cuban big bands with the addition of Vodou drums, but the melodic contours, rhythms, and texts come from Vodou and peasant dances" (2008:136–137). Romero explicates how in the Peruvian Andes a new genre emerged called *chicha* combines *cumbia* (with brass-dominated ensembles "called jazz bands by the people of Cusco") and traditional *huayno*: "*Chicha* style and the instrumental makeup of its musical groups reflect the influence that since the early 1960s international Latin American popular styles and American and British rock have had on young Andean migrants" (2008:455).

The following excerpt from Gioia's final words in his *History of Jazz* is profoundly telling:

> The genealogies of the players themselves will almost certainly be less crucial to the history of jazz than the intermingling of the panglobal sounds they have inherited...With the passing years, *jazz has become more an attitude than a static body of practices, more an openness to the possible* than a slavish devotion to the time honored, and no single city or country or region can contain its omnivorous appetite. Looking back at the first century of jazz's history, its most identifiable trademark may simply be this unwillingness to sit still, this mandate to absorb other sounds and influences, this destiny as a music of flux and fusion.
>
> (2011:388, emphasis added)

The idea that jazz is an attitude links it to the ethos of America, emphasizing that American musics are, essentially, musics of revolution, or at least of evolution. They are musics of freedom and growth rather than musics of stagnancy and limitation. Fred Wei-han Ho emphasizes this same point by suggesting that "jazz" is merely a shorthand for African-American music in toto (1995:284). Further along the spectrum, American musics can be seen as representative of outright rebellion, as in the youth culture that gave rise to rock in the 1950s. This ethos has been just as true of Latin America as of the United States, perhaps most clearly embodied in *nueva cancion* ("new song"), a broad, pan-Latin American protest movement emerging first out of Chile in the 1970s—a rejection of "North American imperialism" that nevertheless reflects the overall American synthesis by integrating indigenous South American, African, and Spanish musical elements (Fletcher 2001:528). Musical groups formed from out of the movement in Peru (admittedly after becoming less politicized), for example, have risen to global commercial fame (Romero 2008:458–459).

Indeed, representation along the continuum from freedom to rebellion applies to all of America's original musics, but emerged as especially powerful in the pop genres.

> What matters…is that all countries' popular musics are shaped these days by international influences and institutions, by multinational capital and technology, by global pop norms and values. Even the most nationalistic sounds—carefully cultivated 'folk' songs, angry local dialect punk, preserved (for the tourist) traditional dance—are determined by a critique of international entertainment. No country in the world is unaffected by the way in which the twentieth-century mass media (the electronic means of musical production, reproduction and transmission) have created a universal pop aesthetic.
>
> (Frith 1989:2)

While it is true that "imported pop is a resource, a supply of new sounds and instruments and ideas which local musicians can use in their own ways to make sense of their own circumstances" (Frith 1989:4), the "universal pop aesthetic" nevertheless came (and generally continues to come) first directly from the Americas. Timothy Taylor also rightly affirms that this universal pop aesthetic flowing from America (and, he feels, the United Kingdom) to the rest of the world continues to thrive in an atmosphere of "syncretisms and hybridities" that promote endless global creativity (1997:ix). This orientation itself is part of what is inherited from the American convergence.

Andy Bennett has traced "how Anglo-American popular musics and their attendant, primarily [youth-oriented] styles have been appropriated, reworked and effectively 'localized' in non-Anglo-American contexts" (2001:2), especially from the 1960s onward. Ska and reggae, for example, which emerged from Jamaican musicians originally influenced by Rhythm and Blues (Bennett 2001:75), may be an ideal example of a pan-American global phenomenon: "Reggae is transmogrified American 'soul' music with an overlay of salvaged

African rhythms, and an undercurrent of pure Jamaican rebellion" (Hebdige 2003 [1976]:140). Among the cultures deeply affected by it has been that of Aboriginal youth in Australia (Bennett 2001:85–86). Meanwhile, "Afrocentric hip hop contests the popular western idea that, prior to its colonization, Africa was a barbaric land." At the same time it is not unlikely that hip hop and rap emerged from a multiethnic New York City environment that included blacks, whites, and Latinos (Bennett 2001:91–92). Marcyliena Morgan and Dionne Bennett note that

> It is nearly impossible to travel the world without encountering instances of hip-hop music and culture…The International Federation of the Phonographic Industry (iFPI) reported that hip-hop music represented half of the top-ten global digital songs in 2009. Hip-hop refers to the music, arts, media, and cultural movement and community developed by black and Latino youth in the mid-1970s on the East Coast of the United States.
>
> (2011:176)

The global manifestation of hip hop is complex: "Primary exponents of much western European rap are second generation immigrants from Africa, the West Indies, Turkey, Morocco and parts of Asia" (Bennett 2001:95), while hip hop plays out as a cultural phenomenon differently in Japan and Oceania, for example (100–101), as one would expect.

South Asian *bhangra*, originally a folk music from the Punjabi regions of Indian and Pakistan celebrating the sugar cane harvest and the new year cycle, came into contact with Western pop through the 1970s, 80s, and 90s and took on some of its key trappings, including electric/electronic instruments and a heavy rock beat (Bennett 2001:105–106), becoming "exactly what the new generation [of South Asians in Britain] wanted…[,]*as genuinely Indian as it was recognisably disco*" (Banerji and Baumann 1990:140, emphasis added). Bhangra continued to evolve into an array of styles such as "fusion"—not to be confused with jazz-rock fusion—integrating "house" and "techno" music, and "ragga"—an intentional pun on the Indian origins—incorporating rap and reggae, giving way later to "raggamuffin" and "bhangramuffin," with strong Jamaican undercurrents (Bennett 2001:108–109).

Pop music superstar personalities continue to reflect the synthetic processes pioneered by American music that have come to define global music overall, including the absorption of Asian influences as the twentieth century evolved into the twenty-first. Others, from Algerian Rai singer Khaled Hadj Ibrahim (b. 1960) to worldwide best-selling Japanese rock duo B'z (active since 1988) and Bollywood (Indian) music and film star Himesh Reshammiya (b. 1973), are derivative of, inspired by, or at least heavily influenced by pan-American originals. In many ways these results were spurred by the intercultural accelerations arising from the age of imperialism and exoticism, including such examples as The Beatles' studies with Indian Ravi Shankar in the 1960s[9] and the deliberate Japanese embrace of American jazz and pop throughout the twentieth century (see Yano and Shūhei 2008). The new transculturality has even been re-exported back to Africa. As evidence, consider the popular genre in Senegal known as *mbalax*, consisting of a

> combination of Cuban rhythms and *kora*-based traditional melodies sung in high pitched style. So influential was Cuban music in Senegal that only with independence from French colonial rule (in the 1970s) did local musicians begin to substitute traditional melodies and vernacular lyrics for Cuban covers sung in Spanish.
>
> (Impey 2000:119)

Richard Shain neatly sums up this phenomenon as "Roots in Reverse: *Cubanismo* in Twentieth-Century Senegalese Music" (2002), noting that Senegalese music negotiates African and Caribbean elements such that the two styles "do not silence one another; instead, they reinforce and complement one another." Among other things, this demonstrates that "hybridity in Africa does not always entail a clash between either the West or the Islamic world and local African cultures" (2002:101).

Songül Karahasanoğlu and Gabriel Skoog document yet another set of syntheses in Turkish popular music late in the twentieth century, summarizing thus:

> The 1990s, marked in particular by the opening of radio and television air ways to private companies, saw a rise in a general cosmopolitanism among Turkish musicians and consumers…Cosmopolitan culture does not negate the local, nor is it a counter to it, because while it might have a historical place of origin, its global ubiquity frees it from any exclusive claims to ownership, allowing it to be integrated into multiple contexts. These objects, ideas, and cultural positions, in being integrated into local contexts, are colored by particular histories and circumstances. Turkey, and in particular Istanbul, is not immune to the influencing tides of cosmopolitanism. New local and international print, radio, and television outlets expose many urban Turks to a wide range of popular music and other artistic media, and this cosmopolitanism fuels acts of affiliation such as the performance of Heavy Metal (and all its substyles), Hip-Hop, and Jazz.
>
> (2009:62)

The authors go on to describe Turkish popular music as now incorporating everything from traditional makam to elements of Caribbean ska (2009:68). They generally frame its development in a political-historical context in which "music is a complex cluster of connotative and denotative meanings" by which Turks "continue to negotiate and synthesize their sense of local identity in relationship to globalizing pressures" (70).

All of these situations have resulted in something new, which may be the most fundamental way of seeing the musical legacy of the New World convergence: it is an optimism about the future and its creative possibilities as human expressions of musical universals are resynthesized and recombined across space, time, and cultural lines. Looking back from this moment, it is increasingly clear that such has been the case for global music history all along—it is only the opportunity to see it, understand it, and embrace it that has changed.

Spotlight: The emergence of a global transcultural singing style[10]

Much of the discussion in this chapter has focused on instrumental genres. Yet transcultural elements could just as clearly be heard in the transformation of singing styles into and through the twentieth century. Henry Pleasants (1973) provides a brief history of the development of European singing style from the rise of Western opera around 1600 CE, generally labeled *bel canto* ("beautiful singing"), and its relationship to jazz and pop singing, suggesting that the textual and ornamental clarity of these later styles actually reflects the ideals articulated in eighteenth-century singing commentaries better than the practice of opera established in the nineteenth century does—and further that the dominance of singing in twentieth-century popular music more closely approximates the status of singers in the earlier era as well. Over her nearly 60-year professional career, the exemplary jazz singer Ella Fitzgerald (1917–1996) stood out as able to retain these ideals of clarity while bringing African tuning and ornamental elements to bear at the same time.

The two natural registers of the voice most relevant to singing across cultures (Bozeman 2013:20–31; Miller 2008:49–58) are the "hoot" (sometimes called "whoop"), typically used for celebration, and the "yell," typically used for urgent, loud communication such as sounding an alarm. Yodeling, also found in different forms across cultures, is the rapid alternation of the hoot and the yell. In other traditional singing parlance, hoot and yell correspond roughly to "head voice," or "falsetto," and "chest voice" respectively. Because of the relationship between the vocal formant and harmonic partials in the vibration of the vocal folds, the pitch extent of the yell is typically half the frequency of the highest hoot formant. As a result, carrying the chest (yell) voice up into ranges more natural to head/falsetto (hoot) voice creates certain timbral, tuning, and physical tension issues, all of which affect the sound. These acoustic principles operate significantly differently in various singing styles. European bel canto takes advantage, for example, of natural resonance while focused on adjustments that smooth out transitions between registers for dynamic control and refined hybridity of timbre. Other styles often value timbral elements that do not so align, such as staying in the upper portion of the chest register for a more visceral sound across ranges.

Grant Olwage (2004) has discussed the clash of timbral and other stylistic elements between the "refined" choral style of English singing and what at the time was characterized as the "harsh," "loud," "rough," "nasal" sounds of African singing (also, incidentally, associated with the white lower classes in England itself and heard in the poor rural regions of the United States, such as Appalachia) in the late nineteenth and early twentieth centuries, at the height of British colonialism. Olwage notes that black South African choirs adopted something of a hybrid approach in order to sing European literature while retaining aspects of an authentic "black" voice. Thus the socialized conflict between "civilized" and "primitive" singing was quite palpable early in the twentieth century, even in the United States—though the particular American transcultural context seems to have modified the trajectory such that the issue evolved differently from other intercultural milieus. Americans largely rejected, for example, the Native American singing sounds they encountered during colonization and further westward expansion, whereas black vocal sound slowly worked its way into the American musical psyche over centuries.

Indeed, black-influenced singing style was very popular for many decades preceding and continuing into the twentieth century in America, as has been shown. Nevertheless, the bel canto ideal was retained from its European origins in American art music singing. The story of the development of a transcultural pop singing style thus parallels the rise of American pop music and its global influence, for the singing style was essential to the nature of the music. Something of a hybrid developed for the purposes of American musical theater, which has proven to be another original and powerful genre, due in part to the element of drama and stagecraft (as in film). Certain aspects of bel canto are retained, while a wide range of more flexible techniques are allowed in musical theater singing, including and especially the pushing up of the chest voice into higher registers and the delay of vibrato on held notes. Indeed, variety in the use of vibrato is a key distinguishing factor across time, space, and culture, as in, for example, its varying widths and speeds in Indian *gamaka*; less vibrato also often clarifies pitch in complex tuning contexts.

The coming of the microphone as an amplifying device allowed singers to focus more on subtleties of tone and phrasing since they could now be heard well without having to rely so much on the carrying power of the high range—a particular concern of professional opera singers due to the demands of their repertoire. The amplification and projection of the voice have been of considerable interest for some time: ancient Greek theaters and the masks that performers wore in them were effectively designed for this purpose (see Montgomery 1959). Later, the reformers who imagined the birth of seventeenth-century European opera were keen to reproduce these qualities in the nature of the singing style.[11] The designs of medieval European cathedrals too caused speaking and singing voices to be amplified and projected in various ways, with long reverberations that carried the sound (albeit delayed) some distance across the structure to listeners. Carole Pegg relates from her research in Mongolia how overtone singing is valued for its carrying power in the context of the natural mountain environment (1992:35–39). Meanwhile, the especially distinctive singing styles in Chinese and Japanese opera demonstrate further how language can affect technique. In the development of European classical singing into and beyond the nineteenth century, the "beautiful sound" is expected to take precedence over textural clarity when necessary (though these elements need not necessarily be mutually exclusive). But the microphone as a recording device also demanded the attention of all singers to certain details that might not always be captured in purely acoustic performance spaces, and thus affected singing style and technique even more broadly.

Intriguingly, as the twentieth and twenty-first centuries unfolded, the notion of the "crossover" singer—jazz, art music, musical theater, pop—also coalesced, and some singers came to benefit from the flexibilities it required. Soprano Kristin Chenoweth (b. 1968) and voice performance artist Bobby McFerrin (b. 1950), both American, are only two of the best examples of such singers. Chenoweth, for whom the extremely vocally diverse and demanding role of Glinda in Steven Sondheim's musical theater piece *Wicked* (2003) was written, was trained as a classical coloratura and sings light opera fare in addition to musical theater and ballad pop numbers in her concerts. Chenoweth regularly performs with symphony orchestras and has been one of only a few artists to stage a solo concert at the Metropolitan Opera (broadcast live in 2007). Meanwhile, McFerrin's incredible versatility and creativity across nearly every genre have been on display since the early 1980s. Singing solo *a cappella* (with multiple parts overdubbed in recordings), or in collaboration with jazz and classical partners (including both Marsalis and Ma), McFerrin demonstrates the artistic and the commercial value of transcultural musical ability coupled with strategic use of media technology in the twenty-first century. His reggae-inspired "Don't Worry, Be Happy" also hit the top of the pop charts, winning Grammy awards for Song and Record of the year in 1989.

The world of new art music has not been immune from this trend. The singing in John Cage's vocal work *Aria* (most often performed simultaneously with the electronic piece *Fontana Mix*, both from 1958), requires mixing a vast array of transcultural vocal styles and languages—classical, jazz, pop, and non-Western—which American mezzo-soprano Cathy Berberian (1925–1983) brought to fruition in her 1961 recording of the work, one of many such projects showcasing her versatility. In an article on singing a work by contemporary Japanese composer Koji Nakano, Canadian soprano Stacey Fraser examines the various Japanese traditional musical sounds and gestures that come to play for the singer, summing up the opportunities and challenges for the performer:

> As a singer who has been trained in the *bel canto* tradition, I have invested many years to establish a reliable technique that not only corresponds to the aesthetic expected in Western opera and concert music, but also allows me to maintain healthy vocal cords. Although I am a performer of standard repertoire, I have an interest in music that goes beyond the traditional techniques of the Western art-music tradition. I have become interested in music that integrates these different aesthetics because of my attraction to the unconventional use of vocal timbre to produce emotional and dramatic effects. This means that I must find a way to interpret extended techniques in a way that is not harmful to my voice. I believe that with a firm technical foundation, one can explore these expressive vocal timbres.
>
> (2010:357)

This comment goes to the heart of the tension for singers in a transcultural age, and not every performer concludes that such an approach is desirable or even possible. Nevertheless, the many examples of highly versatile singers over the last century suggest the possibility of success. Australian voice pedagogue Irene Bartlett has, for example, outlined some of the techniques used in negotiating popular (she terms it "commercial") singing in its particular environments, suggesting from her own professional performing experience as well that it can be done in a sustainable way (2014). Most of the singing styles of cultures outside of Western European bel canto preceded it by centuries, and even within living memory performers such as the traditional Indian singer M.S. Subbulakshmi (1916–2004) have had long careers without loss of technique. Differences in aesthetic, however, must be expected and accepted. With the advent of amplification and recording technology, the voice can be supported and enhanced far more readily than in the past. Meanwhile, the Afro-Arab singing style now at the center of global pop, as detailed by Peter van der Merwe (e.g., 1989:12–13, 30, etc.) and supported heavily by technology, may in fact be the resurrection of a sensibility that permeated the Silk Road and had influence on the earliest stages of Western music (see Chapter 4). If that is the case, we are merely in a later stage of an era that has been underway for some time, and bel canto is simply an additional color being added to the transcultural vocal milieu. Hooting and yelling may thus be seen as another set of qualified musical universals, natural vocal registers that are nevertheless manifested differently in different cultural contexts.

Notes

1 Donald L. Miller (2014) provides a compelling narrative case for this transformation.
2 See Southern (1982:355–554), Crawford (2001:557–851), van der Merwe (1989), Palmer (1981, on the Blues), Fletcher (2001:580–595), Bennett (2001, on rock and its derivatives), along with the numerous journal articles referenced in this work; for jazz particularly, Gioia (2011) is superlative, while for Euro-American art music in the twentieth century Alex Ross's socio-integrative approach (2007) is inspiring.
3 That Jefferson was a Texas bluesman rather than from Mississippi is a distinction Palmer (1981) rightly makes, along with contrasts between Blues coming from Memphis and Kansas City, in various combinations of urban (Northern) and rural (Southern) styles. Certainly urban, electrified Blues gave more direct rise to rock 'n' roll.
4 For a fascinating take on the process by which black American rock music was integrated into (or appropriated by) white culture, see Hamilton 2016.
5 See van der Merwe (1989:118–134), who also notes that Arabic music influenced the Africans who brought these sensibilities to the New World. Interestingly, Kubik (2005) has suggested that blues/jazz harmony can even be seen in an indigenous African tuning context that relies on neither Europe nor the Arab world for its definitive features.
6 Michael Tenzer (2006:22–35) helpfully discusses the notion of musical repetition in terms of "periodicity," a mathematical concept that brings questions of exposition, repetition, variation, and contrast into new light.
7 Though music for religious purposes across the globe has tended to retain traditional, conservative styles, folk and rock idioms have increasingly influenced Christian music in the West, and this trend has been exported by missionaries to the rest of the world. A smaller counter-trend to this, known as ethnodoxology, has valued and embraced indigenous musics for non-indigenous religious purposes. Even in these contexts, though, new fusions are tending to arise.
8 Ever the advocate, in 2011 Marsalis enticed rock guitarist Eric Clapton to team up with him for a straight jazz-blues concert and album titled *Wynton Marsalis & Eric Clapton Play the Blues*.

9   Reck (1985) provides details of this phenomenon, and effectively situates it in the wider sweep of the present study.
10   I am deeply grateful to Kelley Hijleh for the insights into voice acoustics at the heart of this section.
11   Montgomery also points out that this vision informed the design of Richard Wagner's Festspielhaus at Bayreuth, Germany late in the nineteenth century (1959:245).

References

Averill, Gage, and Lois Wilcken. 2008. "Haiti." In Olsen, Dale, and Daniel Sheehy (eds.), *The Garland Handbook of Latin American Music* (2nd ed.), New York: Routledge, 126–142.

Banerji, Sabita, and Gerd Baumann. 1990. "Bhangra 1984–8: Fusion and Professionalization in a Genre of South Asian Dance Music." In Oliver, Paul (ed.), *Black Music in Britain: Essays in the Afro-Asian Contributions to Popular Music*, Birmingham: Open University Press, 137–152.

Bartlett, Irene 2014. "Reflections on Contemporary Commercial Singing: An Insider's Perspective." *Voice and Speech Review* 8.1: 27–35.

Bennett, Andy. 2001. *Cultures of Popular Music*. Philadelphia: Open University Press.

Bozeman, Kenneth. 2013. *Practical Vocal Acoustics*. Hillsdale, New York: Pendragon Press.

Bromell, Nick. 2000. ""The Blues and the Veil": The Cultural Work of Musical Form in Blues and '60s Rock." *American Music* 18.2: 193–221.

Broze, Yuri, and Daniel Shanahan. 2013. "Diachronic Changes in Jazz Harmony: A Cognitive Perspective." *Music Perception* 31.1: 32–45.

Canton, Niel (Producer), and Robert Zemeckis (Director). 1985. *Back to the Future* [Motion Picture]. United States: Universal Pictures.

Capuzzo, Guy. 2004. "Neo-Riemannian Theory and the Analysis of Pop-Rock Music." *Music Theory Spectrum* 26.2: 177–199.

Cowen, Tyler. 2002. *Creative Destruction: How Globalization Is Changing the World's Cultures*. Princeton, New Jersey: Princeton University Press.

Crawford, Richard. 2001. *America's Musical Life: A History*. New York: W.W. Norton.

Fletcher, Peter. 2001. *World Musics in Context*. New York: Oxford University Press.

Fraser, Stacey. 2010. "Confluences of Vocal Techniques in Koji Nakano's "Time Song II: Howling Through Time."" *College Music Symposium* 49/50: 356–362.

Frith, Simon. 1989. "Introduction." In Frith, Simon (ed.), *World Music, Politics and Social Change: Papers from the International Association for the Study of Popular Music*, Manchester: Manchester University Press, 1–6.

Gioia, Ted. 2011. *The History of Jazz* (2nd ed.). New York: Oxford University Press.

Hamilton, Jack. 2016. *Just Around Midnight: Rock and Roll and the Racial Imagination*. Cambridge, Massachusetts: Harvard University Press.

Hebdige, Dick. 2003 [1976]. "Reggae, Rastas and Rudies." In Hall, Stuart, and Tony Jefferson (eds.), *Resistance through Rituals: Youth Subcultures in Post-War Britain*, London: Routledge, 135–153.

Ho, Fred Wei-han.. 1995. "What Makes "Jazz" the Revolutionary Music of the Twentieth Century, and Will It Be Revolutionary for the Twenty-First Century?" *African American Review* 29.2: 283–290.

Impey, Angela. 2000. "Popular Music in Africa." In Stone, Ruth (ed.), *The Garland Handbook of African Music*, New York: Garland, 113–135.

Karahasanoğlu, Songül, and Gabriel Skoog. 2009. "Synthesizing Identity: Gestures of Filiation and Affiliation in Turkish Popular Music." *Asian Music* 40.2: 52–71.

Miller, Donald G. 2008. *Resonance in Singing*. Princeton, New Jersey: Inside View Press.

Miller, Donald L. 2014. *Supreme City: How Jazz Age Manhattan Gave Birth to Modern America*. New York: Simon and Schuster.

Montgomery, Henry. 1959. "Amplification and High Fidelity in the Greek Theater." *The Classical Journal* 54.6: 242–245.

Morgan, Marcyliena, and Dionne Bennett. 2011. "Hip-Hop & the Global Imprint of a Black Cultural Form." *Daedalus* 140.2: 176–196.

Olwage, Grant. 2004. "The Class and Colour of Tone: An Essay on the Social History of Vocal Timbre." *Ethnomusicology Forum* 13.2: 203–226.

Owsley, Dennis. 2006. *City of Gabriels: The History of Jazz in St. Louis, 1895-1973*. St. Louis, Missouri: Reedy Press.

Palmer, Robert. 1981. *Deep Blues*. New York: Penguin.

Pegg, Carole. 1992. "Mongolian Conceptualizations of Overtone Singing (xöömii)." *British Journal of Ethnomusicology* 1: 31–54.

Pleasants, Henry. 1973. "Bel Canto in Jazz and Pop Singing." *Music Educators Journal* 59.9: 54–59.

Reck, David. 1985. "Beatles Orientalis: Influences from Asia in a Popular Song Tradition." *Asian Music* 16.1: 83–149.

Rodriguez, Olavo. 2008. "Cuba." In Olsen, Dale, and Daniel Sheehy (eds.), *The Garland Handbook of Latin American Music* (2nd ed.), New York: Routledge, 105–125.

Shain, Richard. 2002. "Roots in Reverse: Cubanismo in Twentieth-Century Senegalese Music." *The International Journal of African Historical Studies* 35.1: 83–101.

Southern. Eileen. 1983. *The Music of Black Americans* (2nd ed.). New York: W.W. Norton.

Romero, Raul. 2008. "Peru." In Olsen, Dale, and Daniel Sheehy (eds.), *The Garland Handbook of Latin American Music* (2nd ed.), New York: Routledge, 438–462.

Ross, Alex. 2007. *The Rest is Noise: Listening to the Twentieth Century*. New York: Picador.

Stokes, Martin. 2004. "Music and the Global Order." *Annual Review of Anthropology* 33: 47–72.

Taylor, Timothy. 1997. *Global Pop: World Music, World Markets*. New York: Routledge.

Tenzer, Michael. 2006. "Introduction: Analysis, Categorization, and Theory of Musics of the World." In Tenzer, Michael (ed.), *Analytical Studies in World Music*, New York: Oxford University Press, 3–38.

van der Merwe, Peter. 1989. *Origins of the Popular Style: The Antecedents of Twentieth-Century Popular Music*. New York: Oxford University Press.

von Eschen, Penny. 2006. "Globalizing Popular Culture in the "American Century" and Beyond." *OAH Magazine of History* 20.4: 56–63.

Ward, Geoffrey, and Ken Burns. 2000. *Jazz: A History of America's Music*. New York: Knopf.

Yano, Christine, and Hosokawa Shūhei. 2008. "Popular Music in Modern Japan." In Tokita, Alison, and David Hughes (eds.), *The Ashgate Research Companion to Japanese Music*, Aldershot: Ashgate, 345–362.

Yurchenco, Henrietta. 1995. ""Blues Fallin' Down Like Hail": Recorded Blues, 1920s–1940s." *American Music* 13.4: 448–469.

9 Technology, convergence, and the age of instantaneous exchange

The fact that, since the 1950s, the habitat of musical experience was a techno-logically defined one can and indeed must be traced to a specifically humanistic context... The problems of musical technology concern the more general notion that the experience of art is as a measure of the freedom of invention and expression.
—Agostino Di Scipio (2000:262–263)

Music makes the world go 'round.
—Ubiquitous unattributed saying

Between c. 1850 and 1900, transatlantic cabling and the use of Morse code initi-ated acceleration of communication that radio, sound recording technology, the telephone, film, increasing air travel, and television augmented worldwide into the mid-twentieth century. The advent and widespread consumption of musical recordings from around 1900, followed by regular musical broadcasts on commer-cial radio starting around 1920, and ever-faster and cheaper broadcast technology through the twentieth and into the twenty-first century, gave rise to global musical interchange at exponentially greater levels. Music became a globally mediated commodity at a level not previously reached. New technologies assumed the role that the Silk Road, the Andalusian phenomenon, and the special economic/impe-rial nature of the New World held in earlier eras. A number of commentators, including Fletcher (2001) and Taylor (2007), have viewed this state of affairs negatively, suggesting that the commodification of music has led to a stultifica-tion of creativity, in which diversity is stifled and the powerless are exploited. Yet, first analogue and then digital technologies made possible combinations of the creation, capture, manipulation, and broadcast/distribution of musical sound in ways limited only by human imagination and perception, in an increasingly democratized fashion. The same applied to moving images and their combina-tion with music. In particular, the synthesis of American musics that had been developing over the previous 300 years became the most popular and the most commercially successful, eventually catapulting African-influenced musics to the top of the global popularity scale. Asian-influenced musics also worked their way further into the worldwide psyche, especially through the entertainment media.

Expanded musical freedom: from print to analogue to digital

Stephen Pope helpfully identifies three degrees of freedom expanded by musical technologies over the last 50 years: sound creation and manipulation; higher-quality, lower-cost sound capture and editing; and immediate widespread distribution to listeners (1999:49). These apply both to creative artists and to consumers, though in different ways, and they can be traced as accelerations in various combinations.

Reebee Garofalo (1999) observes that the shift to a "music industry" as we understand it today—in which the music itself is a commodity rather than a service transmitted by performers—first stemmed from music notation and publishing. Even "throughout the early development of sound recording," Garofalo notes, "sheet music was the main vehicle for the mass dissemination of music and music publishers were at the center of the music business" because "the centerpiece of middle-class home entertainment was the piano" (1999:319). One could go back much further than this—for example, to the exclusive license granted to English composers Thomas Tallis (c. 1505–1585) and William Byrd (c. 1540–1623) by Queen Elizabeth I for printing and publishing polyphonic music from 1575–1596—but it is reasonable to conclude that perhaps not until after the Industrial Revolution in the West (c. 1750–1850) did the commodification of the musical product as notation on paper begin in earnest. Britain, for example, did not enact an international copyright law for music until 1842, which the Berne Convention expanded to multiple nations starting in 1886; this protection applied, for example, to international publishing of lucrative American popular music such as the songs of Stephen Foster (Garofalo 1999:321). Importantly, "artists or countries with musical traditions based on rhythm rather than melody or those that valued improvisation over notation were excluded from the full benefit of copyright protection right from the start"(323), though this would not last long into the twentieth century due to the shift from notation to recording as the main way to capture and distribute music. Since consumers no longer had to own a musical instrument or acquire the skill to play it in order to have music at home, and as the price of the necessary playback technology fell—the radio was especially attractive as a "music machine," funded by on-air advertising—the recording industry broadened its customer base considerably: "It appeared as though the market for recorded music was virtually unlimited. Gross revenues in the United States hit an all-time high of $106 million in 1921, with comparable growth being reported elsewhere in the industrialized world" (Garofalo 1999:328). As the 1950s dawned, radio and recording companies formed a partnership in which physical recordings were advertised by virtue of their "free" play on the radio. Into this milieu, rock 'n' roll was born.

Palm-sized cassette tapes—introduced in 1963 along with the machines to record and play them back that gradually shrunk in size and cost—provided unprecedented and comprehensive portability, becoming by far the most ubiquitous personal electronic musical technology internationally by the 1980s and creating a significantly democratized musical ecosystem (Garofalo 1999:341).

These advantages kept cassettes in a dominant position globally well after digital audio in the form of the compact disk—with far superior sound quality—was introduced: for one thing, only professionals could create CDs at first, and the production price was high. Still, audio recorded on the metal-oxide tape inside a cassette eventually wore away as it was played over and over, whereas a digital recording—consisting of information rather than electro-magnetic waves captured as particle patterns on a surface—was far less prone to such degradation. But the next set of confluences in digital music technology removed some of the most significant economic barriers to experiencing musics across time, space, and culture: the rise in the 1990s of ubiquitous personal computers; the compression codec MPEG (Moving Picture Experts Group) audio layer 3 (known as MP3) needed to create and isolate manageable musical file sizes from commercial recordings; the Internet and the World Wide Web; the invention of very small and relatively inexpensive MP3 playing devices to which headphones could be connected (eventually absorbed into the capabilities of smartphones); and the advent of digital music file sharing and purchasing services such as Napster (1999) and iTunes (2003). As Garafalo points out (1999:350), MP3 is an open format that cannot effectively be regulated, providing an even greater level of democratization in the music "industry," and the rise of the "prosumer" (see below).

Music now exists as relatively tiny chunks of information over which nearly anyone can exercise an enormous amount of control if they possess the right tools. As a result, Richard Povall has astutely noted that electronically mediated art and music is "trapped within its own means of presentation" (1997:19), from which it follows that the limitations of digital transmission and reproduction itself—Internet bandwidth, the frequency range of speakers or headphones, consequences of audio compression, etc.—can be just as consequential to the experience of music as the limitations of live performance. It is as subject as any other medium to Marshall McLuhan's oft-quoted 1964 observation that "the medium is the message." Yet it is also obvious that the level of access and manipulative power inherent in digital media—its ability to be both personalized and creatively explored at an unprecedented level of convenience—is widely perceived as definitively trumping its limitations. These dynamics in turn continue to have a profound effect on the nature of musical art, from conception to consumption.

Inter/transcultural mediamorphosis

Late in the twentieth century, media sociologist Kurt Blaukopf coined the term "mediamorphosis" to describe the "electronic mutation of music" (1994:340) or what happens to music and musical contexts when the traditional means of conveyance—live performance and notation—are marginalized or effectively eliminated for music consumers, noting further that this mediamorphosis "tends to intensify intercultural exchange" (341) because it recontextualizes a wider variety of musics in ways more consistent with non-notated (oral) traditions. Blaukopf gives as examples both traditional Javanese and Indian music, which use non-12-EDO tuning/timbre systems and therefore would suffer should Western notational constraints be imposed: electric/electronic sound and visual contexts effectively allow such musics to exist in comparable spheres with Western classical music in the mediated world. Indeed, Blaukopf notes that the advent of film had an even more profound impact on globalized music, implying that this stems from the capture of visual aspects essential to the music that would be lost in sound-only recordings (339).

Technology not only repositioned music as a super-commodity, but also affected its stylistic development—with commodification and style often becoming mutually affective. The typical three-minute length of popular songs and even many early jazz pieces was, for example, partly a result of the amount of time available on one side of the popular 10-inch version of a 78-rpm record early in the twentieth century, which was replicated later by the ubiquitous 45-rpm single with the same three minutes on a smaller disc. But length was only one element so affected by recording technology; indeed, the processing of every aspect of musical audio has become an essential element in defining particular genres over the last several decades. Albin Zak III (2005) has, for example, noted how capturing various ways in which technology is used to create the sonic and timbral space of any given instance of a rock song recording—including reverberation and echo as sonic effects that take on aesthetic meaning—would be essential to creating an "edition" of any particular piece, since each recording would mediate the music in specific ways and create something new.[1]

Agostino Di Scipio insightfully refers to "the emancipation of timbre" (2000:254) as one crucial result of twentieth-century music technology, further implying that the concept applies to both art musics and popular musics since all these involve recording technology whether or not electronics are used in the initial sound production (as in, for example, synthesis). This aspect is but one among many that can be grouped under the category of musical "reality" vs. "ideality," the latter of which is expanded greatly by the use of technology to mitigate human limitations on display in sound creation and live performance. Yet a quest to have the creative options available live as much as in recordings has not abated, and technology has become an increasingly important part of performance as audiences expect the same hyper-reality face to face as they do when listening or watching in more personal contexts. One apt example is the absolutely controlled sound mixing of live and often pre-recorded human and computer-generated sound in pop performances.

New aesthetic philosophies and sociologies have always to some degree arisen from new music technologies and the stylistic possibilities they offer, but electronic techniques have broadened and accelerated the conceptual possibilities precipitously. John White (1997) has demonstrated how radio "formats," meaning styles marketed to specific listener demographics for commercial purposes, can be conducive to stylistic transformations of the same piece of music, citing the case of the 1965 hit song "Downtown," the distinctive 1960s easy rock style of which was modified for a different format audience—Country and Adult Contemporary, with echoes of Disco—in 1984. The commercial nature of the radio advertising medium drove this stylistic transformation, and White suggests that the overall stylistic familiarity to the target demographic was far more important than any artistic diminishment that may have resulted (1997:11). A variation on this same philosophy can be seen in the short-lived but highly popular rendition of portions of the first movement of Beethoven's *Symphony #5* as the disco tune "A Fifth of Beethoven" by Walter Murphy and the Big Apple Band in 1976, attempting with some success to wed the stylistic and traditional familiarity of two musical genres in a way dependent on the control afforded by synthesizer and recording technology.

One especially clear example is the use of sampling as an artistic technique. Sampling means taking a digital recording of a small bit of sound or music and mixing it into another musical context, usually utilizing the additional powers of digital technology to alter one or more aspects of the original: changing the pitch level or speed or some timbral quality, for example. Timothy Taylor (2007:146–160), discussing the development of South Asian *bhangra* as a global pop style, utilizes the term "bhangra remix" (with reference to "Hindi remix") precisely to emphasize its key feature of electronically sampled sounds from films and other sources. Andrew Bartlett has explored the audio sample as a socio-artistic device in hip hop music, noting that the inherent notion of borrowing heard sounds from the environment, musical and non-musical, was a part of African-American musical sensibility—seen in Duke Ellington's music, for example, though without the digital technology of sampling involved—and that the concept of varying the musically familiar in performance can be connected with West African drumming and subsequent African-American musics (1994:640ff.). Thinking about "samples" a different way, Bartlett explains that "the turntable places the record at the center of the hip hop performance, turning the notion of musical virtuosity on its head by using pre-recorded material not only as rhythm but also as melody and harmony" (647). Furthermore, sampling itself "is a high-tech and highly selective archiving"(647) of cultural material in various states of representation and dialogue. Perhaps another way of saying this is that sampling creates a kind of transcultural music history as sound bits are archived in constantly changing contexts—and, in that spirit, hip hop sampling in the 1980s started largely with snippets from jazz as a way of recovering a lost African-American musical legacy (Perchard 2011:285, e.g.). Jazz recordings had not disappeared—or else much of the sampling would have been impossible—yet the technological form of archiving as straight recordings was not sufficient to maintain a vital connection with a key part of jazz's constituency; a new, creatively innovative form of technologically enabled archiving was needed. On the other hand,

> It's easy to see why hip hop producers in their early twenties and even late teens at the turn of the 1990s, those born at the moment of jazz's apparent demise, were construed as acting with acute historical consciousness: not because of their closeness to jazz source materials, but precisely because of their distance from them.
>
> (Perchard 2011:286)

That is, the new technology also gave musical artists the creative distance necessary to feel liberated in that particularly complex historical moment. Richard Perchard arrives at a revealing conclusion:

> The depth of its historical grounding, the brilliance of its experimental methods, and the liveliness of its insider debate meant that hip hop was a musical culture far more alive to the benefits, demands, and impositions of memory and history than simply atavistic or simply pragmatic theorizations could describe.
>
> (2011:300)

It was music technology that allowed for that moment. Sampling may represent a profound phenomenon, indeed: the opportunity for a kind of creative, preservative historicity in the midst of increasing transculturality. If so, it epitomizes the thesis of this book, for it means that music history itself can in fact be inherently transcultural and yet coherently meaningful.

Robert Fink's narrative of the early orchestral sample ORCH5 (a massive chord from Stravinsky's 1910 ballet *Firebird*) and its use in hip hop (2005) offers another especially fascinating example—in this case, black music c. 1982 appropriated a Western classical musical moment and transmogrified it with digital technology into something completely different, yet still a ghost of itself. The upshot of this is that digital technology greatly facilitates the use of disparate musical materials—which rely for meaning and effect on their immediate sonic qualities, not merely what is captured in notation—for transcultural artistic purposes.

Stylistic micro-mediamorphosis became (and remains) the order of the day. Using statistical analysis of some 17,000 examples of pop music produced between 1960 and 2010, in conjunction with the United States *Billboard Hot 100* during the same period, Matthias Mauch and several colleagues (2015) have determined that "while musical evolution was ceaseless, there were periods of relative stasis punctuated by periods of rapid change," notably around 1963, 1984, and 1991, the latter representing the rise of rap, hip hop and related genres—which are among the most deeply technologically mediated and appear to have had the most profoundly evolutionary impact on style over the last 30–50 years. In this new milieu, genres and sub-genres continued to crop up and then combine at an increasing pace. As of this writing well over 100 subgenres each of rock and electronic pop music, and more than 45 sub-genres of hip hop alone, can be identified in the media with unique names, each micro-stylistically different in its combination of elements. In many cases, the distinctives have to do with the way various layers are arranged rhythmically and/or by perceived tempo. Dub (named for a type of heavily manipulated remix of existing tracks) grew out of reggae starting in the late 1960s, with exploration of the temporal relationship between the bass line and the percussion. As the 1980s unfolded, the idea of music created entirely by mixing as a new type of "performance," both live in real time and via recording, coalesced into House music, usually entirely instrumental (with vocal tracks of previous material removed). A similar technique with a different outcome in mind is used to create the many forms of Electronic Dance Music (with a steady, high-energy beat). By way of example, the blog of a band called The Maniac Agenda (Gonzalez n.d.) outlined several "New Music Genres You Need To Hear in 2016," including Air Pop which "combines elements of ambient, Trip-hop, Pop, and Psy Rock...[while] Big dirty hiphop [sic] breaks, 808s [drum machines] or live bass control the bottom usually with the vocals being calm, dark, soft, or mysterious," and Glitch Soulazz, "an amalgamation of glitch-hop or DJ-produced electronic music with traditional jazz or blues elements." Trip-hop, also known widely as "downtempo," grew out of later House styles with an electronic but non-dance-oriented focus, while Glitchhop features sounds from electronic sonic malfunctions; interestingly, computer music theorist Kim Cascone has called Glitch music "post-digital," due to its implicit embrace of the foibles of electronics (2000). In 2017 something called "future bass" emerged, which one commentator described this way: "future bass takes the ecstatic drops of dubstep or trap, but provides a warm bounce rather than a lumbering bruteness. Basslines are provided by harsh, detuned synths that buzz and purr instead of gulp and whomp" (Turner 2017). Dubstep itself, as the name suggests, was an evolution of Dub while Trap is a House subgenre featuring complex layers of synthesized percussion and sustained string-like patches. All these subgenres of the most influential breakthrough categories over the last 50 years (i.e., hip hop and rap) are almost entirely defined by electronic elements and contexts—which allows transcultural development at a level of granularity well beyond anything previously found in global music history.

A number of scholars (e.g., Martin 2002:164–176; Dibben 2006; Webb and Lynch 2010; Malawey 2001) have demonstrated interest in the expressive and sociological elements of the quirky but highly successful Icelandic singer/songwriter/performance artist known as Björk (Björk Guðmundsdóttir, b. 1965), whose music and career exist in a heavily electronically mitigated space between pop and art music, and who *Time* magazine called one of the 100 most influential people of 2015. Alex Ross (2007:590) suggests that some of Björk's work sounds more like art music than that of some composers intending to write art music. Indeed, electronic composition and production techniques are not found solely the realm of pop music: a number of electronic art music composers have been active since the 1940s, among them Halim El-Dabh (1921–2017, Egyptian), whose *The Expression of Zaar* (1944) and *Leiyla and the Poet* (1959) use multicultural materials and themes. El-Dabh moved to New York in 1950 and worked at the Columbia-Princeton Electronic Music Center, which was to become one of two main global centers for the genre. (The other was in Cologne, Germany). By about 1970, use of electronic sound synthesis was vibrant in both art music and pop music styles, especially in America. That year, New Yorker Charles Wuorinen (b. 1938) won the Pulitzer Prize for music composition with his all-electronic work *Time's Encomium* and Robert Moog's (1934–2005) Mini-Moog was released as the first relatively compact analogue synthesizer with an integrated keyboard. The Japanese company Korg followed with a similar format soon after, later becoming a leader in the field, and by 1975 Japan's Yamaha conglomerate had obtained the rights to John Chowning's new digital frequency modulation (FM) synthesis method (developed at Stanford University in California), releasing what was to become the iconic DX-7 keyboard in 1983.

Fabian Holt argues that popular musical genre goes beyond commercial concerns (a type of brand differentiation) into the historical and socio-political concerns of real human lives, making it "a fundamental structural force in musical life" that "has implications for how, where, and with whom people make and experience music" (2007:2). The Internet now allows human communities to be formed and reformed around nearly limitless numbers of musical genres and sub-genres instantaneously, without significant regard to time or space. This does not constitute the erasure of difference, but it does challenge the assumptions of those who claim that "their" musics are unique. There is a higher standard for what may be regarded as different in a world where micro-differences differentiate and re-differentiate very rapidly indeed.

Music, moving images, and interactivity

Beginning in about the 1940s, the full integration of music with moving images—what Miguel Mera and Anna Morcom have called "screened music"—became the dominant transcultural art form globally (2009:4). Mera and Morcom put it plainly:

> Global perspectives are fundamental to the very nature of screened music, whichever part of the world it is from. As mediated, and hence trans-contextual, and as actively or purposely de- and re-contextualised, screened music is inherently multi-contextual and cross-cultural…All music has a history involving change, syncretisation and some degree of migration (even if people are not aware of it). However, with screened music, these characteristics have many and, in some cases, potentially infinite new layers on top of a 'traditional' history, making screened music fundamentally different from non-screened performances and performance traditions.
>
> (2009:5, 6)

The American composer John Williams (b. 1932) represents perhaps the highest level of sustained achievement to date in transcending what were previously rigid categories of art music and entertainment music at a certain level of sophistication, through the multi-medium of film. Having written the scores for 20 of the 100 top-grossing films of all time worldwide (as of this writing and adjusted for inflation), far more than any other single composer, it is nearly certain that Williams's music has been heard by more people on the planet than any other living art music composer. As film music, it straddles the art and pop categories while making use of a global language drawn from Williams's extensive training as a Western classical and jazz musician and the array of transcultural styles and techniques discovered or developed in the late nineteenth through the twentieth centuries, in which he has been steeped. The contexts of many films also require Williams to evoke exoticisms from around the world, such as in *Seven Years in Tibet*, *Indiana Jones and the Temple of Doom* (India), *Memoires of a Geisha* and *Empire of the Sun* (Japan), *Raiders of the Lost Ark* (Middle East), and *Schindler's List* (Jewish traditional music). Mera and Morcom, citing a number of other scholars, are deeply concerned with what could be viewed as musical stereotyping of cultures in such contexts (2009:7–9), but the artistry and sensitivity with which Williams approaches the task transcend the most urgent of those concerns. This is likely one reason his music is so globally popular: there are in fact qualified human musical and dramatic universals that can appeal without extensive cultural translation to a very wide range of the world's people.

The wedding of music with film in India as a popular genre offers another highly relevant example of transcultural momentum. Films for Hindi speakers developed into the sub-genre eventually called "Bollywood," while films for Southern Indian Tamil speakers developed their own conventions, yet music was highly transcultural from the beginning in both of these contexts. Stephen Hughes notes that early Tamil cinema, with sound capability dating from 1931, was so focused on music that two-thirds of each film often consisted of songs—50, 60, and even 100 of them in a single production (2007:3). The ancient relationship between Indian drama and music (going back to the *Natyasastra*) was naturally extended to the expanded capabilities of film, but the conventions of sound recording and the gramophone shaped the way song was integrated into Tamil film (2007:4–5ff.). Hughes also notes that "in south India, the stage music of the early twentieth century was a locally adapted mix of Karnatic music, Hindustani *ragas*, Parsi drama music, and Maharastrian *bhavgeet* influences that combined to create a cosmopolitan, uncomplicated, and accessible music" (7)—that is, a genre ripe for inter/transcultural recontextualization in the midst of a British colonial setting (see Chapter 7). The dominance of music in early Tamil sound films was seen as bridging some of the language/cultural gaps that remained obvious even within native India itself, let alone in a broader global context (Hughes 2007:13). In that sense, both music and visual images likely helped to broaden the cultural appeal of films in India's cosmopolitan milieu, transcending specificities into a more universal human realm of existence. And "one of the ways in which gramophone records influenced musicians and the music-listening public in India was by bringing a new open-mindedness to the mixing of Eastern and Western music" (27). This then spilled over into Tamil films, which were at first heightened versions of the same Indian musical dramas that constituted the content of sound-only recordings.

Meanwhile, Hindi films developed in different directions. By the 1970s both the term "Bollywood" and the conventions it represented as a commercial art form were established, and Hindi film songs have become a highly recognizable global phenomenon ever since (Morcom 2016:1). Designed to appeal to a very broad audience, Bollywood films feature several songs, each of which interrupts the narrative for what is usually a production-number tour de force, complete with elaborate group dances, in many ways like American musical theater. Like Tamil cinema, Hindi films were at first essentially filmed versions of Indian musical dramas (Morcom 2016:3), and, also like their Tamil counterparts, it is nearly certain that they took some of the American musical theater elements noted from the first Hollywood sound films that were shown in India as the 1930s commenced (Hughes 2007:11). Thus, again, the transculturality of the medium was established early, at least in terms of musical style:

> Since the 1930s, [Indian] film songs have been characterized by musical hybridity and a thirst for the new and the modern. Unlike most traditional genres, there were no restrictions on experimentation and the use of foreign genres in film music. Rather, a modern style was appropriate to the new Western and technological medium of films. By the mid-1940s film songs had begun to display an exotic and eclectic array of styles, with songs being written in a jazz style, as waltzes, or in the style of other Western and also Latin American popular genres. This reflection of global musical fashions has continued in [Indian] film songs up through the present day.
>
> (Morcom 2016:4)

It seems clear that in the film genre that most approximates the global reach of Hollywood, inter/transcultural sensibilities have been embraced and facilitated, and that this is understood to be in keeping with the technological advancement inherent in the medium. The Indian composer A.R. Rahman (born A.S. Dileep Kumar, 1967) has been particularly successful at operating in both the various Indian and U.S./global cinematic arenas by effectively integrating musics from his native culture as well as Western film music styles and traditional and popular idioms from around the world—taking his cues, so to speak, from composers such as John Williams, though perhaps even more so due to his being of the next generation. It is perhaps not surprising that early in his career Rahman founded Panchathan Record Inn/AM Studios, advanced recording and production facilities that continue to incorporate the newest technologies. The *New York Times* put it this way on the eve of Rahman's first Academy Award for the score to the film *Slumdog Millionaire*: "One of the first major composers in India to embrace digital technology, [Rahman] is in his natural habitat at the computer," while in the same breath quoting ethnomusicologist David Novak: "He shifted things from a simple East-West mode to a multicultural, global mode" (Sisario 2009).

"Screened music" encompasses a far wider range of products, including television and video/computer games. But it is the element of interactivity in screened contexts that has most recently come to the fore. At first this was a kind of limited interactivity, coded into video games and DVD-ROMs, for example, where the user could direct the flow of information or move to some extent in one of many desired directions. The more recent ability to stream real-time audio and video to multiple users in both directions simultaneously eliminated the geographical constraints and reinvigorated not only musical performance, but the live interactions conducive to an oral-aural musical culture rather than one defined by notation or even by fixed audio recording. The American art music composer Eric Whitacre (b. 1970) demonstrated this further evolution when he created a virtual choir in 2009: each member sang asynchronously to Whitacre's recorded conducting of his work *Lux Aurumque* and uploaded their individual performances (audio and video), which were then edited together for the final recording posted on the Internet. Whitacre followed up in 2013 with a live virtual choir from across the globe that joined a live choir on stage at the Technology, Entertainment, and Design (TED) annual meeting that year, all mixed visually and audibly for a live audience. The video elements of that event are highly creative, not merely functional, reflecting the restoration of full audio-visual reconvergence in live performance, now technologically enhanced. But Whitacre's example is merely a sophisticated art-music version of a phenomenon that has arisen in the form of web services such as eJAMMING AUDiiO and JamKazam, which allow users to collaborate musically in real time. These services are aimed primarily at jazz and pop musicians, but the technology is stylistically neutral since users can provide any kind of musical input, including through a microphone.

Another result of the full integration of advanced audio-visual technologies with the arts has been the rise of the "producer" as an artistic partner. One especially versatile and creative figure in this regard has been the American musician Quincy Jones (b. 1933), whose career has encompassed everything from playing trumpet with some of the major jazz figures cited, to milestones as a songwriter and film/television music composer, to serving as producer for international pop superstars such as Michael Jackson. In the age of instantaneous exchange, however, such roles have evolved further into the idea of "prosumption," the production and consumption of music by the same persons or partners. Don Tapscott and Anthony Williams have explored the history and implications of this concept for music, noting new Internet platforms "where music fans take over the A&R functions of major labels," and "where amateur community members remix one another's artistic works into powerful new combinations," among many other scenarios. In summary, many more "musicians choose mass collaboration" in our time (2012:227, 231).

Another broad term being used as of this writing is the "sharing economy," which most famously applies to finding places to stay outside of traditional hotels when traveling and getting a local ride without using a traditional taxi service: homeowners and renters are making their rooms available and car owners/drivers are providing local transport through web-enabled sites and services, disrupting traditional business models. The same phenomenon applies to music prosumption, where the distinction between artists, producers, and consumers is considerably blurred, both creatively and economically. Wendell Hanna and Kevin Kelly (2013) discuss the return to oral-aural musical contexts due to technology, while Evan Tobias (2013) outlines musical activities in an active "participatory cultural" (as opposed to a passive "consumer culture"). Both of these studies indirectly (and correctly) make the point that prosumption is actually a collaborative music learning context. Such a context fits well in a global musical culture in which styles and products are in constant evolutionary interaction.

Two case studies: music and technology in Japan and Indonesia

Two contemporary Asian contexts help to illuminate how some of these elements can play out in different milieus. Emmanuelle Loubet has chronicled the recent rise of different categories of technologically enabled Japanese musicians, for example:

> The 1990s witnessed an explosion in the number of Japanese "digital per-formers" coming from virtually nowhere—or, more accurately, born directly from digital technology and hardware. Most of them had no musical back-ground. They were graphic designers, programmers, rock musicians, or sim-ply fans of 1970s progressive rock or 1980s alternative rock...This was a generation not particularly interested in music, but one that enjoyed editing digital files that contain sounds (among other things). For them, the music of diverse cultures and historical periods are all situated on the same ahis-torical plane, a flat space that simply crosses the year 2000...Japanese musi-cians have at their disposal an infinite array of samples waiting only for the inspired mix to give them local commercial value.
>
> (Loubet 2000:19)

Moreover, "Japanese artists...have little chance of success without first export-ing their art to foreign lands. Then, their art can be re-imported to Japan with the aura of a foreign product" (Loubet 2000:20). That is, for better or for worse—and in what can be seen as a fascinating twist—without something of a transcultural imprimatur, music in this context is not considered to be authentic.

Interestingly, Loubet identifies the karaoke industry—creating the informa-tion for popular song accompaniments in the form of Musical Instrument Digital Interface (MIDI) data that play back through sound-producing synthesizers in real time as opposed to being any form of an audio recording—and music for computer games—such as those of global gaming giants Nintendo and Sega—as the two leading professional contexts for "computer music" (outside of the regular digital audio recording industry) in Japanese culture in the year 2000. Use of com-puters for sound production in new popular music comes in at third place, while those seeking to focus on less commercially focused projects tend to aim them at foreign markets (2000:26).

The philosophy of creativity in contemporary Japanese techno-contexts takes a decidedly non-Western direction:

> Japan is witnessing the emergence of a new concept of the "artist." Neither the work nor the artist are born of an expressive will or from the articulation of an original thought. Originality is a handicap to the social processes envi-sioned in the musical activity...The sonic result emerges from the global pro-cess, and the artist emerges from the basin of community action—through the reiteration of the performative act. It is a...non-directional, non-intentional culture...[that maintains] a state of perpetual action in which a marketable product finally emerges.
>
> (Loubet 2000:21–22)

This actually represents a departure from some of the tenets of musical Westernization that Japan embraced in the wake of the Meiji period of cultural openness (1868–1912).[2] In that light something like the intentional re-emergence of ancient Japanese *gagaku* in the decidedly globally pop-influenced music of Tôgi Hideki (b. 1959)—complete with all the tech trappings one would expect, and relying on recording techniques to effectively blend ancient and modern—takes on a new level of inter/transcultural significance. Moreover, which element is now seen as the Other is not entirely clear, as Hideki has a deep background in both musical worlds (Lancashire 2000).

Meanwhile, discussing popular music in Indonesia since 1998, Bart Barendregt and Wim van Zanten (2002) focus on the relationship between audio-visual technology and fusion of at least three cultural streams: Islamic popular music (and the complexities inherent in that genre as the religious context is navigated); Indie (independent) artists and labels; and incorporation of traditional Indonesian elements along with more globalized styles from jazz and rock to rap and house. Two older Indonesian popular styles, *kroncong* and *dangdut*, also figure into this mix. Kroncong has a particularly long history, originating from sixteenth-century Portuguese settlers and evolving into something of a sentimentalized ballad-type form featuring vocal/choral elements and European harmonies and instruments combined with Indonesian versions of ukuleles (themselves originally Hawaiian versions of Portuguese lutes). Some of the textural arrangements and other trappings of the genre are similar to those of Indonesian gamelan, a deliberate attempt to legitimize kroncong as the twentieth century unfolded (Becker 1975:16).

One especially interesting feature of Indonesian pop is that, at the turn of the twenty-first century, it was video CDs rather than audio-only CDs that served as the dominant digital medium (along with the ubiquitous analogue cassette tapes)—perhaps suggesting that the visual elements of music are especially important in this context, but also likely driven by the fact that video CDs were cheaper than their audio counterparts, sometimes nearly twice as much, and that MP3 versions of music appealing to Indonesian listeners were far less accessible at the time (Barendregt and van Zanten 2002:68, 88, 98). The focus on local/regional musical sensibilities is perhaps more prevalent in this culture, though "urban Indonesia has had its fair share of rockers, mods, hippies, disco-queens and Madonna and Michael Jackson 'wannabees'" (2002:101).

Barendregt and van Zanten conclude that Indonesian pop over the last 20 years uses "new forms of orality made possible by VCDs and the Internet" (2002:101), thereby drawing attention again to the fact that the latest global technology in many ways pulls musical endeavors back towards non-Western (oral) traditions. That is, by its very nature the Internet is re-transculturalizing the music that now flows freely across it in audio-visual forms—from Atlantic to Pacific and back again, in both directions.

The end of music history?

What amounts, then, to a final(?) inter/transcultural (global) musical convergence is as yet too new to be treated "historically." It can be summarized as a technologically enabled age of instantaneous exchange that has both diversifying and homogenizing effects: diversifying in that more people (can) create and listen to more different kinds of music than ever before, and homogenizing in that these musics are always instantly influencing one another, however subtly, and are therefore transforming each other at the fastest pace yet seen. This may in fact mean "the end of music history" as we have come to know it both traditionally and by virtue of the analysis presented herein. If music history consists of the development of musics in cultures (civilizations), then the continuous transformation of musics across cultures at the speed of electricity obviates such a definition. It may be instead that music history will now be reimagined around the infinite ways these transformations may be manifested transculturally within a global culture (civilization) that retains many local expressions. In that spirit, the concluding chapter to follow reconsiders the very culturality of music itself.

Notes

1 By contrast, a notated score presumably transmits everything necessary; however, all Western classical musicians know that this is not really true, since performance nuances necessary to the vitality of the music are not so captured, and must be learned. Still, the mediation of art musics tends to be done through performance and not production.
2 See, e.g., Lancashire 2003:22–24; Yano and Shūhei 2008.

References

Barendregt, Bart, and Wim van Zanten. 2002. "Popular Music in Indonesia since 1998, in Particular Fusion, Indie and Islamic Music on Video Compact Discs and the Internet." *Yearbook for Traditional Music* 34: 67–113.

Bartlett, Andrew. 1994. "Airshafts, Loudspeakers, and the Hip Hop Sample: Contexts and African American Musical Aesthetics." *African American Review* 28.4: 639–652.

Becker, Judith. 1975. "Kroncong, Indonesian Popular Music." *Asian Music* 7.1: 14–19.

Blaukopf, Kurt. 1994. "Westernisation, Modernisation, and the Mediamorphosis of Music." *International Review of the Aesthetics and Sociology of Music* 25.1/2: 337–345.

Cascone, Kim. 2000. "The Aesthetics of Failure: "Post-Digital" Tendencies in Contemporary Computer Music." *Computer Music Journal* 24.4: 12–18.

Dibben, Nicola. 2006. "Subjectivity and the Construction of Emotion in the Music of Björk." *Music Analysis* 25.1/2: 171–197.

Di Scipio, Agostino. 2000. "The Technology of Musical Experience in the 20th Century." *Rivista Italiana di Musicologia* 35.1/2: 247–275.

Fink, Robert. 2005. "The Story of ORCH5, or, the Classical Ghost in the Hip-Hop Machine." *Popular Music* 24.3: 339–356.

Fletcher, Peter. 2001. *World Musics in Context*. New York: Oxford University Press.

Garofalo, Reebee. 1999. "From Music Publishing to MP3: Music and Industry in the Twentieth Century." *American Music* 17.3: 318–354.

Gonzalez, Antonio, and Dennis Gonzalez (a.k.a. "The Maniac Agenda"). n.d. "6 New Music Genres You Need To Hear in 2016." Accessed 10-30-2017 at https://www.maniacmusic.net/blog/blog/6-new-music-genres-you-need-to-hear-coming-in-2016.

Hanna, Wendell, and Kevin Kelly. 2013. "Web2.0: A Return to Participatory Oral Traditions in Music Education." *American Music Teacher* 63.2: 29–33.

Holt, Fabian. 2007. *Genre in Popular Music*. Chicago: University of Chicago Press.

Hughes, Stephen. 2007. "Music in the Age of Mechanical Reproduction: Drama, Gramophone, and the Beginnings of Tamil Cinema." *The Journal of Asian Studies* 66.1: 3–34.

Lancashire, Terence. 2003. "World Music or Japanese—The Gagaku of Tôgi Hideki." *Popular Music* 22.1: 21–39.

Loubet, Emmanuelle (trans. Marc Couroux). 2000. "Laptop Performers, Compact Disc Designers, and No-Beat Techno Artists in Japan: Music from Nowhere." *Computer Music Journal* 24.4: 19–32.

Malawey, Victoria. 2001. "Musical Emergence in Björk's "Medúlla."" *Journal of the Royal Musical Association* 136.1: 141–180.

Martin, Bill. 2002. *Avant Rock: Experimental Music from the Beatles to Björk*. Chicago: Open Court Publishing.

Mauch, Matthias, Robert MacCallum, Mark Levy, and Armand Leroi. 2015. "The Evolution of Popular Music: USA 1960-2010." *Royal Society Open Science* 2:150081. Accessed 10-27-2017 at http://dx.doi.org/10.1098/rsos.150081.

Mera, Miguel, and Anna Morcom. 2009. "Introduction: Screened Music, Trans-contextualisation and Ethnomusicological Approaches." *Ethnomusicology Forum* 18.1: 3–19.

Morcom, Anna. 2016. *Hindi Film Songs and the Cinema*. New York: Routledge.

Perchard, Tom. 2011. "Hip Hop Samples Jazz: Dynamics of Cultural Memory and Musical Tradition in the African American 1990s." *American Music* 29.3: 277–307.

Pope, Stephen. 1999. "Web.La.Radia: Social, Economic, and Political Aspects of Music and Digital Media." *Computer Music Journal* 23.1: 49–56.

Povall, Richard. 1997. "Sociological, Artistic, and Pedagogical Frameworks for Electronic Art." *Computer Music Journal* 21.1: 18–25.

Ross, Alex. 2007. *The Rest is Noise: Listening to the Twentieth Century*. New York: Picador.

Sisario, Ben. 2009. "'Slumdog' Fusionist in Oscar Spotlight." *New York Times*, Feb 21, 2009:C1. Accessed 11-3-2017 at http://www.nytimes.com/2009/02/21/arts/music/21rahm.html.

Tapscott, Don, and Anthony Williams. 2012. *Macrowikinomics: New Solutions for a Connected Planet*. New York: Portfolio/Penguin.

Taylor, Timothy. 2007. *Beyond Exoticism: Western Music and the World*. Durham, North Carolina: Duke University Press.

Tobias, Evan. 2013. "Toward Convergence: Adapting Music Education to Contemporary Society and Participatory Culture." *Music Educators Journal* 99.4: 29–36.

Turner, David. 2017. "Future Bass: Get Familiar With EDM's Sound of 2017." *Rolling Stone.com*, February 14, 2017. Accessed 10-3-2017 at http://www.rollingstone.com/music/features/future-bass-get-familiar-with-edms-sound-of-2017-w466963.

Webb, Peter, and John Lynch. 2010. ""Utopian Punk": The Concept of the Utopian in the Creative Practice of Björk." *Utopian Studies* 21.2: 313–330.

White, John. 1997. "Radio Formats and the Transformation of Musical Style: Codes and Cultural Values in the Remaking of Tunes." *College Music Symposium* 37: 1–12.

Yano, Christine, and Hosokawa Shūhei. 2008. "Popular Music in Modern Japan." In Tokita, Alison, and David Hughes (eds.), *The Ashgate Research Companion to Japanese Music*, Aldershot: Ashgate, 345–362.

Zak, Albin III. 2005. "'Edition-ing' Rock." *American Music* 23.1: 95–107.

10 Conclusion

Global music history—intercultural or transcultural?

Music history is too often treated as a kind of Mercator projection of the globe, a flat image representing a landscape that is in reality borderless and continuous.
—Alex Ross (2007:589)

It would be enough if music could make people listen,…if they felt that for a moment they had been dreaming of an imaginary country, that's to say, one that can't be found on the map.
—Claude Debussy (1901)[1]

It is fitting to conclude with a brief discussion, in light of the historical conception presented in this study, of where the distinction between intercultural and transcultural musical development might lie, and to consider examples of how these concepts are manifested in real musics. Though that has been a significant aim of the entire study, clarifying the terms further in retrospect and in the context of musics that have not been as significant in the story told thus far will provide considerable additional value for the paradigm going forward.

The insightful work of world music educator Huib Schippers (2010) on these issues may help guide the consideration. Schippers notes that there is something of a continuum along which musical practices may lie, whether conceptually or in reality. At one end of that continuum is musical monoculturality, which (in theory) means that "the dominant culture…is the only frame of reference. Other musics and approaches to music are marginalized." Multiculturality means that "different peoples and musics lead largely separate lives," though coexisting in the same society: "Blacks are taught African music, Moroccans learn Arabic songs, and whites study Mozart," for example. Crossing into a different realm on the spectrum, one in which "loose contacts and exchanges between cultures…[result in] simple forms of fusion," one arrives at Schippers's notion of interculturality, while transculturality "refers to an in-depth exchange of approaches and ideas…in which many different musics and musical approaches are featured on an equal footing" (2010:30–31).

Yet in these comments Schippers continues to reinforce the notion or the perception that differences are more important among musics (and peoples) than potential similarities, connections or syntheses. His terms are useful, but need some re(de)fining, both individually and relationally, in the context of music history. Working backwards, transculturality may be more helpfully seen as a state reached in which a new music emerges from a high level of fusion among several different musics, transcending (though not necessarily *denying*) the cultural moorings of all of its constituent origins. This does not mean that the new music then floats in a completely undefined cultural soup; rather, it defines a new culture around itself, one that very often speaks to human commonalities rather than differences. This study has asserted that global music history has been on a trajectory towards increasing transculturality. The interculturality that precedes it better matches Schippers's description of musics in dialogue with only the beginnings of fusion—but not yet transcendent fusion. Multiculturality in this context would seem to suggest a kind of enforced emphasis on difference, while monoculturality would imply deliberate isolation. Again, this study posits that truly monocultural musical isolation may never have existed, and certainly not from the beginnings of recorded civilization, despite the best efforts of some cultures to make it so.

To state this a little differently, musical development may appear to begin monoculturally, then proceed to multiculturality, then interculturality. That said, it has also been hypothesized herein that even musical monocultures tend to have been created by some process of fusion before settling into clear differentiation, rather than arising spontaneously in isolation. Identifying the point at which a music transcends a single original culture—that is, becomes truly transcultural in that it speaks to multiple cultures simultaneously, accessing qualified human musical universals at some level—is likely to be more strongly disputed; indeed, some will say that a music can never become truly transcultural in that sense. Introduced in Chapter 1, and used at various times throughout this study, the term "inter/transcultural" represents some of the complexities of these categorical boundaries—yet another reminder that the categories are not really bounded very much at all, but rather form a continuum.

Three example contexts

The example from Chapter 1 of musics of certain Central African forest peoples may serve to clarify these concepts. Were any of these musics truly monocultural at any point, and if so, how long did they remain so? Evidence suggests that even if they were less susceptible to outside influence due to geographical isolation, these musics were nevertheless themselves influential across at least some local cultural lines before becoming more so globally later in history—which means that they are part of some process of interculturation if not transculturation. If this music did not embody something more universal, why has it gained a level of popularity so quickly upon broader exposure, and why have some musicians been able to integrate it into modern pop genres or seen its sensibilities reflected in or at least commensurate with some contemporary art music as well? The example of the music of these Central African peoples may be more in line with a theory of monoculturality (long ago) evolving into transculturality (much more recently), but even so, the categories of the continuum are more fluid than not. Across enough time, it is simply a matter of the rate of change, not the nature of the change.

Likewise in Chapter 1, it was noted that the musics of Oceania were not as relevant to the outline of a global music history—that is, until much later in the trend towards our current age of instantaneous exchange. Wild and Kaeppler (1998) demonstrate that aboriginal Australian music remains a thriving set of traditions that have almost certainly retained key characteristics across millennia, especially in the central and northern parts of that continent: each region has its own distinctives, yet all are focused on the role of song in society. Typical instruments include idiophonic rattles and rasps in addition to clapper sticks that sometimes double as paired boomerangs; the famed aerophonic didjeridu (especially in the northern-situated Arnhem Land); and, only in the extreme northeast (nearest New Guinea), cylindrical or hourglass drums. In the southern region, the area settled earliest and most heavily by the British beginning in 1788, European influence has been significant, perhaps even definitive, while indigenous musics are found more intact further inland as one travels north and west. Asian music has played a role as well during the nineteenth century and since the 1960s. Since the 1930s, both Western and indigenous musics have been on the country's radios through the Australian Broadcasting Corporation. Western popular musics have been ubiquitously embraced across the regions, and in the 1980s, aboriginal musicians began to bring their distinctives to these pop-rock genres as well (Wild and Kaeppler 1998:414). In this context, "a cosmopolitan nation with musics of indigenous peoples coexisting and intermingling with musics of immigrants is the destiny of Australia in the twenty-first century" (1998:407).

Thus, Australian music (and to a large extent Oceanic music generally) is a good *example* of the resultant processes of global music history, especially since c. 1500 CE, but not a prominent *contributor* to the currents of global music history to date. At the same time, Australia can be considered in two highly interesting ways that are also relevant to this study: first, as a contrast to the Americas in terms of the interactions of indigenous musics with foreign transplants, and second, as a locus on the cutting edge of music education from a multi/inter/transcultural perspective. In 1975 the Australian scholar Catherine Ellis established the first aboriginal music study center at the University in Adelaide, enhancing a general push towards excellence in music education. More recently, the international collection of studies in *Sound Musicianship* (2012, edited by Andrew Brown out of Queensland Conservatorium in Brisbane) is but one example of many scholarly works demonstrating this trend, including viewing music as a global phenomenon and supporting experimental work, for example, in digital music applications, music sociology and psychology, and various forms of fusion. An intentional spirit of embrace of the multicultural nature of Australia's history and its music fuels this trajectory. Unlike in the United States, however, indigenous musics in Australia have not been marginalized to the same extent as that of Native North Americans. In another contrast, African musical influence came quite late to Australia—after the 1950s, and not very profoundly in the form of African-*American* musics until the 1990s (Stratton 2015:395). This produced a milieu in which the trajectory towards musical transculturality unfolded very differently from that of the New World convergence; yet now these two milieus are themselves converging in interesting ways across the musical spectrum, caught up in the forces detailed in Chapters 8 and 9.

Finally, revisiting Central Asia—the vast locale of the first pivotal convergence in global music history (flowing out of pre-history)—is also instructive. Both the *maqām/maqom* tradition that developed from considerable Islamic influences after the turn of the first millennium and the remnants of traditions and connections that pre-date Islam remain relevant. Yet, as Will Sumits puts it, "since musical traditions are continuously evolving it is seldom possible to indicate their historical starting points, and this is particularly true of Central Asia" (2015:343). The city of Herat was a major locus of musical development during the reign of Husayn Bayqara from 1470–1506 CE, just at the time that Western European music was coalescing around what would become its distinctive features. Bayqara, also a trained musician, supported a lavish array of musician-poets at court in keeping with other Islamic rulers. Following his reign, this situation diminished and many of the Herat artists exited to other important ancient cities including Bukhara and Samarkand while the thrust of this influence also extended to Turkey and into India (Sumits 2015:345–346). On this basis Central Asia continued its inter/transcultural musical development around the *maqām/maqom* traditions even into twentieth-century Soviet Russian era, during which a variety of cultural changes were imposed and long-held traditions tended to be marginalized or treated as specializations in the wake of a Western modernistic musical approach (Sumits 2015:352). At the local level, music helps to redefine cultural identity in light of the collapse of the Soviet Union, wars, the pursuit of independence, and globalization:

> Today, the West and the East have become closer than we think... "What is music in the Central Asian region today?" "What are the musical features of the new 21st century?" "How is 'the old', the 'traditional' in music rendered compatible with the 'new', with 'modern' qualities?" "What are the sources of new appearances in music: the media, new technology or new social events?"
>
> (Sultanova 2005:133)

Razia Sultanova goes on to demonstrate how famous singers, especially those for weddings as a shared cultural feature, represent both tradition and change: "Uzbek traditional music of the recent past (at the beginning of the twentieth century) was represented by professional court music in a form of *Shashmaqom* (Six Maqams), *katta ashula* (large song) and folk music. Singers were the bearers of the oral musical tradition" (2005:135). More recently, however, for example,

> Sherali Juraev (b. 1947)...became a special kind of Uzbek professional artist, who devoted himself to wedding musical performance, making each wedding

a unique presentation with dramatic flavour. His repertoire includes about 600 songs, half of which are his own compositions. He works in a wide range of styles, including Uzbek classical songs on the poetry of medieval poets with a mystical flavour and modern lyrical songs, which are often hits, dance songs, and songs influenced by the music of neighbouring countries like Afghanistan, India, Turkey and Pakistan.

(2005:137)

Even more recently, Uzbek pop music artist Yulduz Usmonova (b. 1963) offers "an exceptional fusion of folk and international pop music [which] she composes on the basis of old folk songs that are still being sung in the villages of Uzbekistan. Traditional instruments, such as the *tambur* (long-necked lute) or the *doira* (frame drum), are combined with modern electronics" (Sultanova 2005:138). Seeing these developments in the light of a transcultural global music history illuminates both the ways in which they are exceptional and the ways in which they reflect larger trends.

A new defining paradigm

And so a metaphorical set of musical circumnavigations of the globe is now complete: it is most likely that human musics emerged (with the humans that practiced them) from the western portions of Afro-Eurasia, traveled east towards Oceania and simultaneously north towards Europe proper, came to the Americas both early on (from the Pacific) and later in history (from the Atlantic), coalescing all the while around patterns of intercultural convergence, fusion, and transformation, and finally were (re)broadcast continuously throughout the globe at accelerating speeds. Yes, music makes the world go 'round—but music also has gone and now perpetually goes 'round the world, East to West and West to East, across places and times, ever evolving.

Perhaps the best way to conclude this study, then, consists of a summative rationale for why understanding music as being within the flow of the entire continuum of culturality is an appropriate historical paradigm for our time: transculturality may in fact simply be a new type of identifiable culture in itself—a global culturality in an age in which *the speed of change makes continuous transformation the defining paradigm of human musical culture.* Seeing music history as a series of developments leading to—or perhaps even progressively revealing—such a paradigm clarifies its outline greatly. That is important (rather than merely clever or interesting) because music is a universal human activity and therefore ought to be understood to reflect something fundamental about humanity. If music has always flourished in a milieu of intercultural convergence, fusion, and transformation, and the pace of those interrelated phenomena have merely been accelerating, then that itself suggests just how adaptable human musicality really is—that it does not after all thrive primarily on fixedness but rather on dynamic synthesis. To be sure, synthesis does require some measure of stability. But, like humans themselves, human musics are either growing or they are dying.

The lesson of global music history is that this dynamic growth is spurred by the courage to interact, integrate, and transcend infinite shades of mono/multi/inter/ transculturality. The eternal infinity of the human musical spirit demands it, and will not be confined.

Note

1   From a letter to fellow composer Paul Dukas (Lesure and Nichols 1987:118).

References

Brown, Andrew (ed). 2012. *Sound Musicianship: Understanding the Crafts of Music.* Newcastle upon Tyne: Cambridge Scholars Publishing.

Lesure, François, and Roger Nichols (eds.; trans. Roger Nichols). 1987. *Debussy Letters.* Cambridge, Massachusetts: Harvard University Press.

Ross, Alex. 2007. *The Rest is Noise: Listening to the Twentieth Century.* New York: Picador.

Schippers, Huib. 2010. *Facing the Music: Shaping Music Education from a Global Perspective.* New York: Oxford University Press.

Stratton, Jon. 2015. "Popular Music, Race and Identity." In Bennett, Andy, and Steve Waksman (eds.), *The SAGE Handbook of Popular Music*, London: Sage Publications Ltd., 381–400.

Sultanova, Razia. 2005. "Music and Identity in Central Asia: Introduction." *Ethnomusicology Forum* 14.2: 131–142.

Sumits, Will. 2015. "Uzbekistan and Tajikistan." In Church, Michael (ed.), *The Other Classical Musics*, Woodbridge, Suffolk: Boydell and Brewer, 341–360.

Wild, Stephen, and Adrienne Kaeppler. 1998. "The Music and Dance of Australia." In Kaeppler, Adrienne, and J. Love (eds.), *The Garland Encyclopedia of World Music, Volume 9: Australia and the Pacific Islands*, New York: Garland, 407–417.

Index